John Wiley & Sons, Inc.

Contents

Email (for orders and customer service enquiries): cs-books@wiley.co.uk. Visit our Home Page on www.wiley.com

Editorial Director: Kelly Regan
Production Manager: Daniel Mersey
Editor: Fiona Quinn
Content Editor: Sarah Pavey
Photo Research: Cherie Cincilla
Cartography: Andrew Dolan

Wiley publishes in a variety of print and electronic formats and by print-on-demand. Some material included with standard print versions of this book may not be included in e-books or in print-on-demand. If this book refers to media such as a CD or DVD that is not included in the version you purchased, you may download this material at http://booksupport.wiley.com. For more information about Wiley products, visit www.wiley.com.

British Library Cataloguing in Publication Data

A catalogue record for this book is available from the British Library
ISBN 978-0-730-37560-9 (pbk), ISBN 978-0-730-37561-6 (ebk),
ISBN 978-0-730-37563-0 (ebk), ISBN 978-0-730-37562-3 (ebk)

Typeset by Wiley Indianapolis Composition Services

Printed and bound in China by RR Donnelley
5 4 3 2 1

A Note from the Editorial Director

Organizing your time. That's what this guide is all about.

Other guides give you long lists of things to see and do and then expect you to fit the pieces together. The Day by Day guides are different. These guides tell you the best of everything, and then they show you how to see it *in the smartest, most time-efficient way*. Our authors have designed detailed itineraries organized by time, neighborhood, or special interest. And each tour comes with a bulleted map that takes you from stop to stop.

Hoping to discover more about the endangered Tasmanian Devil, looking to sample some of the country's finest wines, or wander into the bush past lakes and mountains, or along deserted beaches? Whatever your interest or schedule, the Day by Days give you the smartest routes to follow. Not only do we take you to the top attractions, hotels, and restaurants, but we also help you access those special moments that locals get to experience—those "finds" that turn tourists into travelers.

The Day by Days are also your top choice if you're looking for one complete guide for all your travel needs. The best hotels and restaurants for every budget, the greatest shopping values, the wildest nightlife—it's all here.

Why should you trust our judgment? Because our authors personally visit each place they write about. They're an independent lot who say what they think and would never include places they wouldn't recommend to their best friends. They're also open to suggestions from readers. If you'd like to contact them, please send your comments our way at feedback@frommers.com, and we'll pass them on.

Enjoy your Day by Day guide—the most helpful travel companion you can buy. And have the trip of a lifetime.

Warm regards,

Kelly Regan

Kelly Regan, Editorial Director
Frommer's Travel Guides

About the Author

Lee Atkinson is a freelance travel writer and guide book author based in Australia. Her travel stories regularly appear in the travel sections of various newspapers and glossy travel magazines in both Australia and internationally. She is the author of seven travel guide books, including *Frommer's Sydney Day by Day*, *Frommer's Sydney Free and Dirt Cheap* and a contributor to *Frommer's Australia*.

Acknowledgments

Thank you to all the people in Tasmania who provided food and a bed for the night and, most importantly, who shared their stories about both the present and the past. Thanks to Bill for joining me for some of my journey around the island state, and special thanks to all my fellow hikers on the Overland Track: We know how special Tasmania really can be.

Ratings, Icons & Abbreviations

Every hotel, restaurant, and attraction listing in this guide has been ranked for quality, value, service, amenities, and special features using a **star-rating system.** Hotels, restaurants, attractions, shopping, and nightlife are rated on a scale of zero stars (recommended) to three stars (exceptional). In addition to the star-rating system, we also use a **kids icon** to point out the best bets for families. Within each tour, we recommend cafes, bars, or restaurants where you can take a break with a $ sign to indicate price. Each of these stops appears in a shaded box marked with a coffee-cup-shaped bullet.

The following **abbreviations** are used for credit cards:

AE	American Express	DISC	Discover	V	Visa
DC	Diners Club	MC	MasterCard		

A Note on Prices

Cost	Hotels	Restaurants
$	under $150	under $20
$$	$150–$250	$20–$30
$$$	$250–$350	$30–$40
$$$$	$350–$450	$40–$50
$$$$$	over $450	over $50

Travel Resources at Frommers.com

Frommer's travel resources don't end with this guide. Frommer's website, **www.frommers.com**, has travel information on more than 4,000 destinations. We update features regularly, giving you access to the most current trip-planning information and the best airfare, lodging, and car-rental bargains. You can also listen to podcasts, connect with other Frommers.com members through our active-reader forums, share your travel photos, read blogs from guidebook editors and fellow travelers, and much more.

Advisory & Disclaimer

Travel information can change quickly and unexpectedly, and we strongly advise you to confirm important details locally before traveling, including information on visas, health and safety, traffic and transport, accommodations, shopping, and eating out. We also encourage you to stay alert while traveling, and to remain aware of your surroundings. Avoid civil disturbances, and keep a close eye on cameras, purses, wallets, and other valuables.

While we have endeavored to ensure that the information contained within this guide is accurate and up-to-date at the time of publication, we make no representations or warranties with respect to the accuracy or completeness of the contents of this work and specifically disclaim all warranties, including without limitation warranties of fitness for a particular purpose. We accept no responsibility or liability for any inaccuracy or errors or omissions, or for any inconvenience, loss, damage, costs, or expenses of any nature whatsoever incurred or suffered by anyone as a result of any advice, or information contained in this guide.

The inclusion of a company, organization or website in this guide as a service provider and/or potential source of further information does not mean that we endorse them or the information they provide. Be aware that information provided through some websites may be unreliable and can change without notice. Neither the publisher nor author shall be liable for any damages arising herefrom.

How to Contact Us

In researching this book, we discovered many wonderful places—hotels, restaurants, shops, and more. We're sure you'll find others. Please tell us about them, so we can share the information with your fellow travelers in upcoming editions. If you were disappointed with a recommendation, we'd love to know that, too. Please e-mail: frommers@wiley.com or write to:

Frommer's Tasmania Day by Day
John Wiley & Sons, Inc. • 111 River St. • Hoboken, NJ 07030-5774

18 Favourite **Moments**

18 Favourite Moments

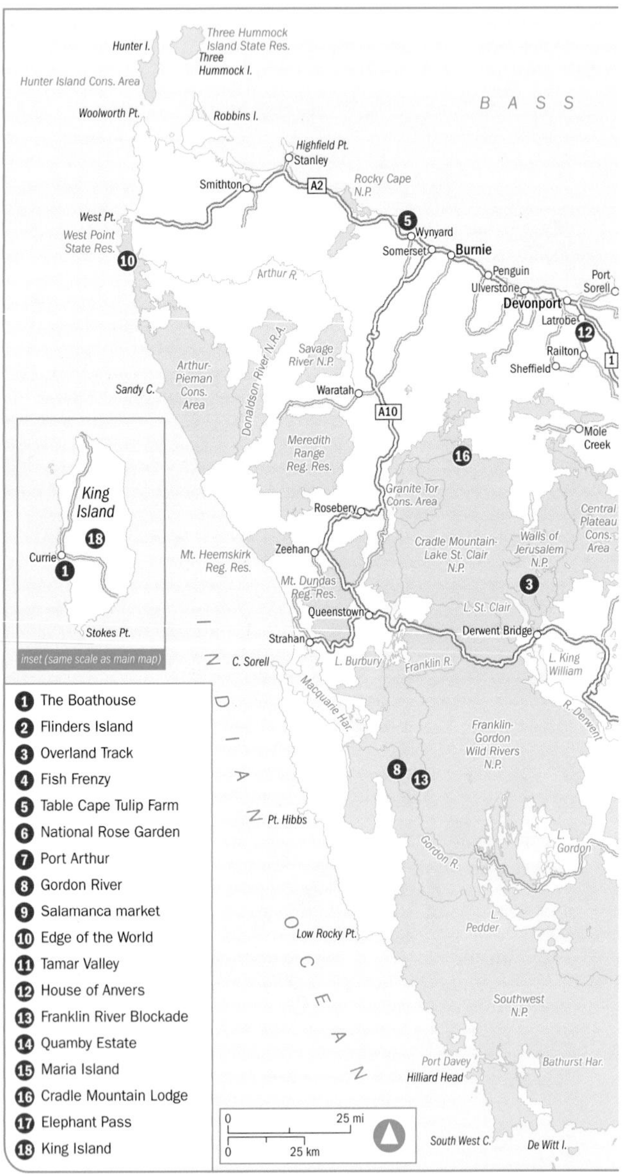
Hunter I.
Three Hummock Island State Res.
Three Hummock I.
Hunter Island Cons. Area
B A S S
Woolworth Pt.
Robbins I.
Highfield Pt.
Stanley
Smithton
A2
Rocky Cape N.P.
West Pt.
West Point State Res.
Wynyard
Somerset
Burnie
Penguin
Ulverstone
Port Sorell
Devonport
Latrobe
Arthur R.
Railton
Sheffield
1
Savage River N.P.
Arthur-Pieman Cons. Area
Donaldson River N.R.A.
Sandy C.
Waratah
A10
Mole Creek
Meredith Range Reg. Res.
King Island
Currie
Stokes Pt.
inset (same scale as main map)
Granite Tor Cons. Area
Rosebery
Central Plateau Cons. Area
Cradle Mountain-Lake St. Clair N.P.
Walls of Jerusalem N.P.
Zeehan
Mt. Heemskirk Reg. Res.
Mt. Dundas Reg. Res.
Queenstown
L. St. Clair
Derwent Bridge
Strahan
C. Sorell
L. Burbury
Franklin R.
L. King William
Macquarie Har.
R. Derwent
I N D I A N O C E A N
Franklin-Gordon Wild Rivers N.P.
Pt. Hibbs
Gordon R.
L. Gordon
L. Pedder
Low Rocky Pt.
Southwest N.P.
Port Davey
Hilliard Head
Bathurst Har.
South West C.
De Witt I.
0 25 mi
0 25 km
1 The Boathouse
2 Flinders Island
3 Overland Track
4 Fish Frenzy
5 Table Cape Tulip Farm
6 National Rose Garden
7 Port Arthur
8 Gordon River
9 Salamanca market
10 Edge of the World
11 Tamar Valley
12 House of Anvers
13 Franklin River Blockade
14 Quamby Estate
15 Maria Island
16 Cradle Mountain Lodge
17 Elephant Pass
18 King Island

Port Arthur.

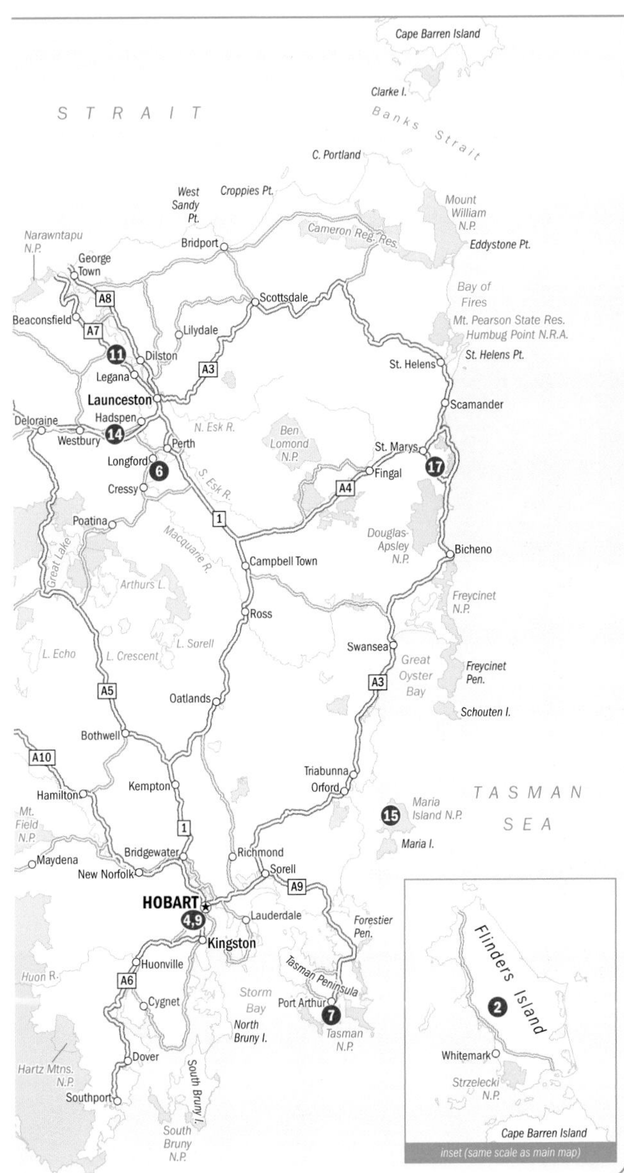
Cape Barren Island
Clarke I.
STRAIT
Banks Strait
C. Portland
West Sandy Pt.
Croppies Pt.
Mount William N.P.
Narawntapu N.P.
Bridport
Cameron Reg. Res.
Eddystone Pt.
George Town
A8
Scottsdale
Bay of Fires
Beaconsfield
A7
Lilydale
Mt. Pearson State Res.
Humbug Point N.R.A.
11
Dilston
St. Helens Pt.
St. Helens
Legana
A3
Launceston
Scamander
Deloraine
Hadspen
N. Esk R.
Ben Lomond N.P.
Westbury
14
Perth
St. Marys
Longford
6
Fingal
17
Cressy
S. Esk R.
A4
1
Poatina
Macquarie R.
Douglas-Apsley N.P.
Bicheno
Great Lake
Campbell Town
Arthurs L.
Freycinet N.P.
Ross
L. Sorell
L. Echo
L. Crescent
Swansea
Great Oyster Bay
Freycinet Pen.
A3
A5
Oatlands
Schouten I.
Bothwell
A10
Triabunna
Kempton
Orford
TASMAN SEA
Hamilton
Maria Island N.P.
15
Mt. Field N.P.
1
Maria I.
Bridgewater
Richmond
Maydena
New Norfolk
Sorell
A9
HOBART
4,9
Lauderdale
Forestier Pen.
Kingston
Huonville
Huon R.
A6
Tasman Peninsula
Cygnet
Storm Bay
Port Arthur
7
North Bruny I.
Tasman N.P.
Dover
Hartz Mtns. N.P.
South Bruny I.
Southport
South Bruny N.P.
Flinders Island
2
Whitemark
Strzelecki N.P.
Cape Barren Island
inset (same scale as main map)

Tasmania may be part of Australia but it has its own way of doing things, which makes it such a special place. It produces some of the country's finest food and wine, is laced with rich seams of history, and has magnificent wild landscapes, but it's the warm welcome and unique outlook of the locals that set it apart. Here are 18 Tasmanian moments you just can't find anywhere else.

Woolmers National Rose Garden.

❶ **Having the best meal of your life at a restaurant with no food.** There's nothing better than sitting down to a feast of just-caught King Island crayfish, melt-in-the-mouth beef, and sinfully rich local cheese at **The Boathouse** on Currie Harbour. You have to supply your own food and drinks, cook and serve it yourself, but the views and atmosphere are unbeatable. *See p 133.*

❷ **Staring out to sea on the prettiest beach you've ever seen.** Tassie has more than its fair share of breathtakingly beautiful beaches, but the beaches on **Flinders Island** are picture-perfect—and deserted. Even better, some of them are littered with diamonds. *See p 66.*

❸ **Conquering Cradle Mountain.** The 6-day Overland Track is one of the world's great wilderness walking trails. The scenery is splendid and reward enough for the hard slog, but nothing beats the sense of achievement you feel when you make it to the other end—despite the weather, blisters and aching muscles. *See p 17.*

❹ **Eating cheap-as-chips fish and chips on the wharf in Hobart.** Sublime views, sublime food and wallet-friendly to boot. A feeding frenzy at **Fish Frenzy** is always the very first thing to do when you visit Hobart. *See p 134.*

❺ **Tiptoeing through the tulips on Table Cape.** The beautiful tulips on the headland at Wynyard might only be a by-product of the bulb

Cruising down the Gordon River.

Taking a break at the Edge of the World.

business, but they have to be some of the most beautiful by-products around. Now try getting that song out of your head... *See p 60.*

❻ **Stopping to smell the roses at the National Rose Garden.** Life really is extravagantly rosy when you're surrounded by more than 6,000 heavily scented roses in the marvellous rose garden at World Heritage-listed **Woolmers Estate** near Launceston. *See p 35.*

❼ **Seeing ghosts in the dark at Port Arthur.** If you don't believe in ghosts, you will by the time you finish the captivating—and slightly unnerving—night-time tour of the ruins of the convict prison settlement at Port Arthur, where gaolers tried their hardest to break their prisoners' spirits. If you believe the guides, some of those broken spirits never left. The stories they tell about sightings and strange happenings will make your spine tingle and your hair stand on end. *See p 31.*

❽ **Marvelling at the mirror-like reflections on the Gordon River.** It can be hard to tell which way is up on a sunny day on the Gordon River near Strahan in the wild southwest. The dark tannin-stained waters throw up flawless reflections of the rainforest and blue sky. *See p 75.*

❾ **Finding a local bargain at Salamanca market.** More than just a place to pick up a bargain-priced hand-spun, hand-knitted jumper, beautifully turned native Tasmanian timber bowls and other hand-made uniquely Tasmanian souvenirs, these Saturday morning outdoor markets in Hobart are a great opportunity to taste the fruits of local growers' labours: artisan smoked meats, hand-made cheeses, flaky pastries and old-fashioned fruits. It's a Saturday-morning ritual for locals and visitors alike. Don't miss it! *See p 105.*

❿ **Breathing in the world's freshest air at the Edge of the World.** The Edge of the World is a wild and desolate place where monstrous waves crash up against a rocky shore and the bitterly cold wind is so strong it almost blows you off your feet. But that wind has travelled 16,000km (10,000 miles) across nothing but empty ocean, making it the cleanest air on Earth, so breathe deeply. *See p 61.*

⓫ **Getting bubbles up your nose in the Tamar Valley.** Tasmania's sparkling wines are, in a word, divine, and the best of them are made in the Tamar Valley. Fine wine, a long lunch and an even longer view—there's no better way to

Walking on a beautiful beach.

spend a day than on the deck of a Tamar Valley winery. *See p 17.*

⓬ **Having chocolate cake for breakfast at the House of Anvers.** You'll feel like a big kid when you have breakfast at this chocolate factory near Devonport. Nothing could be more delicious than the range of chocolaty treats on the breakfast (and lunch) menu combined with the fact that no one thinks a chocolate binge is something to feel guilty about. *See p 135.*

⓭ **Hugging a 2,000-year-old tree.** The Franklin River Blockade was the birth of the green movement in Australia, so there's no better place to hug a tree than in the rainforest where it all began. *See p 76.*

⓮ **Bedding down in one of the country's grandest manor houses.** If you've always felt that you belong on a grand country estate rather than in an inner-city apartment, you'll feel right at home in Tasmania's gorgeous country house hotels, like **Quamby Estate.** Then again, it might just be the warm Tasmanian welcome that makes you feel so much like one of the family. *See p 158.*

⓯ **Spending 3 whole days walking along a beach.** Bushwalking on Maria Island or in the Bay of Fires takes on a whole new meaning when most of your time is spent walking along some of the most beautiful beaches in the country. *See p 114.*

⓰ **Experiencing four seasons in 1 day.** Is there anything more perfect than sitting in a spa bath at **Cradle Mountain Lodge** with a glass of bubbly watching the snowfall outside? It might be the middle of summer, and you might have planned to be out there bushwalking, but you probably won't care. (At least, not until you have to dig your car out of the snow without gloves the next morning.) *See p 155.*

⓱ **Tilting the horizon on the back of a motorcycle.** Sweeping around one wide curve after another, leaning left then right then left again, watching the road unfurl and the scenery slip by and the views unfold—Tasmania's twisting mountain roads are heaven on a stick for motorcyclists. *See p 46.*

⓲ **Sipping ice-cold cloud juice on King Island.** Everything seems to taste better on King Island, even the rain. Thank goodness someone came up with the bright idea to bottle it. There's 7,800 drops of pure rainwater in every 600ml (1-pint) bottle of cloud juice. It tastes so good it's enough to turn you teetotal. *See p 29.* ●

1 Strategies for Seeing **Tasmania**

Strategies for Seeing **Tasmania**

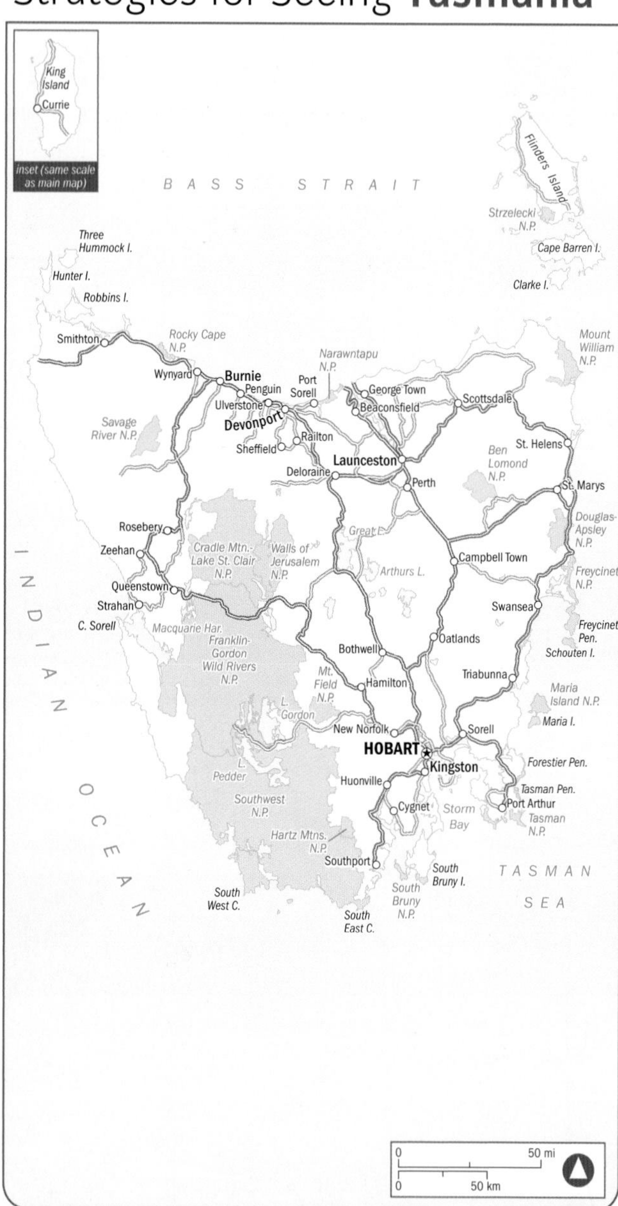

King Island
Currie
inset (same scale as main map)
BASS STRAIT
Flinders Island
Strzelecki N.P.
Cape Barren I.
Clarke I.
Three Hummock I.
Hunter I.
Robbins I.
Smithton
Rocky Cape N.P.
Narawntapu N.P.
Mount William N.P.
Wynyard
Burnie
Penguin
Port Sorell
Ulverstone
Devonport
George Town
Beaconsfield
Scottsdale
Savage River N.P.
Railton
Sheffield
Launceston
St. Helens
Ben Lomond N.P.
Deloraine
Perth
St. Marys
Douglas-Apsley N.P.
Rosebery
Great L.
Zeehan
Cradle Mtn.-Lake St. Clair N.P.
Walls of Jerusalem N.P.
Campbell Town
Arthurs L.
Freycinet N.P.
Queenstown
Strahan
Swansea
C. Sorell
Macquarie Har.
Franklin-Gordon Wild Rivers N.P.
Freycinet Pen.
Oatlands
Bothwell
Schouten I.
INDIAN OCEAN
Triabunna
Mt. Field N.P.
Hamilton
Maria Island N.P.
L. Gordon
Maria I.
New Norfolk
Sorell
HOBART
Kingston
Forestier Pen.
L. Pedder
Huonville
Tasman Pen.
Southwest N.P.
Cygnet
Storm Bay
Port Arthur
Tasman N.P.
Hartz Mtns. N.P.
Southport
South Bruny I.
TASMAN SEA
South Bruny N.P.
South West C.
South East C.
0
50 mi
0
50 km

Previous page: Get up close to cliffs on a Bruny Island Cruise.

Time stands still in Tasmania—or at least stretches and bends—until what should have been a 3-hour drive morphs into 2 days and you've only clocked up 180km (110 miles); it's the Tassie-time theory of relativity, where getting from A to B will always take more time than you think. Tasmania may look small on the map, but it feels huge in real life. Take your time, and don't try to see it all at once.

Rule # 1: Be flexible with your travel arrangements

Tasmania's an island surrounded by one of the world's wildest seas, and the changeable weather can destroy the most carefully laid travel plans. Putting together a travel itinerary with tight connections is an almost guaranteed recipe for disappointment: flight cancellations happen all the time.

Rule # 2: Be prepared for all weather, every day

You'll never get bored with the weather in Tasmania. One minute you'll be basking in sunshine, with thick fog or driving rain the next. Snow, even in summer, is not uncommon in highland areas. Be prepared for all weather, no matter what the time of year. As the saying goes, 'There's no such thing as bad weather. There's only bad clothing.'

Rule # 3: Try to have your own wheels

While it is theoretically possible to explore the island using public transport, you'll see a lot more and spend a lot less time backtracking if you have your own vehicle, so we haven't included public transport details in this guide. Bring your own car (or motorbike) over on the ferry, or hire a car when you arrive—all the major international and national car-hire companies have offices in Hobart, Launceston and Devonport. Remember: driving is on the left. Not all petrol stations open at night or on weekends, so plan ahead and always fill up when you can.

Rule # 4: Avoid driving at night

Tasmania's narrow, winding roads can be tricky at the best of times, especially when wet or icy, but at night they are even more dangerous, when the risk of hitting a nocturnal marsupial on an unlit road is very high.

Rule # 5: Don't drink & drive

Following one of Tassie's wine trails is a fantastic way to explore the

Spirit of Tasmania ferry.

Watch for animals on the road.

island. A few 20ml tastes won't put you over the limit but a day of tasting will. If you can't decide who should be the (sober) designated driver, go on a wine tour. The blood alcohol limit in Tasmania is 0.05 (grams of alcohol per 100ml of blood).

Rule # 6: Be sun smart

Tassie's mild climate and fresh sea breezes can be misleading: it's very easy to get sunburnt here, especially if you are bushwalking in the Cradle Mountain area. Always wear plenty of sunscreen.

Rule # 7: Swim safe

Tasmania has hundreds of gloriously deserted beaches, but isolated beaches are unpatrolled, which means that if you find yourself in trouble help can be a long way away, so take care and never swim alone. Lonely beaches are often in lonely places far away from cafes and kiosks, so stock up on food and water before you go.

Rule # 8: Don't bushwalk alone

Tasmania's wilderness is wild, remote and far from help should you need it. Never walk alone, make sure you have the right equipment, appropriate clothing for all kinds of weather and more water than you think you'll need. Let someone know your plans (friend, family, ranger or B&B host) and report back when you return safely. If there are logbooks along the track, sign them; they are not checked regularly (which is why you need to let someone know your intentions) but they are relied upon in the event of a search if you are reported overdue. *See box Walk Safe, p 113.*

Rule # 9: Get a National Parks Pass

If you are planning on spending more than 1 or 2 days in national parks, a National Parks Pass will save you some serious money. *See box, p 115.*

Rule # 10: Avoid school holidays if you can

Crowds in Tassie are rare, but school holidays can be very busy. If possible, try to plan your trip outside of the main school holidays. If you are travelling during school holidays, make sure you book your accommodation well ahead. *See The Best Time to Go, p 162.* ●

Always walk with someone.

2 The Best Full-Day Tours

The Best in Three Days

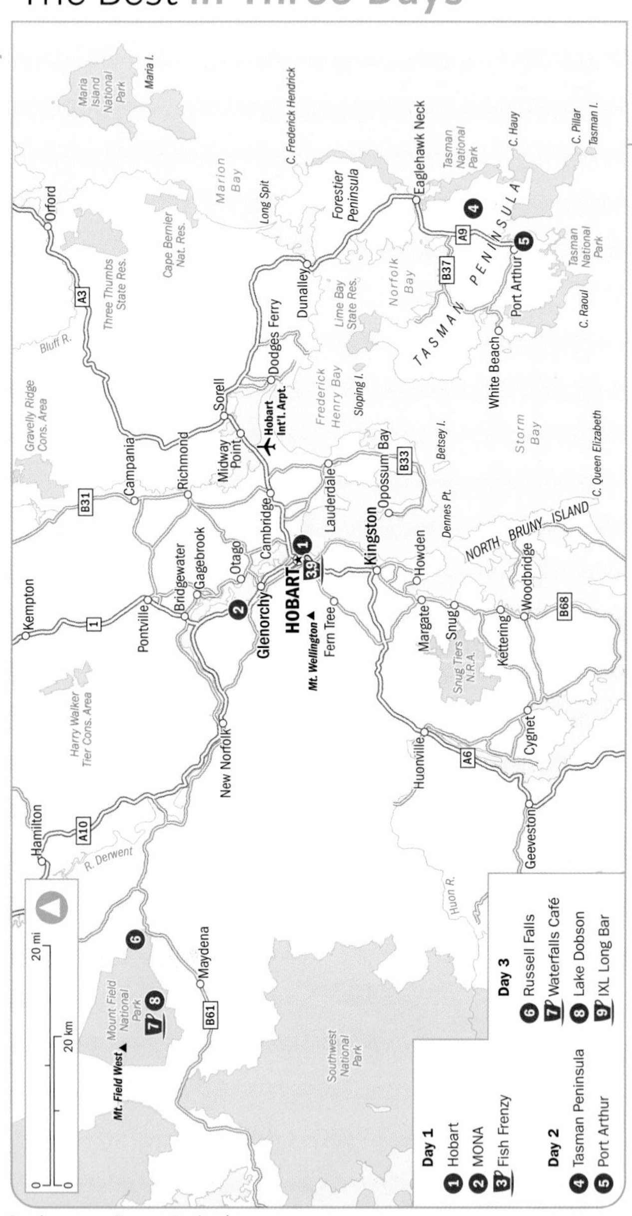

Previous page: Tasman Peninsula.

Convict history, glorious coastal scenery and rugged wilderness. If you only have 3 days to see the best of Tasmania, you want to make sure you get a taste of three of the things that make Tasmania such a unique place to visit. The trick is try not to travel too much, so this tour doesn't venture far from Hobart. So much to do, so little time… START: **Hobart.**

Day One

1 ★★★ Hobart. Hopefully, you've timed your visit to Hobart to begin on a Saturday, which means you can spend the morning at **Salamanca market** (they close at 3pm, see p 105). If not, there's still plenty to look at in this historical old quarter of Hobart, where sandstone warehouses have been converted into galleries, boutiques, cafes and eateries. The area known as **Battery Point ★★★** (p 80, 5) just behind Salamanca is where you'll find many of the city's oldest houses. *2 hr. For more information, see p 79.*

2 ★★★ MONA. This brand-new private art museum, which is larger than the Museum of Contemporary Art in Sydney, is Australia's version of the Guggenheim. The range of art at MONA—the Museum of Old and New Art—has everything from Egyptian tombs and an excrement machine that mimics the human intestinal system to rotting animal carcasses and twirling light installations. It's weird, confronting, often sexually explicit, and certainly thought-provoking (if you have kids there's a special guide you can follow to avoid all the nudity and sex). There are plenty of eating and drinking options once there; my favourite spot is the Wine Bar, where you can discuss the thought-provoking art over a glass of wine or two and a couple of plates of tapas. *3 hr. 655 Main Rd., Berriedale. 03/6277-9900. www.mona.net.au. Adults $20; free children 17 and under, and Tasmanians. Wed–Mon 10am–6pm. Closed Tues. Limited on-site parking. 30-min MONA Roma ferry from the MONA ferry terminal adjacent Elizabeth St. Pier ($15 return; 8 ferries a day from 9:30am–6:45pm).*

MONA.

3 Fish Frenzy. One of Hobart's charms is that it's a working maritime city, and there's no better way to soak in all that seafaring heritage and activity than a seafood dinner on the waterfront. There are plenty of options, but just because you have a million-dollar view doesn't mean you have to pay a million-dollar price tag. Fish Frenzy serves up tasty fish and chips at bargain prices, and if you've lucked it for a balmy evening, there's no better place to be than on one of the outside tables on the wharf. *See p 134. $.*

Day Two

4 ★★★ Tasman Peninsula. Spend your second day exploring the dramatic coastal scenery and atmospheric ruins of convict settlements on the Tasman Peninsula. It's a 90-minute drive from Hobart via the Tasman Highway (A3) and Arthur Highway (A9), but take your time and stop at some of the coastal lookouts in **Tasman National Park** such as the **Tessellated Pavement** (p 83, 1), **Tasman Blowhole,** and the ruins of once huge sea caves at **Tasman Arch** and the **Devil's Kitchen** (p 83, 4). Call into the **Tasmanian Devil Conservation Park** (p 39, 4) to see Tasmanian devils (see box, p 23), some of the world's largest carnivorous marsupials, now sadly on the brink of extinction due to devil facial tumour disease. Your visit here will help fund research into the disease. *2–3 hr. National Park entry fee applies, see box National Parks Pass, p 115.*

The ruins of Port Arthur.

5 ★★★ Port Arthur. The ruins of the 19th-century convict penal settlement at Port Arthur is the main attraction on the Tasman peninsula, and is one of Australia's most important heritage sites. There are more than 30 buildings and ruins (including church, penitentiary, hospital and prison), gardens, an island cemetery (poetically named the Isle of the Dead), Point Puer across the bay, where young boys were imprisoned and a fascinating interpretation centre-cum-museum in the visitor centre. To make the most of your visit, opt for the Bronze pass, with introductory guided tour and a harbour cruise and then spend an hour or so wandering. If you don't mind driving home after dark, stay for the Ghost Tour, but be careful of wildlife on the roads: you don't want to wipe out one of the few remaining devils on the way home. Alternatively, there is accommodation on site at the Comfort Inn, see p 154. *½–1 day. See also p 43, 2.*

Day Three

6 ★★★ Russell Falls. It's a typically Tasmanian quirk of geography that in less than an hour's drive from the centre of Hobart you can find yourself surrounded by alpine wilderness, lush rainforest and ancient plants. If you want to sample how remarkable the Tasmanian wilderness can be, **Mount Field National Park** is the place to visit. There are two sections to the park and you

Take a short walk to Russell Falls.

should try to visit both. First, make the short 25-minute loop walk through the rainforest to Russell Falls near the visitor centre and car park. ◷ ***25 min. For more details see Mount Field National Park, p 41, ❸. National park entry fee applies, see box National Parks Pass, p 115.***

7 Waterfalls Café. There's a cafe at Mount Field National Park visitor centre if you're hungry after your walk. There's an open picnic area beside the visitor centre with picnic tables and shelter, so if it's raining you can unpack a picnic from supplies you picked up in Hobart before you left. ***$.***

❽ Lake Dobson. From the visitor centre, drive 16km (10 miles) up a twisting, gravel road to Lake Dobson. There's a small ski field here, and snow can come at any time, so bring warm and waterproof clothing with you, even if it's a hot sunny day in Hobart. The 4- to 5-hour **Tarn Shelf** walk is a fantastic sub-alpine loop and is breathtaking in autumn (Apr and May). If you don't have the energy for the longer walk, do the 40-minute **Pandani Grove** walk instead. It circles Lake Dobson and weaves through stands of spiky pandani, the largest heath plant in the world and found only in Tasmania. ◷ ***40 min–5 hr. For more details see Mount Field National Park, p 114, ❸. National park entry fee applies, see box National Parks Pass, p 115.***

9 IXL Long Bar. Finish off your time in Tassie with a celebratory cocktail at this little bar oozing with history in the Henry Jones Art Hotel (p 156) on Hobart's waterfront. After all, there's no better place for a jar or two than in an old jam factory, where the signature cocktail is indeed served in an old jam jar. ***See p 143. $$.***

Walking through the Pandani Grove at Lake Dobson.

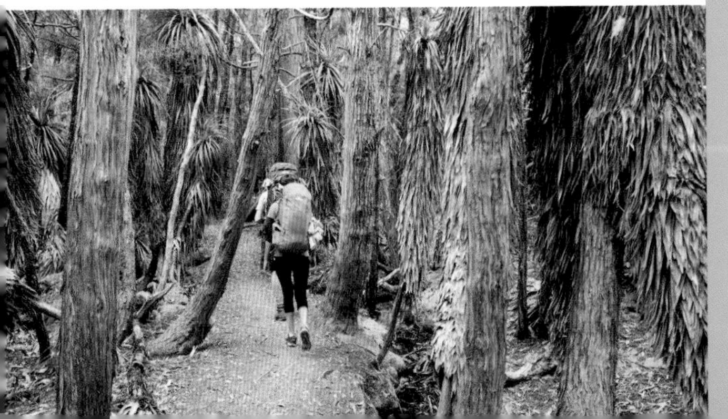

The Best in One Week

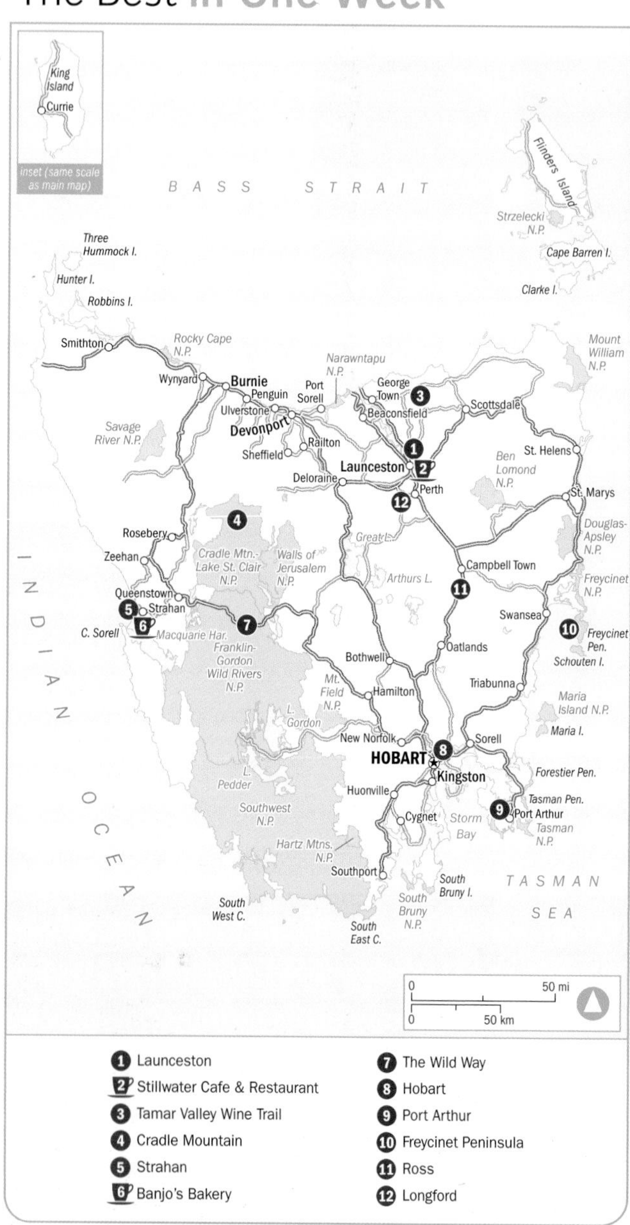

King Island
Currie
inset (same scale as main map)
BASS STRAIT
Flinders Island
Strzelecki N.P.
Cape Barren I.
Clarke I.
Three Hummock I.
Hunter I.
Robbins I.
Smithton
Rocky Cape N.P.
Narawntapu N.P.
Mount William N.P.
Wynyard
Burnie
Penguin
Port Sorell
George Town
Ulverstone
Devonport
Beaconsfield
Scottsdale
Savage River N.P.
Railton
Sheffield
Launceston
Ben Lomond N.P.
St. Helens
Deloraine
Perth
St. Marys
Douglas-Apsley N.P.
Rosebery
Zeehan
Cradle Mtn.-Lake St. Clair N.P.
Walls of Jerusalem N.P.
Great L.
Arthurs L.
Campbell Town
Freycinet N.P.
Queenstown
Strahan
Swansea
C. Sorell
Macquarie Har.
Franklin-Gordon Wild Rivers N.P.
Freycinet Pen.
Schouten I.
Oatlands
Bothwell
Triabunna
Mt. Field N.P.
Hamilton
Maria Island N.P.
L. Gordon
Maria I.
New Norfolk
Sorell
HOBART
Kingston
Forestier Pen.
L. Pedder
Huonville
Tasman Pen.
Port Arthur
Cygnet
Storm Bay
Tasman N.P.
Southwest N.P.
Hartz Mtns. N.P.
Southport
South Bruny I.
South Bruny N.P.
TASMAN SEA
INDIAN OCEAN
South West C.
South East C.
0
50 mi
0
50 km
1 Launceston
2 Stillwater Cafe & Restaurant
3 Tamar Valley Wine Trail
4 Cradle Mountain
5 Strahan
6 Banjo's Bakery
7 The Wild Way
8 Hobart
9 Port Arthur
10 Freycinet Peninsula
11 Ross
12 Longford

A whirlwind week in Tasmania will give you a taste of all the island has to offer. Travelling anti-clockwise, this is a circuit of the island starting and returning to Launceston, but you could easily begin in Hobart, or even Devonport, if you have brought your own car on the ferry. You do need a set of wheels if you want to cover this much ground in a week. **START: Launceston.**

1 ★★ **Launceston.** Get up early and take a misty morning walk along the riverside walking trail and follow it all the way to **Cataract Gorge** (p 52, **6**), which, depending on your strolling pace, will take you around 15 minutes or so. Make time to explore the parklands and take a ride on the chairlift. ½ *day. See also Launceston p. 51.*

2 Head back to the city, stopping for coffee and brunch at **Stillwater Cafe & Restaurant** (p 138) beside Ritchie's Mill. *$$.*

3 ★★ **Tamar Valley Wine Trail.** Spend the afternoon sampling some of Tasmania's best wines on the Tamar Valley Wine Trail. You only have a few hours, so rather than trying to do it all, head up to Pipers Brook, where there are a couple of excellent wineries close together: **Pipers Brook Vineyard** and **Jansz Wine Room.** ½ *day. See p 28,* **7** *&* **8***.*

4 ★★★ **Cradle Mountain.** Plan on spending a full day at Cradle Mountain. It will take just a little over 2 hours to drive from Launceston, via Deloraine. Call into the **Wilderness Gallery** (p 71, **4**) next door to Cradle Mountain Chateau on the way for a look at some of the landscapes you don't have time to see on this trip. If you want a challenge, climb up to **Marion's Lookout** (around 3 hr return) for fantastic views, but be warned: it's steep and involves hauling yourself up some steep sections with chains. Easier alternatives are the 2-hour walk around **Dove Lake** for views of the famous mountain peaks from below and the much shorter 10-minute **rainforest walk** near the visitor centre. Splurge on a **spa treatment** (there is a day spa at Cradle

Enjoy the view on Cradle Mountain.

Saturday's Salamanca market in Hobart.

Mountain Lodge (p 155) and Cradle Mountain Chateau (p 155) and then order some Tasmanian cheese and wine to enjoy beside the fire back at your accommodation. 🕘 *1 day. See p 72,* ❺.

Allow at least 2 hours to drive the winding mountain road from Cradle Mountain to Strahan, and watch out for wildlife and patches of ice.

❺ ★★★ **Strahan.** You could spend 3 or 4 days at Strahan on the wild (and usually wet) west coast, but you only have one, so spend it wisely: take a **Gordon River Cruise** (p 75, ❷) for magnificent river scenery and stops in the rainforest and on Sarah Island (p 33, ❾). In summer (Jan–end Mar) there's an afternoon cruise, but for the rest of the year cruises depart daily at 8:30 or 9am, depending on the company you cruise with, so you'll need to get up early if you leave from Cradle Mountain. If you can't make the early-morning start, there are plenty of other things to see and do in Strahan. 🕘 ½ *day. See p 75,* ❶.

❻ There aren't many eating options between Strahan and Lake St. Clair, so stock up on breakfast, sandwiches, or pies at **Banjo's Bakery** in Strahan (on the Esplanade, next door to Hamer's Hotel) before you hit the road. ☎ *03/6210-5000. www.banjos.com.au. $.*

❼ ★★★ **The Wild Way.** It's a stunning drive across the island between Strahan and Hobart along the aptly named Wild Way that winds through the **Franklin-Gordon Wild Rivers National Park,** where it seems as if a new jagged-edged mountain rises up around every curve of the road. You could do this trip in 4 hours, but it's better to make it last all day. The two best spots to stop and stretch your legs are **Lake St. Clair,** where you can walk around the lake shore at **Cynthia Bay,** and where, if you're lucky, you may even spot an echidna or platypus, and **Mount Field National Park** (p 114, ❸), where the 10-minute walk to pretty Russell Falls is a favourite. 🕘 *½–1 day. National park entry fee applies, see box National Parks Pass, p 115.*

8 ★★★ **Hobart.** Take an early evening walk along the waterfront to **Salamanca Place** and **Battery Point** (p 80, **4** & **5**). There are plenty of great restaurants and bars in this area: try **Fish Frenzy** (p 134) or **Smolt** (p 138). If tomorrow is a Saturday, don't miss the **Salamanca market** (p 27). *For more information, see p 79. For overnight accommodation, see p 153.*

9 ★★★ **Port Arthur.** The atmospheric ruins of the convict penal settlement at Port Arthur are a comfortable day-trip from Hobart, and you can easily spend a whole day here. Stay overnight and you can also join in the **Ghost Tour** of the site. If you do return to Hobart after dark (around a 90-min drive), be very careful of Tasmanian devils and other wildlife on the road. *5–6 hr. See p 31,* **2**.

Allow 3 hours to drive up the coast from Hobart to Coles Bay, an extra 20 minutes if coming from Port Arthur.

10 ★★★ **Freycinet Peninsula.** You'll love getting to Freycinet as much as being there. It's a picturesque drive that meanders beside deserted beaches and offers magnificent coastal views across **Great Oyster Bay** and the rocky pink granite peaks of the Freycinet Peninsula known as **The Hazards.** Stop for morning tea at **Kate's Berry Farm** (p 87, **4**) in Swansea, then once you're in the **Freycinet National Park** walk up to the lookout above **Wineglass Bay** ★★★ (p 114, **2**), one of the most photographed beaches in the state. Drive up to the lighthouse at **Cape Tourville** for sunset. *8 hr. National park entry fee applies, see box National Parks Pass, p 115.*

It will take around 2½ hours to drive from Coles Bay back to Launceston, although that, of course, does not allow for any stops along the way.

11 ★ **Ross.** From Coles Bay cut inland to make your way back towards Launceston. Take a short detour en route to visit Ross with its Georgian architecture and famous convict-built **Ross Bridge** (p 33, **7**). There are 40 historic buildings, in town, so take an hour to wander around. *1 hr. Ross Visitor Information Centre, Church St. ☎ 03/6381-5466. www.visitross.com.au. Daily 9am–5pm.*

12 **Longford.** Spend a few hours exploring the two World Heritage-listed convict sites at **Brickendon** ★ (p 33, **2**) and **Woolmers Estate** ★★★ (p 33, **3**), although if you only have the time (or inclination) for one, I'd head straight to Woolmers and do the guided tour. *3–5 hr.*

Looking out over Wineglass Bay on the Freycinet Peninsula.

The Best in Two Weeks

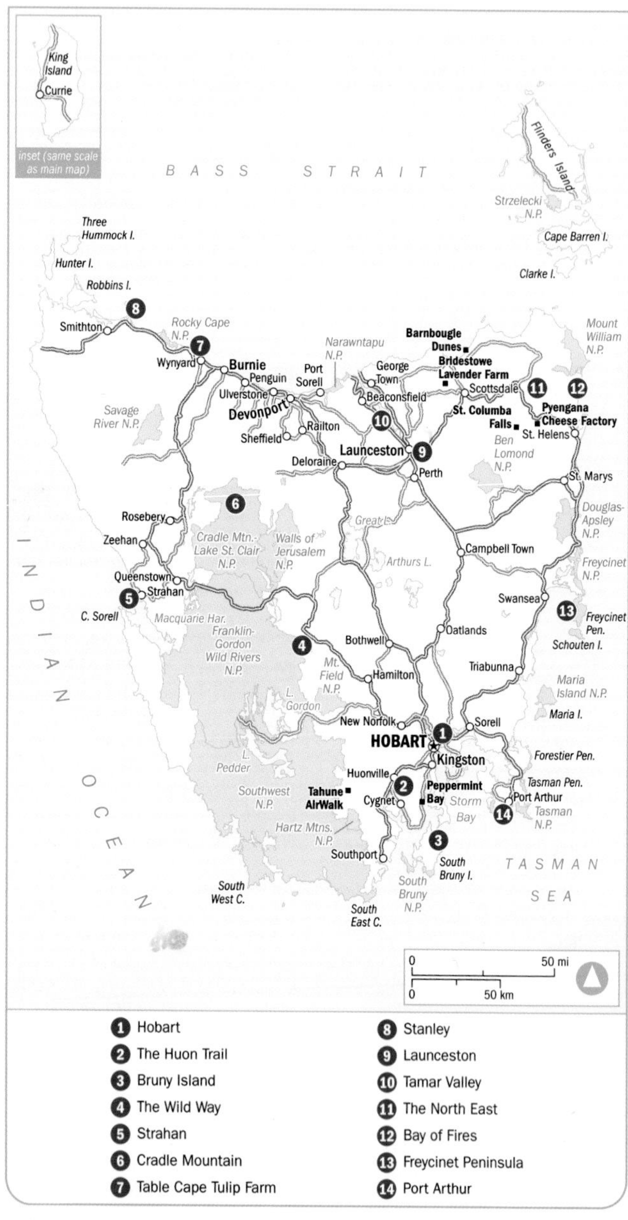

1 Hobart
2 The Huon Trail
3 Bruny Island
4 The Wild Way
5 Strahan
6 Cradle Mountain
7 Table Cape Tulip Farm
8 Stanley
9 Launceston
10 Tamar Valley
11 The North East
12 Bay of Fires
13 Freycinet Peninsula
14 Port Arthur

Two weeks in Tasmania is the optimum, because it means you can see most of the island at an easy pace and not rush too much. This journey traces a clockwise loop around the state, beginning with 3 nights in Hobart but, just like the 1-week tour earlier in this chapter, you can also begin and end the trip in either Launceston or Devonport. START: **Hobart.**

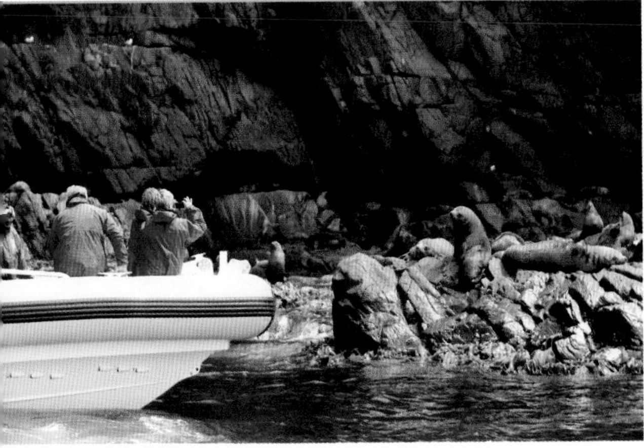

Seal spotting on Bruny Island Cruise.

❶ ★★★ **Hobart.** For details on how to best spend your first day in Tasmania, see the early listings for The Best in Three Days (p 79, ❶, ❷ & ❸). *1 day.*

❷ **The Huon Trail.** Spend a day driving around the apple orchards and bucolic farmland of the **Huon Valley,** south of Hobart. Whatever you do, don't miss the elevated treetop walk at ★★★ **Tahune AirWalk** (p 91, ❸) and allow time for a long lunch with a view at **Peppermint Bay** (p 136). *1 day. For more information, see Down South, p 90.*

❸ ★ **Bruny Island.** Some hire car companies won't let you take your car on the ferry to visit remote Bruny Island, so if you can't drive, take the **Bruny Island Cruise** instead; the full-day tour departs from Franklin Wharf in Hobart. *1 day. See p 95,* ❹.

❹ ★★★ **The Wild Way.** After 3 days in Hobart it's time to head west to Strahan on one of our favourite drives. It's the same route as The Wild Way in 'The Best in One Week' (p 16, ❼), but done in reverse. *1 day.*

❺ ★★★ **Strahan.** Aim to spend 2 days in this charming little town beside the sea at the mouth of Macquarie Harbour, the second-biggest natural harbour in Australia. Take a ★★★ **Gordon River Cruise** (p 75, ❷) and a ride on the restored stream train along the **West Coast Wilderness Railway** (p 77, ❼). *2 days. For more information, see Strahan, p 75.*

❻ ★★★ **Cradle Mountain.** Strap on your walking shoes and pack a raincoat and some winter woollies because the walks around Cradle Mountain are worth doing even if

Table Cape Tulip Farm.

the weather gets nasty; this place really is as beautiful as everyone says it is. 1 day. *See p 72,* **5** *for some suggestions on how best to spend your day.*

From Cradle Mountain head back to the Murchison Highway and head north to Wynyard, a little less than 2 hours' drive.

7 ★★ **Table Cape Tulip Farm.** In September and October, Table Cape headland near Wynyard is covered in spectacular tulips. *45 min. See p 60,* **9**.

It's a scenic drive across the top of the island to Stanley in the far west; allow around 1 hour 45 minutes.

8 ★★★ **Stanley.** Huddled in the shadow of a massive flat-topped circular headland descriptively named **The Nut,** the historic harbourside village of Stanley was established in 1825 by the Van Diemen's Land Company, a group of London merchants who planned a wool-growing venture to supply the needs of the British textile industry. The town is a charming collection of picturesque old warehouses, many now converted into luxury accommodation, restaurants and galleries, quaint cottages and antique shopfronts. *1 day.*

9 ★ **Launceston.** Launceston is a pretty city with winding riverside walks, gorgeous parklands and the famous **Cataract Gorge,** a wild ravine in the centre of the city that you can ride across on the longest single-span chairlift in the world. There are a number of museums in town, but the best two are the **Queen Victoria Museum and Art Gallery,** which spreads across two separate sites, and the **National Automobile Museum of Tasmania.** Don't leave without visiting the **Design Centre,** a showcase of contemporary wood design. *1 day. For more information, see p 51.*

10 **Tamar Valley.** There's more to the Tamar Valley than just fine wine, although that's the main reason why most people go. But, if you can tear yourself away from the wineries,

The Nut at Stanley.

Tasmanian Devil

The world's largest carnivorous marsupial is about the same size as a small dog and has extremely powerful jaws and teeth. It's black with a white band on its chest and hindquarters and has hairless pink ears. Once found all around Tasmania, it's nocturnal and spends the daytime hidden in a den. They love feasting on roadkill, which means they often end up as roadkill themselves. This creature can make a variety of sounds, including snarls and an unnerving screech. Sadly, you no longer hear—or see—them as often as you used to. The wild population has been decimated in recent years by a deadly facial cancer and so far scientists are at a loss as to how to save them. In some areas, more than 90% of the population has been wiped out. To see them, visit either the **Tasmanian Devil Conservation Park** (p 39, ❹) or **Bonorong Wildlife Sanctuary** (p 43, ❷). For more information about Tasmanian devils, see www.tassiedevil.com.au.

their restaurants and cellar doors with stunning river and valley views, you'll discover plenty of non-alcoholic activities to occupy your time, from wetlands and mineshafts to seahorse farms. ◷ *1 day. See p 55.*

⓫ **The North East.** You could zoom across the northeast corner of the state from Launceston to St. Helens in 3½ hours, but it's more fun to make a day of it. Try some hand-made lavender biscuits at the **Bridestowe Lavender Farm** (p 103, ❺), the country's largest lavender farm; play an astonishingly inexpensive round of golf at **Barnbougle Dunes,** one of the most beautiful public links courses and consistently rated in the world's top 100; gaze at one of Tassie's highest waterfalls, **St. Columba Falls** (p 58, ❸); and taste some cheese at **Pyengana Cheese Factory** (p 58, 2). ◷ *1 day. For more information, see p 58.*

The Bay of Fires area is 20km (12 miles) north of St. Helens via a dirt road signposted 'The Gardens'.

⓬ ★★★ **Bay of Fires.** Often lauded as one of the best beaches in the world, the Bay of Fires is a landscape that French Impressionist painter Gauguin would have loved: white sand, cobalt-blue water and bold-orange boulders. There are none of his Tahitian lovelies here,

Cataract Gorge, Launceston.

Barnbougle Dunes golf course.

though; in fact, there's rarely any one here at all and even though locals tend to moan that the place is being loved to death and overrun, there doesn't seem to be any sign of it—except for a few days in the Christmas holidays, perhaps. *3 hr. See p 89,* ⓫.

Allow around 2 hours to drive from the Bay of Fires area to the Freycinet Peninsula; follow the signs to Coles Bay.

⓭ ★★ **Freycinet Peninsula.** Break your journey south at the **Friendly Beaches** (p 124, ❸)—a long stretch of deserted beach heaven that most people overlook in their rush to get to the more famous Wineglass Bay farther down the peninsula. Watch out for the turn-off 20km (12 miles) south of Bicheno on the Coles Bay Road. If you can afford it, stay at Saffire (p 159) overlooking Great Oyster Bay; otherwise, The Edge of the Bay (p 155) at Coles Bay and Freycinet Lodge (p 155) just inside Freycinet National Park are more affordable alternatives. This really is one place where you should splurge out on a room with a view. *1 day. For more information on what to visit, see p 19,* ❿.

Freycinet Lighthouse.

It's a 3 to 3½-hour drive from Coles Bay to Port Arthur via the A3 and A9.

⓮ ★★★ **Port Arthur.** There's so much more to this beautiful fish-hook-shaped pendant of land of the Tasman Peninsula (p 83, ❹) than just the gaol, but for this tour head straight to the convict ruins at Port Arthur. *1 day. For more information, see p 43,* ❷.

Allow 90 minutes to return to Hobart from Port Arthur, and be wary of animals if driving at night. ●

3 The Best Special-Interest Tours

For Food & **Drink Lovers**

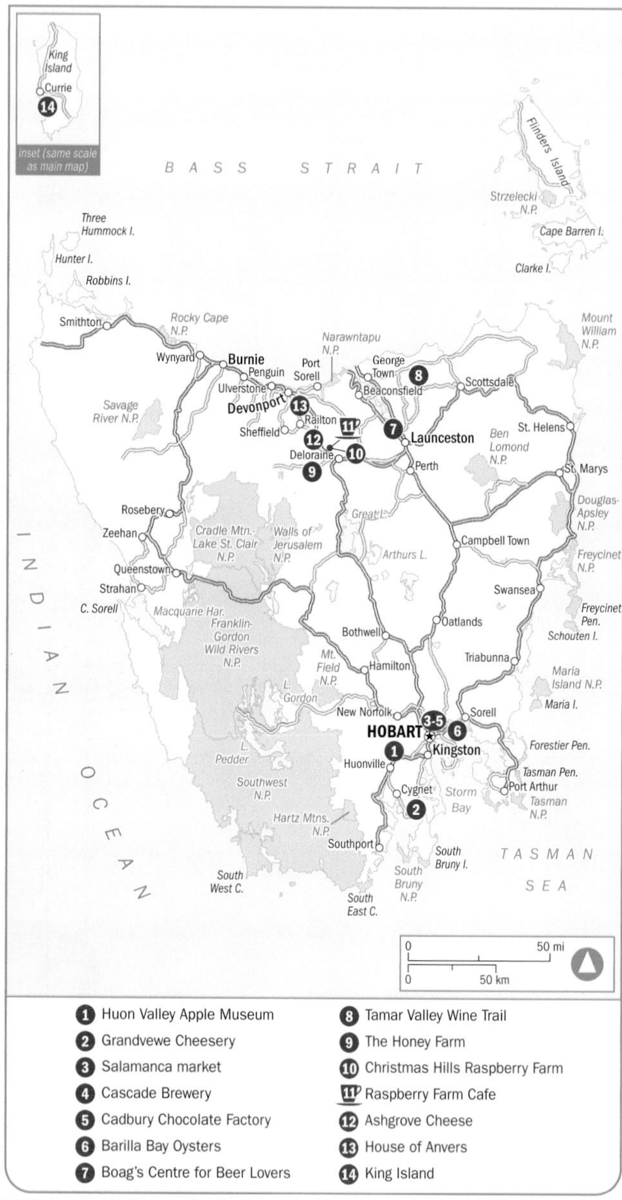
King Island
Currie
inset (same scale as main map)
BASS STRAIT
Flinders Island
Strzelecki N.P.
Cape Barren I.
Clarke I.
Three Hummock I.
Hunter I.
Robbins I.
Smithton
Rocky Cape N.P.
Narawntapu N.P.
Mount William N.P.
Wynyard
Burnie
Penguin
Port Sorell
Ulverstone
Devonport
George Town
Beaconsfield
Scottsdale
Savage River N.P.
Railton
Sheffield
Launceston
Ben Lomond N.P.
St. Helens
Deloraine
Perth
St. Marys
Rosebery
Zeehan
Cradle Mtn.-Lake St. Clair N.P.
Walls of Jerusalem N.P.
Great L.
Arthurs L.
Douglas-Apsley N.P.
Campbell Town
Freycinet N.P.
Queenstown
Strahan
C. Sorell
Macquarie Har.
Franklin-Gordon Wild Rivers N.P.
Swansea
Freycinet Pen.
Schouten I.
Oatlands
Bothwell
Mt. Field N.P.
Hamilton
Triabunna
Maria Island N.P.
Maria I.
L. Gordon
New Norfolk
Sorell
HOBART
Kingston
Forestier Pen.
L. Pedder
Huonville
Tasman Pen.
Port Arthur
Tasman N.P.
Southwest N.P.
Cygnet
Storm Bay
Hartz Mtns. N.P.
Southport
South Bruny I.
South Bruny N.P.
INDIAN OCEAN
TASMAN SEA
South West C.
South East C.
0 50 mi
0 50 km
1 Huon Valley Apple Museum
2 Grandvewe Cheesery
3 Salamanca market
4 Cascade Brewery
5 Cadbury Chocolate Factory
6 Barilla Bay Oysters
7 Boag's Centre for Beer Lovers
8 Tamar Valley Wine Trail
9 The Honey Farm
10 Christmas Hills Raspberry Farm
11 Raspberry Farm Cafe
12 Ashgrove Cheese
13 House of Anvers
14 King Island

Previous page: Wallaby on Cradle Mountain.

Tasmania is a gourmand's paradise where you can indulge almost every culinary passion. Its lush pastures produce excellent cheeses and tender beef. Artisan farmers grow everything from raspberries, saffron, wasabi and truffles. Cool-climate vineyards produce fine wines, the beers are legendary and the oceans teem with seafood. START: **Hobart. Trip Length: 1 week.**

The Old Apple Shed.

1 Huon Valley Apple Museum. The Huon Valley is the fruit bowl of Tasmania; almost all of the state's apples and stone fruits are grown in this region. There are dozens of shed-door stalls where you can buy apples (see the Farm Gate Guide, p 28), but if you really want to learn about the apple industry, and taste a few of the rarer varieties of apples, visit this little museum at **The Old Apple Shed.** *45 min. 2064 Huon Hwy., Grove. 03/6266-4345. www.applemuseum.huonvalley.biz. Adults $5.50, children 15 and under $3. Daily 9am–5pm.*

2 ★★ Grandvewe Cheesery. Tasmania's only organic sheep dairy. Taste (and buy) some of their 15 cheeses, yoghurt and ice cream while admiring the ocean view. If you're here at 4:30pm (daily Sept–Mar), watch the sheep being milked *30 min. 59 Devlyns Rd., Birchs Bay. 03/6267-4099. www.grandvewe.com.au. Free admission. Daily 10am–5pm (4pm in winter).*

3 ★★★ Salamanca market. Don't miss these wonderful Saturday-morning markets in Hobart, with stalls selling handcrafted gourmet goodies (think fresh breads, speciality pies, smoked fish and game). *See p 105.*

4 ★★ Cascade Brewery. Australia's oldest brewery has a museum and three acres of beautiful gardens, but most people just come here for the beer. There are three tours: a 2-hour Brewery tour, 1-hour Heritage tour and a great-value 45-minute Beer and Food matching experience—and all include at least one glass of the amber fluid (this is not a place for the underage). You'll need to wear flat, covered shoes and long trousers (no thongs, sandals, shorts or

Cascade Brewery.

Barilla Bay Oysters.

skirts). 🕘 *45 min–2 hr. 140 Cascade Rd., South Hobart. ☎ 03/6224-1117. www.cascadebreweryco.com.au. Brewery tour: adults $22, seniors and students $17, children (5–17) $11, family $47. Heritage tour: adults $15, children 17 and under $12, family $42. Beer & food matching: $55; bookings essential. Mon–Fri 9:30am–4:30pm, Sat–Sun 9:30am–3:30pm during summer.*

❺ kids **Cadbury Chocolate Factory.** Give in to your chocoholic cravings. 🕘 *1 hr.* *See p 43,* ❶.

❻ ★★★ **Barilla Bay Oysters.** The cold clean Southern Ocean waters produce some of the best-tasting oysters in the world, and if you're an oyster lover, you'll love Barilla Bay. Tour the farm (you'll need to book ahead), browse the shop, which not only sells ready-packed oysters but also a whole range of Tasmanian food products, or gorge on the famous $39 'shucking awesome' platter of 30 oysters in the restaurant (p 132). Forget the old wives' tale of only eating oysters in months with an 'r'; they're good all year round. 🕘 *1 hr. 1388 Tasman Hwy., Cambridge. ☎ 03/6248-5458. www.barillabay.com.au. Free admission; tours: adults $15, children 10–16 $7.50, children 9 and under free. Mon–Fri 9:30am–5:30pm, Sat–Sun 10:30am–4:30pm, 45-min farm tours Thurs & Sun 11am.*

❼ **Boag's Centre for Beer Lovers.** Tasmania's other famous brewery (aside from Cascade, above) is Boag's, which has been brewing on the banks of the Esk River since 1883. There are two tours available (Mon–Fri; the Beer Lovers tour is the best) and an 'Amber Ticket' guided tasting session of seven beers (only on Sat). 🕘 *1–2 hr. 39 William St., Launceston. ☎ 03/6332-6300. www.boags.com.au. Free admission to the museum. Beer lovers tour: adults $28, children (5–17) & seniors $25, family $80. Discovery tour: adults $20, children (5–17) & seniors $18, family $60; bookings essential. Mon–Fri 8:45am–4:30pm, Sat 10am–4pm.*

❽ ★★★ **Tamar Valley Wine Trail.** The trail follows the course of the Tamar River with 30 wineries, all clearly signposted. 🕘 *1–2 days.* *See 'Tamar Valley Wine Route,' p 55 for the full tour.*

Farm Gate Guide

If you want to eat your way around the island, pick up a free copy of the Tasmanian Fruits **Farm Gate Guide** (available at visitor information centres or download from www.fruitgrowerstas.com.au). It details more than 40 farms and growers that welcome visitors or have farm gate market stalls.

Ashgrove Cheese farm.

9 kids The Honey Farm. Tasmania produces gorgeous honey, and you'll often see roadside stalls selling jars of the golden nectar. Leatherwood honey, unique to the island, makes a great gift or souvenir. At the rather touristy Honey Farm you can taste up to 50 varieties as well as test a range of honey products and cosmetics; kids love trying the honey ice cream and watching the bees at work in their honeycomb. *30 min. 39 Sorell St., Chudleigh. 03/6363-6160. www.thehoneyfarm.com.au. Free admission. Sun–Fri 9am–5pm (4pm Apr–Sept).*

10 ★★ Christmas Hills Raspberry Farm. You can buy fresh berries during raspberry season (mid-Dec to mid-May), but it's worth visiting the riverside cafe (see 11) at any time just to pick up a bag of chocolate-dipped raspberries, which are simply divine. *45 min. 9 Christmas Hills Rd., Elizabethtown. 03/6362-2186. www.raspberryfarmcafe.com. Free admission. Daily 7am–5pm.*

11 Raspberry Farm Cafe. There's a full menu of light meals on offer but dessert's the thing—try the raspberry pancakes or splash out on a raspberry cocktail. *9 Christmas Hills Rd., Elizabethtown. 03/6362-2186. www.raspberryfarmcafe.com. $.*

12 ★ Ashgrove Cheese. You can't miss the life-size statues of colourful cows at Ashgrove, painted by local schoolchildren, but don't let them distract you from the cheese. Specialising in hard and semi-hard cheese, there is a staggering range available to taste and buy. Don't leave without trying the wasabi cheese: it's unique. They also sell Tasmanian gourmet goodies, and the ice cream is so good it may make you swoon. *30 min. 6173 Bass Hwy., Elizabethtown. 03/6368-1105. www.ashgrovecheese.com.au. Free admission. Daily 7:30am–5pm (6pm Oct–Apr).*

13 ★★ House of Anvers. You haven't lived until you've had breakfast in a chocolate factory—brioche with choc-hazelnut spread and thick hot chocolate with Aztec chilli and spice is the perfect way to start the day. Watch chocolate being made, indulge in a chocolate platter or buy some to take away. It's better value than the Cadburys visit (p 43, 1). *30 min. 9025 Bass Hwy., Latrobe. 03/6426-2958. www.anvers-chocolate.com.au. Free admission. Daily 7am–7pm.*

14 ★★★ King Island. King Island is famous for soft cheeses (see King Island Fromagerie, p 65, 9) and melt-in-the-mouth beef. Keep an eye out for bottled Cloud Juice (pure delicious rainwater). *For the full tour of King Island, see p 62.*

King Island Fromagerie.

The Convict Trail

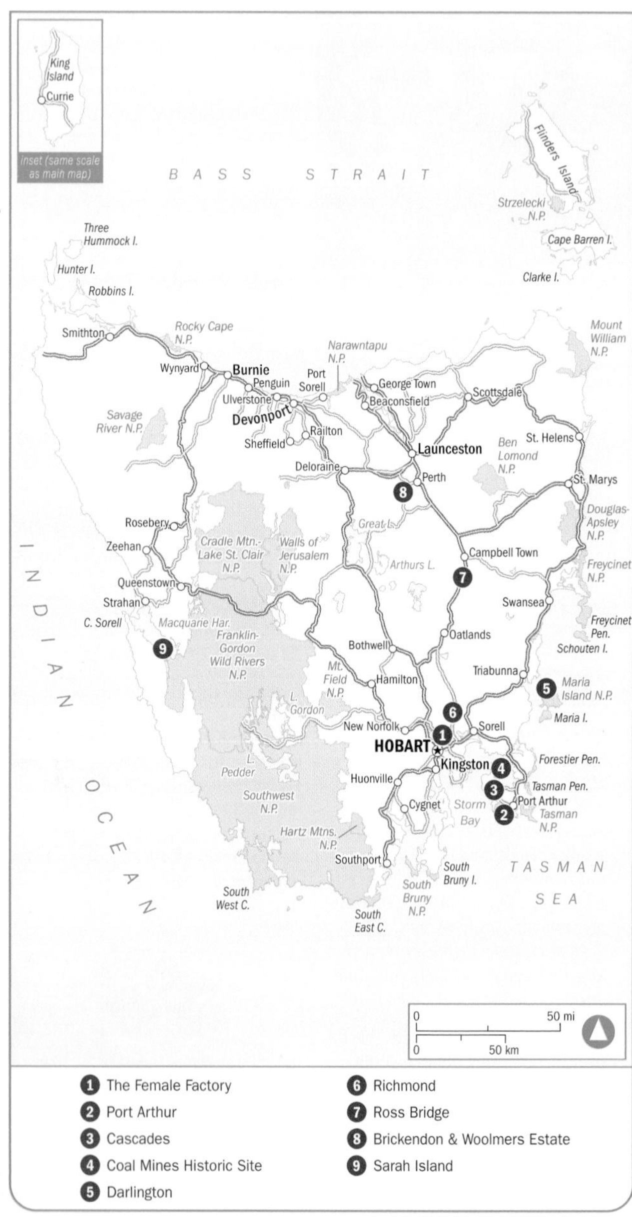

1. The Female Factory
2. Port Arthur
3. Cascades
4. Coal Mines Historic Site
5. Darlington
6. Richmond
7. Ross Bridge
8. Brickendon & Woolmers Estate
9. Sarah Island

In Tasmania, the past is never very far away, particularly its convict past. Of the 11 World Heritage-listed convict sites in Australia, five are in Tasmania: Port Arthur and the Coal Mines Historic Site on the Tasman Peninsula, the Female Factory in Hobart, Darlington Probation Station on Maria Island and Woolmers and Brickendon Estates near Launceston. **START: Hobart.**

1 The Female Factory. More than 5,000 female convicts spent time at the Female Factory between 1828 and 1856, either serving a sentence, waiting to be assigned a workplace or having a baby. But unless you take the 90-minute tour, you won't glean much about its fascinating past as there's not really much left of the original buildings. *90 min. 16 Degraves St., South Hobart. ☎ 03/6233-6656. www.femalefactory.com.au. Tours: adults $15, children 5–17 $5. Mon–Fri 9am–5pm, 90-min tours depart 9:30am & 2pm (9:30am only on Fri). Bookings essential.*

2 ★★★ kids Port Arthur. Established in 1833 as a 'place of terror' for repeat offenders, Port Arthur was Australia's most notorious convict prison (for more on convicts, see box, p 32). Tasmania's biggest tourist attraction covers more than 40 hectares and has 30 of the original buildings and ruins, including fully restored and furnished houses.

Port Arthur Ghost Tour.

Buildings worth seeing include the **Model Prison,** built in 1848, where prisoners were forced to endure solitary confinement, silence and had to exercise with head masks on; the **Isle of the Dead** cemetery tour; and a cruise to **Point**

Ghost Tour of Port Arthur

Led by guides dressed in black and carrying glass lanterns, you learn about the most documented ghost sightings and unexplained happenings in many of the houses and cells. Almost all the guides insist they believe in ghosts and will enthral you with their own on-site encounters with the supernatural. If you didn't believe in ghosts when you arrived, you will by the time you leave. The price for adults is $25, children aged 4 to 17 cost $15. A family of two adults and up to six children can save a minimum of $15 by buying a family ticket for $65.

Coal Mines Historic Site.

Puer, the prison home between 1834 and 1849 to more than 3,000 boys ranging in age from 9 to 18. The **Interpretation Centre** is an interactive museum chronicling the lives of many convicts and is popular with kids.

You can easily spend a day here. There is a range of passes available; the most concise is the Bronze pass, which includes a 40-minute guided walking tour and a 30-minute harbour cruise. One tour not to miss is the night-time **Ghost Tour** (see box above). *1–1½ days. Arthur Hwy., Port Arthur. ☎ 1800/659-101. www.portarthur.org.au. Bronze pass: adults $30, seniors $25, children 4–17 $15, family (2 adults and up to 6 children) $75. For other passes, please visit website. Daily 8:30am–dusk.*

3 ★★ **Cascades.** Spend the night in a former Convict Probation Station, built in 1841. The officer's quarters have been restored into very comfortable self-catering cottages. *See p 154.*

4 ★★ **Coal Mines Historic Site.** Tasmania's first operational mine was developed both to limit the colony's dependence upon imported coal from New South Wales as well as used as a place of punishment for the 'worst class' of convicts from Port Arthur. It provides a very different experience from the more popular Port Arthur site. You can wander freely among the evocative ruins of **Saltwater River Convict Station** with its cramped and gloomy underground cells. Go early in the morning and you'll more than likely have the site to yourself. *90 min. Coal Mine Rd., 20km (12½ miles) off the highway at Taranna via Premaydena. www.portarthur.org.au. Free admission. Daily 24 hr.*

Convicts

Between 1787 and 1868, around 165,000 men, women and children as young as 9 years old were sent to Australia from England and Ireland as convicted felons (many for minor crimes or as political prisoners). Some ended up living and working on farms and grand estates, some endured forced labour in chain gangs, and others reoffended and languished in prisons such as Port Arthur. In 2010 UNESCO accorded World Heritage Status to 11 convict sites in Australia (five in Tasmania: Port Arthur, the Coal Mines Historic Site, Cascades Female Factory, Woolmers and Brickendon Estates, and Darlington Probation Station on Maria Island) because they are 'the best surviving examples of large-scale convict transportation and the colonial expansion of European powers through the presence and labour of convicts'.

5 ★★★ Darlington. Maria Island was established as a penal colony in 1825 and you can wander around the extensive ruins at the convict settlement of Darlington. *See p 109, 1.*

6 ★★ Richmond. In the 1820s, Richmond was one of the colony's most important convict stations and military posts, and most of the convict-built buildings in this well-preserved town predate Port Arthur by a decade or so. Take an hour to admire the sandstone architecture, including the historic churches, the courthouse, gaol and **Richmond Bridge**—the oldest bridge in Australia that is still in use and reputedly haunted. *1 hr. www.richmondvillage.com.au.*

7 Ross Bridge. Another well-preserved 19th-century village, Ross was home to a Female Factory (p 31, 1), although little remains above ground that you can see. A much more enduring legacy of the convict era is Ross Bridge over the Macquarie River. It was built by convicts in 1836—making it the third-oldest bridge still standing in Australia—and features 186 flamboyant carvings of birds, fish, animals, insects, plants and ghoulish faces on its sides, which you can see easily from the river bank. *10 min. Ross Visitor Information Centre, Church St. 03/6381-5466. www.visitross.com.au. Daily 9am–5pm.*

8 ★ Brickendon & ★★★ Woolmers Estate. Whereas the other World Heritage-listed convict sites in Tasmania were primarily places of punishment, these two neighbouring farming estates represent the assignment side of the convict system. Between the two estates, which were owned by two brothers, more than 100 convicts lived and worked, the second-largest pool of convict labour in private hands in the colony. *5 hr. See p 35, 2 & 3.*

9 ★ Sarah Island. This infamously brutal gaol was the first penal colony in Tasmania, established in 1822. It was also the most remote: any convict trying to escape had to swim across Macquarie Harbour and then hack his way through impenetrable forests only to find himself stranded in the middle of wilderness on the unpopulated west coast. It was a place of banishment for the 'worst description of convicts', up until it was closed in 1833 and replaced by Port Arthur (see p 31, 2) in the east. The only way to visit the island and wander around the ruins is on a 6-hour **Gordon River Cruise** to Strahan. *1 day. See p 75, 2 for Gordon River Cruise.*

Convict-built Ross Bridge.

The Heritage Highway

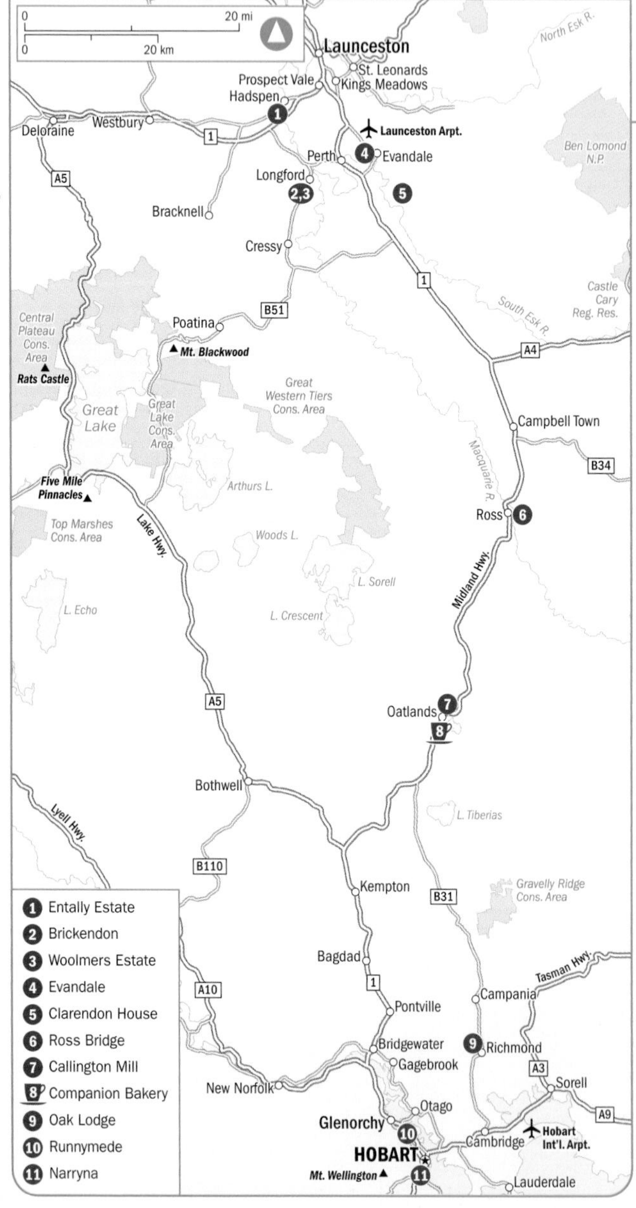

0 20 mi
0 20 km
Launceston
St. Leonards
Kings Meadows
Prospect Vale
Hadspen
Westbury
Deloraine
Launceston Arpt.
Perth
Evandale
Longford
Bracknell
Cressy
Poatina
Mt. Blackwood
Central Plateau Cons. Area
Rats Castle
Great Lake
Great Lake Cons. Area
Great Western Tiers Cons. Area
Five Mile Pinnacles
Arthurs L.
Top Marshes Cons. Area
Lake Hwy.
Woods L.
L. Sorell
L. Crescent
L. Echo
North Esk R.
Ben Lomond N.P.
Castle Cary Reg. Res.
South Esk R.
Campbell Town
Macquarie R.
Ross
Midland Hwy.
Oatlands
Bothwell
L. Tiberias
Lyell Hwy.
Kempton
Gravelly Ridge Cons. Area
Bagdad
Tasman Hwy.
Campania
Pontville
Bridgewater
Gagebrook
Richmond
Sorell
New Norfolk
Otago
Glenorchy
Cambridge
Hobart Int'l. Arpt.
HOBART
Mt. Wellington
Lauderdale
1
A5
B51
A4
B34
B110
B31
A10
A3
A9
1 Entally Estate
2 Brickendon
3 Woolmers Estate
4 Evandale
5 Clarendon House
6 Ross Bridge
7 Callington Mill
8 Companion Bakery
9 Oak Lodge
10 Runnymede
11 Narryna

Journey into the past from Launceston to Hobart on the A1, nicknamed the Heritage Highway. The road takes you back 200 years as you travel through some of the first lands settled in the early days of the colony. Take the time to explore the villages with their quaint Georgian coaching inns, gracious colonial houses and convict-built bridges. **START: Launceston.**

TRAVEL TIP

The best place to spend the night is at Launceston, as all these towns are only a short drive from the city. See p 153 for accommodation recommendations.

❶ ★★ **Entally Estate.** Entally was built in 1819 by Thomas Haydock Reibey, son of Mary Reibey. Thomas was a convict whose image now graces the Australian $20 note. Reibey, a successful merchant, managed to rid himself of the 'convict stain' and positioned himself as a country squire. Entally is a fantastic example of a colonial gentleman's residence. The stunning gardens are more than 150 years old and include the oldest conservatory in Australia, as well as the oldest cricket grounds, which are often in use during summer. *1 hr. Meander Valley Touring Route, Hadspen. ☎ 03/6393-6201. www.entally.com.au. Adults $10, children 6–16 $8. Daily 10am–4pm.*

❷ ★ kids **Brickendon.** Still owned by the descendants of William Archer, who built the farm and convict village in 1824, Brickendon is one of five World Heritage-listed convict sites in Tasmania; at its peak up to 30 assigned convicts lived and worked on the farm. Kids love the farm animals, and the **Farm Village**—with its Gothic chapel, barns, former blacksmith's shop and cottages—shows how self-sufficient early settlers needed to be. Across the road is the Georgian homestead, where the family still lives. The house is not open, but you can wander around the beautiful flower-filled **Estate Gardens** and through all the other buildings on a self-guided tour. *2 hr. Woolmers Lane, Longford. ☎ 03/6391-1251. www.brickendon.com.au. Adults $12, children 6–16 $4.50, family $35. Tues–Sun 9:30am–5pm.*

❸ ★★★ **Woolmers Estate.** Established by Thomas Archer (brother to William at neighbouring Brickendon) in 1817, Woolmers is also World Heritage-listed, and is one of the best-preserved colonial gentry houses in Australia. All the furniture is original and most dates from the

Farm Village at Brickendon.

Woolmers Estate.

1850s. The 45-minute **Guided Homestead tour** is the only way you can see inside the house and is a must-do. You can wander around the gardens and through the outdoor farm buildings on your own—don't miss the vintage cars in the imposing mansion-like sandstone stables. Also here is the **National Rose Garden**—visit in spring (Sept–Oct), when the perfume from the 6,000 blooms is intoxicating. ◷ *3 hr. 658 Woolmers Lane, Longford.* ☎ *03/6391-2230. www.woolmers.com.au. Adults $20, children 6–16 $7. Daily 10am–4:30pm; tours 11am, 12:30, 2 & 3:30pm (& 10am in summer).*

4 Evandale. The entire village of Evandale is classified by the National Trust, and almost all of the buildings date back to the 1820s, making it one of the most well-preserved Georgian villages in the country. Today, most have been converted into B&Bs or house antiques shops, galleries and bakeries, although many are private houses. One of Australia's most unusual carnivals, the **National Penny Farthing Championships** (www.evandalevillagefair.com), is held here every February. ◷ *45 min. Evandale Visitor Information Centre, 18 High St.* ☎ *02/6391-8128. www.evandaletasmania.com. Daily 9am–5pm.*

5 ★★★ Clarendon House. Built in 1838 for James Cox, wealthy woolgrower and merchant and son of William Cox who pioneered the first road over the Blue Mountains in New South Wales, Clarendon was the grandest house in the colony when it was built and is one of the grandest Georgian houses still standing in Australia. You can take a self-guided tour of the fully furnished house and stroll around the extensive gardens. The cafe serves reasonable coffee and sandwiches. ◷ *1 hr. 234 Clarendon Station Rd., Evandale.* ☎ *03/6398-6220. Adults $10, children 17 and under free. Daily 10am–4pm (by appointment July & Aug).*

6 Ross Bridge. The ornately carved convict-built bridge over the Macquarie River is the most famous attraction in the 19th-century village of Ross. ◷ *10 min.* *See p 33,* **7**.

7 ★ Callington Mill. Oatlands has one of the largest collections of sandstone buildings in Australia, and it's worth taking the time to explore the village, but its pride and joy is Callington Mill. Built in 1837, it's not just the third-oldest windmill in Australia but also, since being restored in 2010, the only authentic mill of its kind in the Southern Hemisphere that is still working and, if

Evandale.

Callington Mill at Oatlands.

you're lucky, you might see the mill in action. *45 min. 1 Mill Lane, Oatlands. 03/6254-1212. www.callingtonmill.com.au. Free admission. Daily 9am–5pm.*

8 You can buy the sourdough bread made from the flour ground at the mill, as well as grab a lunch of sandwiches, pies or pastries from the **Companion Bakery** opposite the mill for less than $10. *106 High St., Oatlands. 03/6254-0088. www.companionbakery.com.au. 10am–5pm Wed–Sat, 10am–4pm Sun. $.*

9 ★★ **Oak Lodge.** Like Ross and Evandale, the everyday village of Richmond (p 33, 6) is home to dozens of original buildings, most dating from the 1820s. It's worth taking a peek inside Oak Lodge to see how the town-based gentry used to live. The private home is now a museum. *30 min. 18 Bridge St., Richmond. 03/6260-4153. Admission by gold coin donation. Daily 11:30am–3:30pm.*

10 **Runnymede.** Hobart was once a whaling town, and the colonial house of Runnymede was the home of a whaling family for more than a century. It's full of material related to the whaling and maritime interests of the family as well as artworks and family possessions of the previous owner, Bishop Francis Nixon, Tasmania's first Anglican Bishop. *30 min. 61 Bay Rd., New Town, Hobart. 03/6278-1269. Adults $10, children 17 and under free. Fri 10am–4:30pm, Sun noon–4:30pm (closed July & Aug).*

11 ★★ **Narryna.** One of Hobart's earliest colonial abodes Narryna, built in 1836, shows what domestic life was like for a wealthy merchant. It's home to one of the most comprehensive collections of 19th-century items in Tasmania, including some exquisite dresses and costumes. Battery Point was once an area of ill-repute full of brothels, convicts, roaming bushrangers, drunken sailors and all sorts of rascals; in the downstairs rooms, keep an eye out for the trapdoors, which were reputedly to aid a quick escape, although there's no record of them ever being used. *30 min. 103 Hampden Rd., Battery Point, Hobart. 03/6234-2791. www.narryna.com.au. Adults $6, children 3–15 $3. Mon–Fri 10:30am–5pm, Sat–Sun 12:30–5pm. Closed July.*

Bedroom at Narryna.

Wildlife Safari

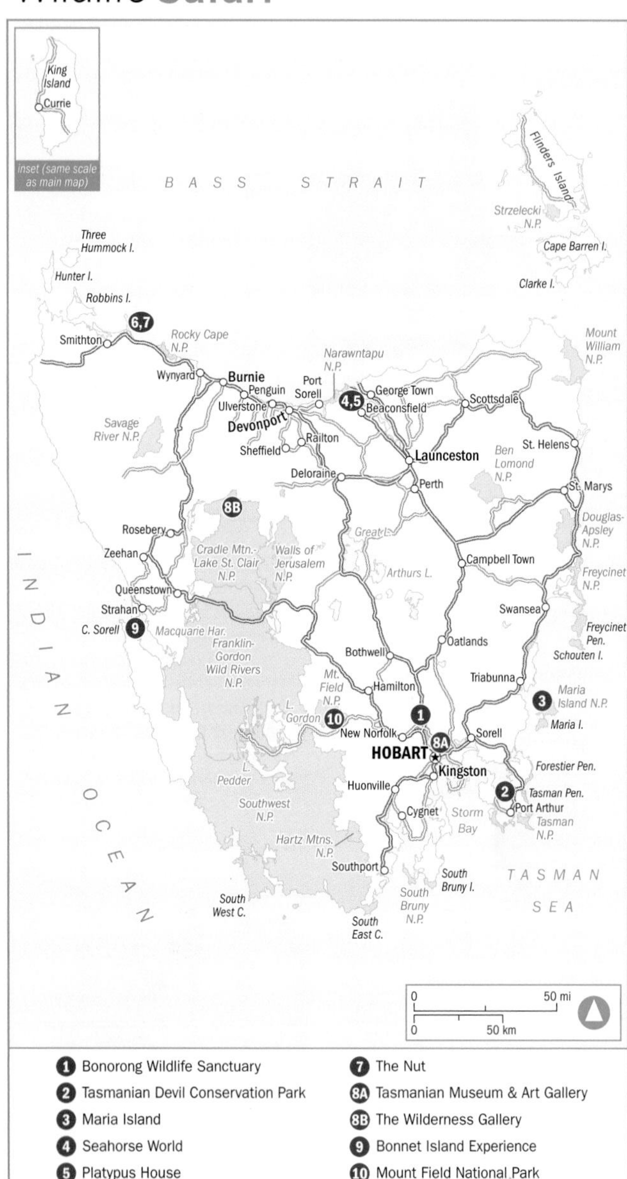

1 Bonorong Wildlife Sanctuary
2 Tasmanian Devil Conservation Park
3 Maria Island
4 Seahorse World
5 Platypus House
6 Stanley Seal Cruises
7 The Nut
8A Tasmanian Museum & Art Gallery
8B The Wilderness Gallery
9 Bonnet Island Experience
10 Mount Field National Park

If you want to see Australian animals in the wild, you've come to the right place. With so much of the state covered in World Heritage wilderness and a lack of introduced predators such as foxes, wildlife is prolific. From wallabies and wombats to penguins and Tasmanian devils, there's a good chance you'll come across them. Tasmanian Tigers, however, are harder to find. **START: Hobart.**

1 kids Bonorong Wildlife Sanctuary. Bonorong helps care for and rehabilitate injured and orphaned wildlife and is an ideal place to get up close and personal with a range of native animals. *2½ hr. See p 43, 2.*

2 ★★★ kids Tasmanian Devil Conservation Park. A few years ago, the night-time screams of Tasmanian devils were enough to make even the most hardened camper nervous, but sadly a contagious facial cancer disease has wiped out more than half the population. No one knows yet what causes the fatal cancer, but there has been some success breeding the meat-eating marsupials in disease-free areas. *1–2 hr. See p 43, 4.*

3 ★★★ Maria Island. Maria Island is home to an astounding array of wildlife as it has no permanent human residents. You are guaranteed to see plenty of birdlife, including the endangered **forty-spotted pardalote** (one of the smallest and rarest birds in Australia; it is thought that half of the world's breeding pairs call the island home). Amazing **muttonbirds** (known in other parts of the world as short-tailed shearwaters) build their summer nests here before flying 15,000km (932 miles) across the Pacific Ocean to the Arctic each year. You'll see colonies of **little penguins** at Fossil Cliffs and Haunted Bay, and you'll come across the comical ground-dwelling **Cape Barren geese** (the world's second-rarest goose) everywhere. Beside birds, you'll also see plenty of **pademelons, wombats, wallabies** (especially near French's Farm) and all sorts of reptiles. *For the full tour, see Maria Island p 108.*

4 kids Seahorse World. Did you know that it is the male seahorse who gets pregnant and gives

Tasmanian Devil.

Cape Barren Goose.

birth to live babies, that they eat sea monkeys, just like those you looked at in comic books as a child, and that, according to Asian herbal apothecaries, dried and ground seahorse is a great aphrodisiac? Learn everything you never knew you needed to know about the native pot-bellied seahorse, weedy sea dragons and pipefish at this commercial seahorse farm. *1 hr. Inspection Head Wharf, Beauty Point. 03/6383-4111. www.seahorseworld.com.au. Adults $20, children 4–16 $9, family (2 adults & all kids) $50. Guided tours daily 9:30am–3:30pm Sept–Apr, 10am–3pm May–Aug.*

5 kids **Platypus House.** One of Australia's strangest creatures, the platypus, with its sleek otter-ish body, webbed feet and duck-like bill, is notoriously hard to spot in the wild. But at Platypus House you can get a good close look through the glass of the indoor ponds, and learn through film all about how this extraordinary monotreme (and its cousin, the **echidna**) eats, lives and breeds. *1 hr. Inspection Head Wharf, Beauty Point. 03/6383-4884. www.platypushouse.com.au. Adults $20, children 4–16 $9, family (2 adults & up to 3 children) $49. Daily 9:30am–3:30pm.*

6 ★★ **Stanley Seal Cruises.** Climb aboard the *Sylvia C* and cruise out to a colony of around 600 **Australian fur seals** that 'haul out' at a tiny speck of an island called **Bull Rock,** some 600m (1,969 ft.) offshore from Stanley. Watch hundreds of seals frolic, bask and bellow in the sunshine, but be warned: you'll need to breathe through your mouth to avoid the overpowering stench of too many seals in a very small space. *75 min. Fisherman's Dock, Stanley. 0419/550-134. www.stanleysealcruises.com.au. Adults $49, children 5–15 $17, children 4 and under $5, family $130. Daily 10am May–Sept, 10am & 3pm Oct–Apr. No cruises during Aug.*

7 **The Nut.** Ten thousand **muttonbirds (short-tailed shearwaters)** nest on The Nut, a 152m (500-ft.) high flat-topped circular headland at Stanley, and when they all take off to go out to sea at once, it's an amazing sight. The best time

Seals basking.

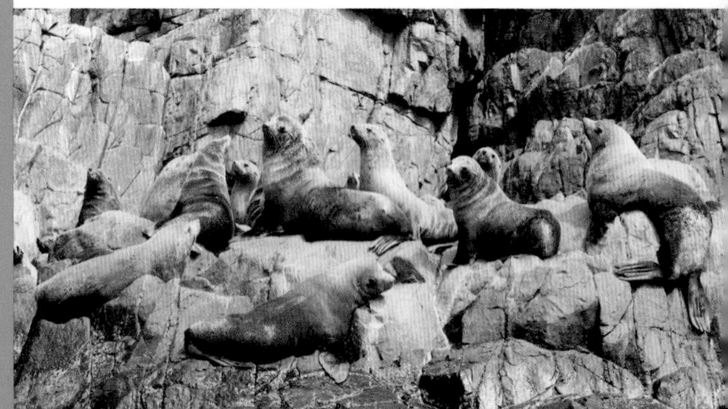

Penguins.

to see them is between September and April, but be careful where you walk: their nests are just holes in the ground. 1 hr. *See p 60,* ⑩ *for details on how to get to The Nut.*

❽ **Tasmanian Tigers.** Tasmania's most famous native animal was the thylacine, or Tasmanian tiger, a large striped dog hunted to extinction by the early European settlers. The last-known thylacine died in Hobart zoo in 1936. However, that doesn't mean there haven't been plenty of weird and outrageous sightings reported in the years since, although whether that's been after staring too long at the twin tigers on the Cascade beer label is hard to tell. Your best chance of seeing them today is at the 8A **Tasmanian Museum & Art Gallery** (p 79, ❷), where there is a stuffed one. 8B **The Wilderness Gallery** (p 71, ❹) at Cradle Mountain also has an excellent permanent exhibition on the thylacine, where you can watch recorded footage of the last known tiger and listen to the stories of old trappers in a recreated trappers hut. *1–2 hr in each.*

❾ **Bonnet Island Experience.** Sometimes called a fairy penguin, the **little penguin** is the smallest of all penguins, although that doesn't seem to stop it scaling great heights each and every night after it returns to its burrow from a day spent fishing at sea. It's estimated there are around 110,000 to 190,000 breeding pairs found along the Tasmanian coastline, including along the River Derwent, at Bicheno, on the Bruny Island Neck and the Bass Strait coast, including the area around George Town, Penguin (no prizes for guessing why the town got its name), and Stanley.

You'll find evening tours that take you out to nesting grounds at most of those places, but the best tour is the Bonnet Island Experience near Strahan, which combines local history with penguin watching and great food. *2½ hr. See p 76,* ❹.

❿ **Mount Field National Park.** A pademelon is a small, slightly chubby wallaby. They're found throughout Australia, but you'll find them in the largest numbers in Tasmania. The **red-bellied,** or **Tasmanian, pademelon** is native to the island. If you want to see them in the wild, you're almost guaranteed to come across them in Mount Field National Park, particularly on the short walk to Russell Falls (p 14, ❻). *25 min. See p 114,* ❸.

Pademelon with joey in pouch.

Tasmania **with Kids**

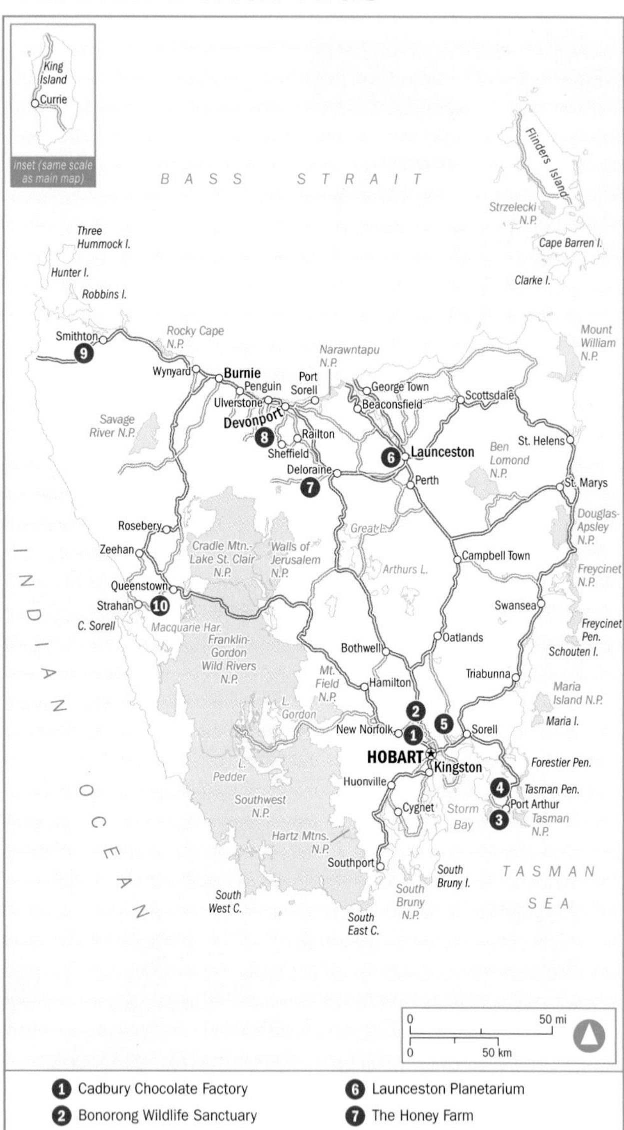

1 Cadbury Chocolate Factory
2 Bonorong Wildlife Sanctuary
3 Port Arthur
4 Tasmanian Devil Conservation Park
5 Old Hobart Town
6 Launceston Planetarium
7 The Honey Farm
8 Tasmazia
9 Tarkine Forest Adventures
10 West Coast Wilderness Railway

Kids seldom get bored in Tassie. Nowhere is very far away from anywhere else, and there's always something fun or interesting along the way. From chocolate factories, confounding mazes and miniature villages to slippery slides, steam train rides and slightly scary ghost tours, there's plenty in Tasmania to keep kids of all ages entertained and enthralled. START: **Hobart.**

1 kids Cadbury Chocolate Factory. You don't have to be a kid to get excited about visiting one of the country's most famous chocolate factories: chocoholics of all ages have been known to get carried away at the visitor centre. Sadly, you can no longer tour the factory to watch chocolate being made, but you can still learn all about it, taste lots of samples and buy up big at the shop. *1 hr. 100 Cadbury Rd., Claremont. 1800/ 627-367. www.cadbury.com.au. Adults $7.50, children under 15 $4, family $17.50. Mon–Fri 8am–4pm (9am–3pm June–Aug).*

2 kids Bonorong Wildlife Sanctuary. Much of Tasmania's wildlife is nocturnal, which means driving at dawn, dusk and night-time can be a dangerous activity. Unfortunately, many animals end up as roadkill. This animal park began as a sanctuary for injured and orphaned wildlife, and the focus is still very much on conservation and rehabilitation. It's not a zoo, so you'll only find local native animals here, but there are always plenty of wallabies, echidnas and Tasmanian devils—the park has been successfully breeding them for more than 20 years. There are three behind-the-scenes tours and kids love the 2½-hour feeding frenzy tour, where they can hand feed the animals. *2½ hr. 593 Briggs Rd., Brighton. 03/6268-1184. www.bonorong.com.au. Adults $22, children 4–15 $9, family $57; behind-the-scenes tours: adults $149–$249, children 3–15 $49–$74. Daily 8am–5pm (9am–3pm June–Aug). 45-min tours 11:30am & 2pm; night tours also available.*

Enjoying chocolate.

3 ★★★ kids Port Arthur. A gaol notorious for its cruelty might seem like a weird place to take kids, but they love it. There are lots of kids activities scheduled in school holidays and older kids get a kick out of the nightly ghost tours. Ask about the free Port Arthur Journey Activity Book when you buy your tickets. *½–1 day.* *See p 31, 2.*

4 ★★★ kids Tasmanian Devil Conservation Park. If you think your kids are devils at feeding time, wait until you see the real things tear a wallaby limb from limb in a feeding frenzy (staff collect roadkill for the animal's supper). A warning: young kids may find feeding time disturbing. This conservation park is the best place to see Tasmanian devils (see box, p 23) and is working hard at creating a disease-free habitat for

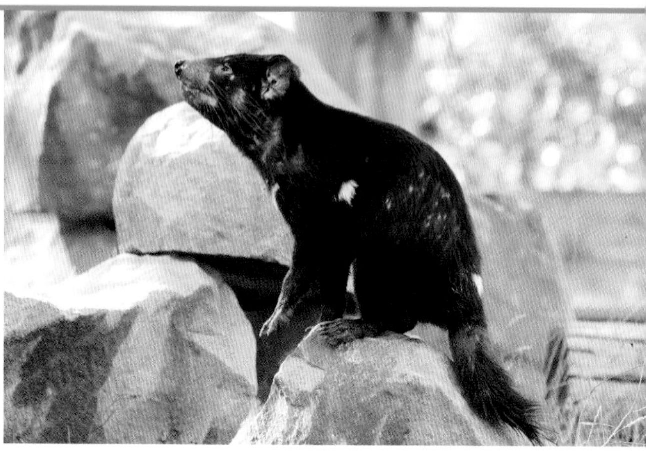

Tasmanian Devil.

the endangered marsupials; the wild population has been decimated in recent years by a mysterious facial cancer. Learn all about their plight and the animals themselves at this excellent centre, which has feeding times on the hour, as well as quoll and kangaroo feeding and falcon free-flight displays. All admission fees help fund much-needed research and you can re-enter the park as many times as you want in 24 hours. *1–2 hr. 5990 Port Arthur Hwy., Taranna. ☎ 03/6250-3230. www.tasmaniandevilpark.com. Adults $32, children 4–16 $17, family (2 adults & up to 4 children) $79. Daily 9am–5pm (later in summer).*

5 kids Old Hobart Town. Little kids will get a kick out of playing Gulliver at this miniature version of Hobart as it was in the 1820s. The scaled-down replica was designed and built from historical plans, and there are free 'treasure hunt' type activities for kids. *45 min. 21A Bridge St., Richmond. ☎ 03/6260-2502. www.oldhobarttown.com. Adults $14, children 4–18 $3.50, under 4s free, family $30–$35. Daily 9am–5pm.*

6 kids Launceston Planetarium. If your kids are fascinated with space, then take them to the Planetarium, part of the Queen Victoria Museum and Art Gallery (p 52, 5). There are two shows: the **Origins of Life** looks at the formation and development of life on Earth, while **What Happened to Pluto** tells the story of the discovery of Pluto and why it was famously demoted from planetary status in 2006. Both shows are 25 minutes long and are followed by a live description of the current night sky. *1 hr. 2 Invermay Rd., Launceston. ☎ 03/6323-3777. www.qvmag.tas.gov.au. Adults $5, children 5–16 $3 (not suitable for children under 5), family $13. Shows Tues–Fri 2 & 4pm, Sat 2 & 3pm.*

7 kids The Honey Farm. Learn how honey is made and watch the busy bees at work in the honeycomb and hives before indulging in a honey ice cream treat. *See p 29, 9.*

8 kids Tasmazia. If you need to steal some time out for yourself, you can set the kids loose here; they love getting lost in this complex of eight mazes, four of which are traditional hedge mazes. The **Great Maze** is reputedly the world's largest botanical maze. Tasmazia is also home to the **Village of Lower Crackpot,** a weird and whimsical miniature village. There is also a **lavender farm** on site. *1–2 hr. 500 Staverton Rd., Promised Land. ☎ 03/6491-1934. www.tasmazia.com.au. Adults $17.50, children 4–15 $10. Daily, 10am–5pm Dec–Apr, 10am–4pm other months.*

Tarkine Forest Adventures Slide.

9 ★★★ kids Tarkine Forest Adventures. A rather magical place that doesn't deserve its harsh name, **Dismal Swamp** is a giant sinkhole filled with ancient blackwood and other forest trees. Owned and operated by Forestry Tasmania, Tarkine Forest Adventures at Dismal Swamp is a strange mix of theme park, art gallery and nature park that somehow manages to meld together. From the top, you can follow the walkway, take the buggy, or slip down a curvy 110m (330-ft.) slide to the swamp floor 40m (130 ft.) below (that's the theme park bit). At the bottom, four meandering boardwalks make it easy to check out life in a swamp without getting your feet wet (the nature side). Local artists display artwork and extraordinary sculptures throughout the site, and it's all a bit *Alice in Wonderland*-ish as you wander through the forest to stumble across trees with eyes, pop-up crayfish and alien-looking swamp creatures. They also serve coffee at the visitor centre. *2 hr. Bass Hwy., 30-min drive northwest of Smithton. ☎ 03/6456-7138. www.adventureforests.com.au. Adults $20, children 4–12 $10, family $50. Daily, 9am–5pm Sept–Nov, 10am–8pm Dec–Feb; 10am–4pm Mar–Aug.*

10 kids West Coast Wilderness Railway. The full-day steam train ride through the rainforest from Strahan to Queenstown (and vice versa) is popular with kids of all ages. *See p 77,* 7.

West Coast Wilderness Railway.

Tasmania on Two Wheels

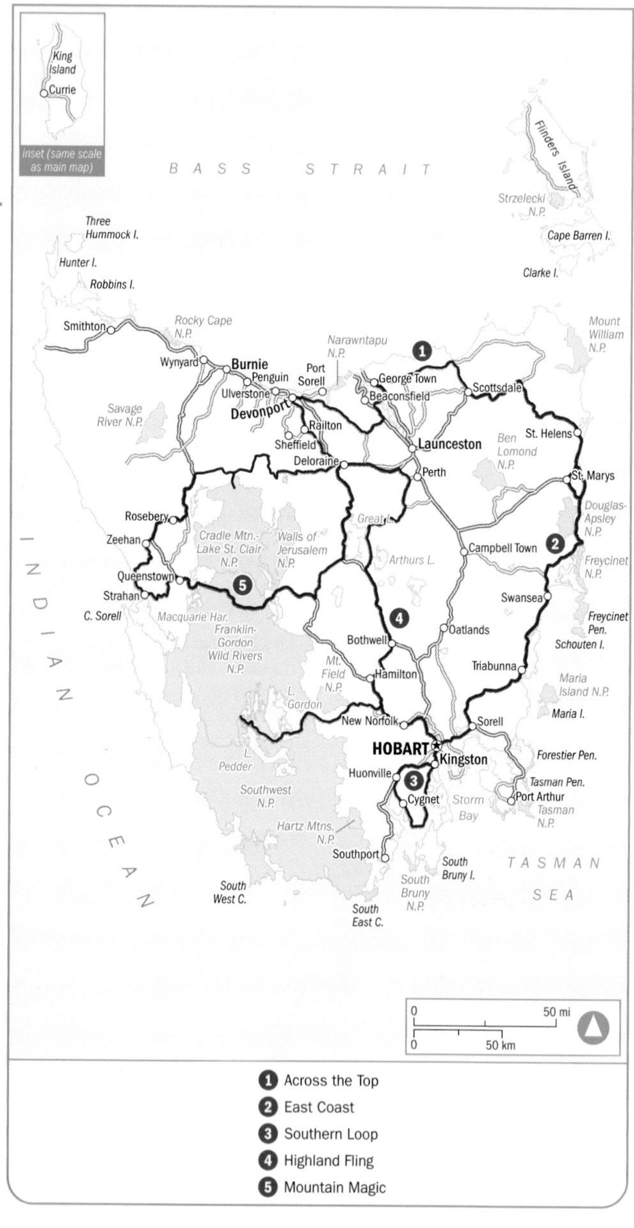

1 Across the Top
2 East Coast
3 Southern Loop
4 Highland Fling
5 Mountain Magic

If your ideal tour is all about the road and the ride, you'll love riding around Tassie. Corners outnumber straights by 20 to one. Distances are short, so there are no long sections between the good bits of road, and there's hardly any traffic compared to what you're probably used to. Do any of these tours as a 1-day ride, or together for 6 days of moto magic. START: **Devonport.**

Tour Tasmania on a motorbike.

❶ **Across the Top.** From Devonport head east on the B71, a lovely winding trip across rolling hills and not much traffic, to **Exeter** on the Tamar River. Cross the Tamar at **Sidmouth** and take the top road (the B82) across the eastern half of the island. Have a break at **Bridport,** then head south to Scottsdale and take the A3 **Tasman Highway,** a fantastic ride that winds through the mountains to reach the coast. Good stops along the way include the **Pyengana Cheese Factory** (p 58) and **St. Columba Falls** (p 58, ❸), before you arrive at the coastal town of **St. Helens** (p 88, ❿). ⏲ *1 day. Distance 270km (170 miles).*

❷ ★★★ **East Coast.** From St. Helens head south on the A3. The road splits 8km (5 miles) south of Scamander and you need to make a choice: either head inland to **St. Marys** via the tight, twisty **Elephant Pass** through the rainforest or take the quieter **coast road** (it has hardly any traffic because they are all stuck behind the caravans inching their way along the Elephant

Getting Your Motorbike There

If you're worried about bringing your bike across the seas on the ferry, don't be. On the *Spirit of Tasmania*, all the motorbikes are parked together and securely lashed to the deck by the crew. ***Tip:*** the bikes go on first when boarding, so wriggle your way through to the front of the queue.

Be careful when cornering.

Pass). It's a hard choice—they are both great rides, although if you really want to do the pass get up early before the grey nomads are on the road. Back on the A3 (Tasman Hwy.) head towards Bicheno and spend half an hour or so admiring the vintage metal on show at the **Bicheno Motorcycle Museum** (35 Burgess St. ☎ 03/6375-1485. $9. Daily 9am–5pm). Take a detour to **Coles Bay** on the Freycinet Peninsula (p 19, ⓾), then enjoy the nice winding stretch between Orford and Runnymede and pull up stumps in **Hobart** (p 13). 🕘 *1 day. Distance 310km (190 miles).*

❸ **Southern Loop.** Spend a day exploring the bucolic **Huon Valley,** tracing the river and coast past apple orchards and through pretty valleys—take the A6 out of Hobart through **Margate, Woodbridge, Cygnet,** and **Huonville.** 🕘 *1 day. Distance 132km (82 miles).*

❹ ★★★ **Highland Fling.** This is a long riding day, but one you won't forget, as you travel through some of the most splendid mountain and lakeside scenery that Tassie has to offer—it's one tour not to miss. Take the A10 from Hobart through the very pretty **Derwent River Valley** and the B61 out of **Strathgordon** through the heart of the southwest wilderness. Retrace your steps through to **Westaway,** rejoin the A10 then the B10 connecting road to **Bothwell** and head up the Lake Highway past the Great Western Tiers. Take the B51 to **Longford** and follow the Bass Highway to **Deloraine.** 🕘 *1 day. Distance 480km (298 miles).*

❺ ★★★ **Mountain Magic.** Saving the very best for last, this ride takes you deep into the mountains and you'll get one magnificent view after another as the road unfurls and you tilt the horizon again and again. It's a 2-day trip you'll do purely for the riding pleasure, and while you could cover the 580km (360 miles) in one very long and exhausting day, you'd be missing out on the chance to see some of Tassie's best spots, like Strahan (p 75), along the way. From Deloraine head west on the B12 through **Mole Creek** to **Cradle Mountain** (p 72, ❺) then continue west to hook up with the A10 (Murchison Hwy.) and point the bike south. Stretch your legs at **Zeehan** and spend a night (or two) at **Strahan.** The Waterfront Executive apartments at Strahan Village have undercover parking for your bike—(it rains a lot on the west coast). Head east to **Queenstown,** up over the hills and into the Franklin-Gordon Wilderness and past **Lake St. Clair.** Turn left at the B11 junction to Miena and **Great Lake.** The road is dirty, so take it slow until you reach the bitumen south of Deloraine. From here, it's an easy run north to Devonport. 🕘 *2 days. Distance 580km (360 miles).* ●

4 The Best Regional & Town Tours

Launceston

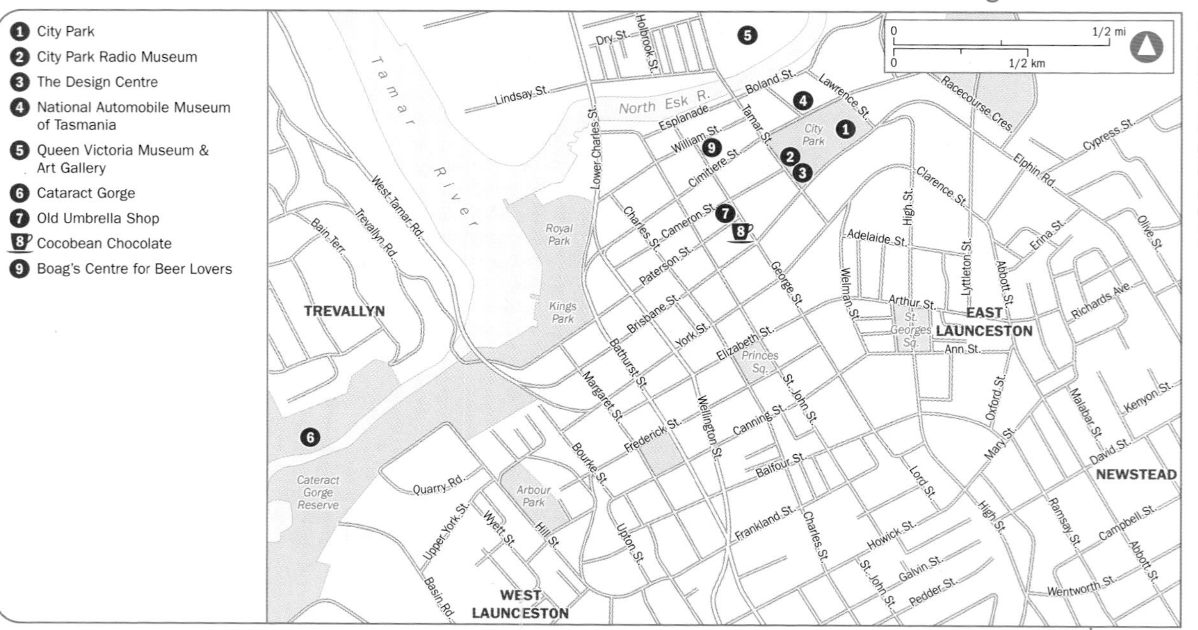

1. City Park
2. City Park Radio Museum
3. The Design Centre
4. National Automobile Museum of Tasmania
5. Queen Victoria Museum & Art Gallery
6. Cataract Gorge
7. Old Umbrella Shop
8. Cocobean Chocolate
9. Boag's Centre for Beer Lovers

Previous page: Mount Wellington and Hobart.

Tasmania's second-largest city is full of surprises. Its mix of Victorian and Georgian architecture and abundance of riverside parks and gardens make it one of the country's prettiest cities. With old towns and world-class wineries on its doorstep, it's a good place to use as a base from which to explore the north. **START: City Park.**

1 ★★ kids City Park. Start your exploration at City Park, the largest and most impressive of Launceston's many beautiful gardens. Originally called the 'People's Park', it was developed in the 1820s by Australia's first horticultural society. You can saunter through Victorian gardens and a beautiful conservatory full of exotic hothouse plants, watch the troop of Japanese macaques at Monkey Island or play on a giant chessboard. On summer Sunday afternoons, relax and listen to a free band performance at the bandstand. *1 hr. Entrances on Tamar St. or corner of Cimitiere St. & Lawrence St. Free admission. Monkey enclosure: daily 8am–4:30pm Oct–Mar (4pm Apr–Sept). Conservatory: daily 9am–5:30pm Oct–Mar, 8:30am–4:30pm Apr–Sept.*

2 City Park Radio Museum. For a nostalgic look at what 'wireless' used to mean before the Internet took over our lives, head to this cute little radio museum at the front entrance of City Park. There are more than 50 antique radios in the collection, housed in the original park caretaker's cottage, and if you ask nicely, they'll even show you around the working community radio studio during broadcasting. *20 min. City Park, Tamar St. ☎ 03/6334-3344. www.cityparkradio.com. Entry by donation. Mon–Sat 9am–2pm.*

3 ★★★ The Design Centre. Australia's only museum collection of contemporary wood design, this gallery-cum-showroom at the entrance to City Park showcases the best of Tasmanian timber design and craftsmanship with changing exhibitions of everything from furniture to sculpture. Pick up a high-quality, original souvenir from the well-stocked shop selling Tasmanian-made art and furniture. *30 min. City Park, corner of Brisbane St. & Tamar St. ☎ 03/6331-5505. www.designcentre.com.au. Free admission. Mon–Fri 9:30am–5:30pm, Sat–Sun 10am–2pm.*

City Park, Launceston.

4 ★ **National Automobile Museum of Tasmania.** A must for car enthusiasts with more than $8 million of motoring metal on show—a terrific collection of vintage, veteran, British and European sports classics. Covering motor cars and motorcycles from the early 1900s through to the 1990s, the display includes more than 50 exhibits. All vehicles are privately owned, which means the collection changes regularly as soon as new exhibits become available. Each season has a different theme, from muscle car legends to motor-racing greats. Along with the beautifully restored cars and motorcycles, the museum features historical displays and a gift shop with a wide range of memorabilia. *1 hr. 86 Cimitiere St. ☎ 03/6334-8889. www.namt.com.au. Adults $11.75, children 15 and under $6.50. Daily 9am–5pm Sept–May, 10am–4pm June–Aug.*

5 ★★★ kids **Queen Victoria Museum and Art Gallery.** Across the river is the **Inveresk Cultural Precinct,** where you'll find the Queen Victoria Museum and Art Gallery (QVMAG), the largest museum and art gallery in Australia located outside a capital city. The museum has two sites: the original purpose-built building in Royal Park and the Inveresk site, formerly the Launceston Railway Workshops. These once-derelict railway workshops have been transformed into an innovative industrial museum. Highlights include the Phenomena Factory (a new interactive science centre that's a hit with kids), blacksmith's shop, railways and migration exhibitions and the **Launceston planetarium** (p 44, 6). The museum's sister site at **Royal Park** houses a dedicated art gallery with Australian colonial art and contemporary craft and design from around the world, as well as a Chinese temple from the 1880s. It's linked to the cultural precinct at Inveresk by a riverside walkway. *3 hr. Inveresk: 2 Invermay Rd.; Royal Park: 2 Wellington St. ☎ 03/6323-3777. www.qvmag.tas.gov.au. Free admission. Daily 10am–5pm.*

6 ★★★ **Cataract Gorge.** No visit to Launceston is complete without spending 2 or 3 hours at the city's favourite playground. Cataract Gorge, a 15-minute walk from the city centre, is a piece of tamed wilderness in the heart of the city. The spectacular gorge extends from the mouth of the South Esk River at King's Bridge and winds its way up the river to the Duck Reach Power Station 5km (3 miles) upstream, around a 45-minute walk. The reserve is popular with walkers, river rafters and rock climbers. The **chairlift** crossing the gorge is the longest single-span one in the world. There is a restaurant, The Gorge Restaurant (p 135), in the grounds, a cafe and kiosk near the main chairlift, and on the southern side of the basin is a 50m (164-ft.) swimming pool, which includes a full-length wading pool for young children. *2–3 hr.*

Queen Victoria Museum & Art Gallery.

Cataract Gorge.

☎ 03/6331-5915. www.launcestoncataractgorge.com.au. Chairlift operates daily 9am–5:30/6pm Dec–Feb, 9am–5pm Mar–May & Sept–Nov, 9am–4:30pm June–Aug; adults $12 one-way, $15 return, children 15 and under $8 one-way, $10 return.

7 Old Umbrella Shop. This quaint shop, listed by the National Trust, was opened in 1860. You can find umbrellas of all types and ages, as well as plenty of tourist trinkets. Step back in time to see what a shop was like 100 years ago. *5 min. 60 George St., Launceston. ☎ 03/6331-9248. www.nationaltrust.org.au. Free admission. Mon–Fri 9am–5pm, Sat 9am–noon.*

8 Cocobean Chocolate. Coffee and chocolate—who needs anything more? Drop into this chocolate cafe for handmade chocolates, a bowl of something sweet, like chocolate mousse or a selection of ice creams, or a cup of hot chocolatey goodness to warm you up. *82 George St. ☎ 03/6331-7016. www.cocobeanchocolate.com.au. Closed Sun. $.*

9 Boag's Centre for Beer Lovers. Launceston's favourite amber fluid has been brewed on site beside the Esk River since the 1880s. Call in for a cleansing ale or take a tour. *1–2 hr.* *See p 28, 7.*

Launceston–Further Afield

Launceston is an ideal base for touring the north of Tasmania. From here, you can visit the **Tamar Valley** (p 54), head to **Hollybank Treetops Adventure** (p 121, 4), **Evandale** and **Clarendon House** (p 36, 5), or visit two of Tasmania's World Heritage-listed convict sites at Longford: **Brickendon** (p 35, 2) and **Woolmers Estate** (p 35, 3).

For more information on Launceston and the surrounding area, visit **Launceston Visitor Information Centre,** Cornwall Square Transit Centre, 12–16 St. John Street, Launceston. ☎ **1800 651 827.** www.visitlauncestontamar.com.au. It's open Monday to Friday 9am–5pm, Saturday 9am–3pm, Sunday and Public Holidays 9am–3pm.

Tamar Valley

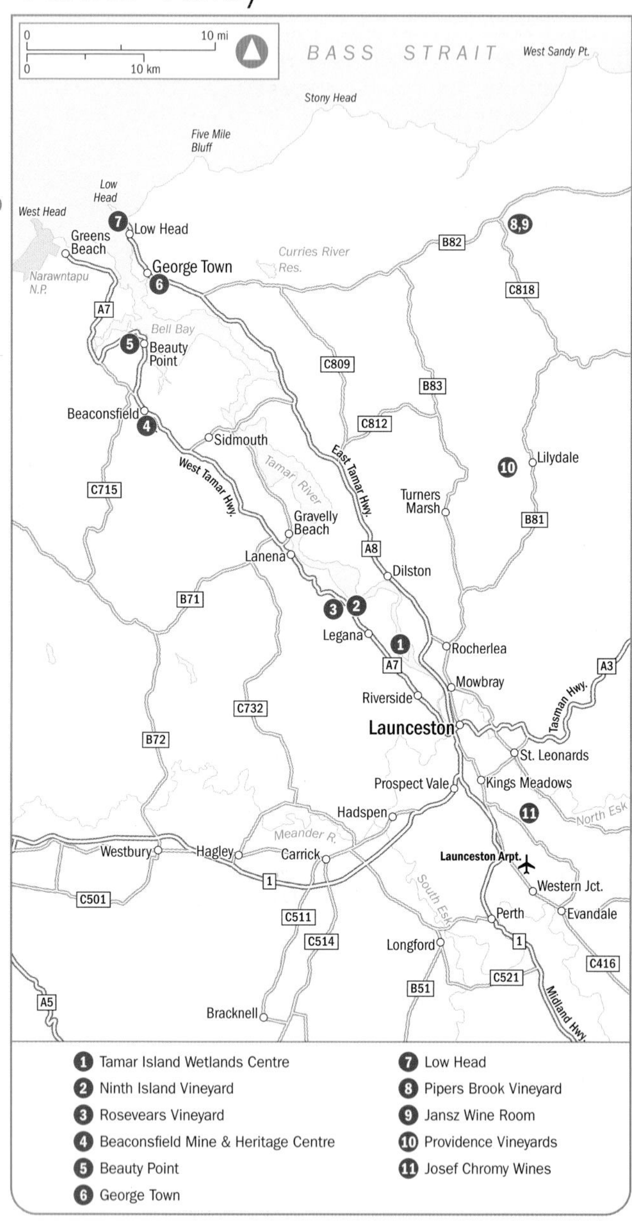

1. Tamar Island Wetlands Centre
2. Ninth Island Vineyard
3. Rosevears Vineyard
4. Beaconsfield Mine & Heritage Centre
5. Beauty Point
6. George Town
7. Low Head
8. Pipers Brook Vineyard
9. Jansz Wine Room
10. Providence Vineyards
11. Josef Chromy Wines

The Tamar Valley is home to some of the best cool-climate wines in the country. As pretty as it is productive, the hills and valleys that flank the Tamar River produce sparkling wines as well as riesling, pinot gris, sauvignon blanc, chardonnay and pinot noir. This tour includes a small selection—there's enough on the trail to fill 2 days. START: **Launceston.**

1 Tamar Island Wetlands Centre. Before you start wine tasting, drop into this wetlands centre—where you can do a spot of bird-watching—just 10 minutes' drive from Launceston. There's an interpretation centre and boardwalk out to **Tamar Island.** To get there from Launceston, head north across the Kings Bridge over the river on the West Tamar Highway (A7), through the northern outskirts of the city, past rambling, sometimes crumbling, hillside manor houses, and across the river flats. *30 min. Free admission. Daily 9am–5pm (10am–4pm Apr–Sept). www.parks.tas.gov.au.*

2 ★★★ Ninth Island Vineyard. The blink-and-you'll-miss-it riverside village of **Rosevears** is just a few minutes up the road and is home to two vineyards. The first, Ninth Island Vineyard, sells two of Tasmania's most well-known wine labels—Pipers Brook and Ninth Island. *30 min. 95 Rosevears Dr., Rosevears. 03/6330-2388. www.kreglingerwineestates.com. Free admission. Daily 10am–5pm.*

Grape-laden vines.

3 ★★★ Rosevears Vineyard. Just up the road is Rosevears, where, if all the imbibing becomes too much, you can stay in one of their luxury cabins (Rosevears Vineyard Retreat, p 159) overlooking the vineyard and river below. *30 min. 1a Waldhorn Dr., Rosevears. 03/6330-0300. www.rosevears.com.au. Free admission. Daily 10am–5pm.*

Tamar Valley Wine Route

For details of the 30 wineries along the trail, pick up a free copy of the Tamar Valley Wine Route Guide from visitor information centres throughout Tasmania and the wineries, or download a copy from www.tamarvalleywineroute.com.au.

Beaconsfield Heritage Centre.

Continue north, taking the meandering waterfront road to Deviot and Beaconsfield.

4 kids Beaconsfield Mine & Heritage Centre. In the early 1880s, Beaconsfield was the richest gold town in Tasmania with more than 53 companies working the goldmines. It hit the headlines again in April 2006 when a rockfall killed a miner and trapped two others in a 1.5m (5-ft.) square wire cage 1km (0.6 miles) underground for 14 days. The rescue had most Australians glued to their television sets. If you're not claustrophobic, you can crawl through a pipe and look into a replica of the crushed cage. There are plenty of other local-history and mining displays to look at in the museum next to the real working mine. *45 min. West St., Beaconsfield. ☎ 03/6383-1473. www.beaconsfieldheritage.com.au. Adults $12, children 15 and under $4, family $30. Daily 9:30am–4:30pm.*

5 kids Beauty Point. Beauty Point is just 7km (4.3 miles) from Beaconsfield, where you can learn about seahorses at **Seahorse World** (p 39, 4), and right next door, platypuses at the **Platypus House** (p 40, 5). *2 hr.*

Backtrack from Beauty Point and cross the river via the Batman Bridge just north of Deviot.

6 ★★ George Town. This cute little town on the eastern side of the wide mouth of the Tamar, established in 1804, is one of the country's oldest settlements, and the first in northern Tasmania. The first Europeans to explore the area were George Bass and Matthew Flinders in 1798 in the rather tiny sloop the *Norfolk*, and you can see a replica at the **★★★ Bass & Flinders Centre,** along with a number of other 18th- and 19th-century craft. *45 min. 8 Elizabeth St. ☎ 03/6382-3792. www.bassandflinders.org.au. Adults*

Low Head Lighthouse.

Pipers Brook Vineyard.

$10, children 15 and under $4, family $24. Daily 10am–4pm (3pm June–Aug).

❼ ★★ **Low Head.** Drive north out to Low Head on the edge of Bass Strait to the red-and-white lighthouse. The old **Low Head Pilot Station,** built by convicts in 1805, is now a **maritime museum** with 12 rooms of historical displays, and if you time your visit right you can hear the fog horn sound on Sundays at noon. Even if you don't visit the museum, it's worth the 5km (3-mile) drive up here just to admire the views and try to spot one of the **little penguins** who burrow in the coastal scrub, although they mostly sleep during the day. *1 hr. Low Head Rd. 03/6382-1143. http://museum.lowhead.com: Adults $5, children 15 and under $3, family $15. Daily 10am–4pm.*

❽ ★★★ **Pipers Brook Vineyard.** Spear east to the area known as Pipers River or Pipers Brook to sample some of the finest sparkling wines produced in Australia. There are half a dozen wineries in the vicinity, but two of the better ones are Pipers Brook Vineyard and Jansz Wine Room, just across the road from each other. Pipers Brook does a tasty lunchtime antipasto platter to accompany their wines. *1 hr. 1216 Piper Brook Rd. 03/6382-7527. www.kreglingerwineestates.com. Free admission. Daily 10am–5pm.*

❾ **Jansz Wine Room.** Jansz Wine Room, across the road from Pipers Brook Vineyard, has an Interpretive Centre where you can learn all about why Tassie is so good at putting the bubbles into wine—Jansz was the first place to make Tasmanian sparkling wine. *1 hr. 1216B Piper Brook Rd. 03/6382-7066. www.jansz.com.au. Free admission. Daily 10am–4:30pm.*

❿ **Providence Vineyards.** You can taste from a selection of their own wines, or up to 60 of the smaller lesser-known Tasmanian vineyards that are not so easy to get to. If you want to ship a box or two home (Australia only), they offer free freight. *20 min. 236 Lalla Rd. 1800/992-967. www.providence-vineyards.com.au. Free admission. Daily 10am–5pm (July & Aug by appointment).*

⓫ ★ **Josef Chromy Wines.** This winery just south of Launceston has some of the best views of vine-clad hills from the tasting-room deck, where you can tuck into a plate of local produce, but the wines are pretty good too. A glass of their Botrytis Riesling is the perfect way to finish a day of wine tasting. *20 min. 370 Relbia Rd. 03/6335-8700. www.josefchromy.com.au. Free admission. Daily 10am–5pm.*

North Coast: Across the Top

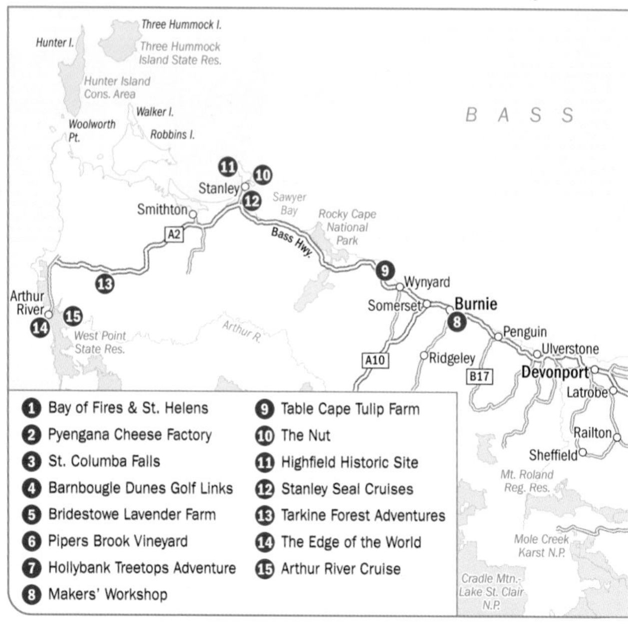

Tasmania's northern coastline is one of its best-kept secrets. From boulder-strewn white-sand beaches in the north-east, the main route across the top of the island travels through rain-forest, some of the state's best wine areas, and along the coastal Bass Highway past pretty fishing villages to reach the wilderness of the west coast and the Edge of the World. **START: St. Helens.**

1 ★★★ Bay of Fires & St. Helens. Start your journey across the top of the island at pretty St. Helens, a charming fishing village surrounded by implausibly beautiful beaches. *3½ hr. See p 88, 10 & 89, 11.*

2 Pyengana Cheese Factory. Head west from St. Helens over the rolling hills and into the rainforest-clad mountains and call into Pyengana Cheese Factory for a taste of their fabulous cheddar—they make around three tonnes of cheese a year. *20 min. St. Columba Falls Rd., Pyengana. ☎ 03/6373-6157. www.pyenganadairy.com.au. Free admission. Daily 9am–5pm (10am–4pm during June–Aug).*

3 ★ St. Columba Falls. Take a short detour to St. Columba Falls. At 90m (295 ft.) high, they are one of Tassie's highest waterfalls. There's a lovely short walk through the forest of tree ferns, sassafras and myrtle to the base of the falls. *30 min.*

4 ★★★ Barnbougle Dunes Golf Links. If you're a golfer, don't pass up the chance to play a round

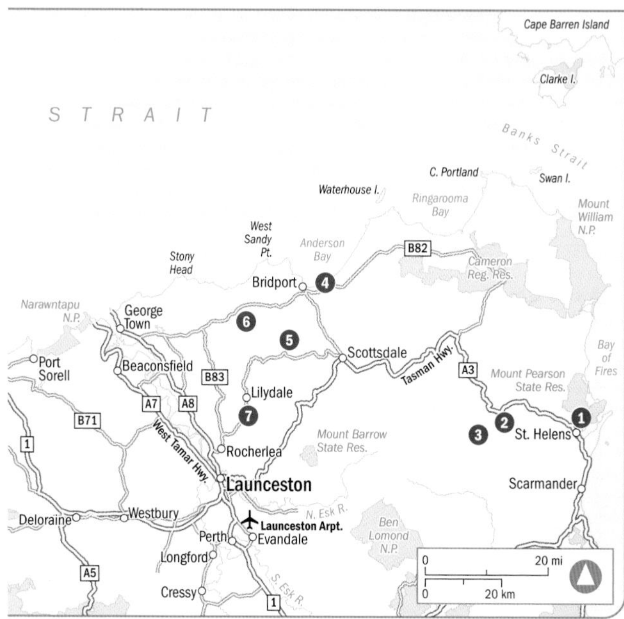

at Australia's top-ranking public golf course. It's one of the most beautiful links courses in Australia and extends across and between the coastal dunes. Even non-golfers will appreciate the view from the clubhouse. *3–4 hr. Waterhouse Rd., Bridport. 03/6356-0094. www.barnbougledunes.com.au. 9 holes $70, 18 holes $98.*

5 Bridestowe Lavender Farm. At its most colourful and fragrant in December and January but interesting all year, you can take a tour of the distillery and then browse the gift shop for all things purple and fragrant. There's a cafe here that serves light lunches, tea and coffee; don't leave without trying the lavender biscuits. *30 min. 296 Gillespies Rd., Nabowla. 03/6352-8182. www.bridestowelavender.com.au. Adults $7, children 15 and under free. Daily 9am–5pm Sept–May, Mon–Fri 10am–4pm June, July & Aug.*

6 Pipers Brook Vineyard. The vineyards and wineries of the Tamar Valley (p 54) are all worth visiting, but Pipers Brook and Jansz Wine Room produce some of the best bubbly in Australia. *1–2 hr. See p 57, 8 & 9.*

7 ★★ kids Hollybank Treetops Adventure. Get a bird's-eye view of the forest as you skim the treetops on the 'Flying Fox' adventure ride. *3 hr. See p 121, 4.*

At Exeter cut northwest towards Devonport on the B71. Follow the coastline through places like the village of Penguin until you get to Burnie.

Barnbougle Dunes golf course.

8 ★ Makers' Workshop. A busy container port, **Burnie** was infamous for its smelly paper mills, until they closed down in 2010. The Makers Workshop, a new museum-cum-art centre, specialises in handmade artisan papers (including some from kangaroo droppings) and paper sculptures and runs regular tours that incorporate a paper-making lesson. *30 min. 2 Bass Hwy., Burnie. ☎ 03/6430-5831. www.discoverburnie.net. Papermaking tour, adult $15, children 5–14 $8. Daily 9am–5pm.*

9 ★★ Table Cape Tulip Farm. If you're here in spring (particularly Sept–Oct), drive out to Table Cape and visit the tulip farm to wander amongst rows of stunning blooms, all the by-product of the farm's main business of growing the bulbs. The farm covers most of the flat-topped circular headland, and if you're lucky enough to be flying over it (Wynyard is the region's main airport) the patchwork of brilliant red, yellow, pink and purple flowers is a breathtaking sight. *45 min. 363 Table Cape Rd., Wynyard. ☎ 03/6442 2012. www.vdqbulbs.com.au. Free admission. Daily 9am–5pm.*

Bridestowe Lavender Farm.

10 ★★★ The Nut. The pretty fishing community of Stanley is most well known for the 152m (499-ft.) high flat-topped circular headland called The Nut that looms above the town. The Nut is actually the stump of a volcano, and it's a steep climb to the top (or take the chairlift), where there's a 40-minute circular track with great coastal and ocean views, and the opportunity to see muttonbirds (shearwaters; p 40, 7). *1 hr. Stanley. ☎ 03/6458-1286. Adults $10, children 12 and under $8. Chairlift operates daily 9am–5pm, closed during winter.*

11 ★ Highfield Historic Site. This beautiful Regency-era home was originally built for Edward Curr, chief agent of the Van Diemen's Land Company not long after the company first established Stanley as the base for their sheep-raising enterprise in 1826. The sensational views across to the Nut and Bass Strait are worth it even if old houses

Table Cape Tulip Farm.

aren't quite your thing. ◷ *45 min. Greenhills Rd., Stanley. ☎ 03/6458 1100. www.historic-highfield.com.au. Adults $10, children 5–18 $5. Daily 10am–4pm, Sept–May, 10am–4pm Mon–Fri June–Aug.*

⓬ ★★ **Stanley Seal Cruises.** Cruise out to Bull Rock, home to a colony of Australian fur seals. ◷ *75 min.* *See p 40,* ❻.

⓭ ★★★ kids **Tarkine Forest Adventures.** Take a slippery ride to the bottom of a giant sinkhole. ◷ *2 hr.* *See p 45,* ❾.

⓮ **The Edge of the World.** The Edge of the World is a stormy lookout over the mouth of the Arthur River, around a 90-minute drive from Stanley across windswept and heath-covered dunes, past picturesque stone cottages with streamers of thick kelp drying on the clotheslines and impossibly green farms. It's worth it for the drive alone. ◷ *15 min. Gardiner Point, Arthur River Rd. www.theedgeoftheworld.com.au.*

⓯ ★★ **Arthur River Cruise.** The Arthur River is one of the few rivers in Tasmania whose banks have never been logged, and the 14km (8½-mile) cruise aboard the *RV George Robinson* to where the Arthur river meets the Frankland River in the heart of the Tarkine wilderness is a great day tour. The cruise includes a 2-hour lunch stop at a clearing in the old-growth forest, where you can go for a short guided walk through the rainforest. ◷ *5 hr. Arthur River wharf. ☎ 03/6457-1158. www.arthurrivercruises.com. Adult $90, children 5–15 $35. Daily 10am, closed June–Aug.*

Stanley in front of The Nut.

King Island

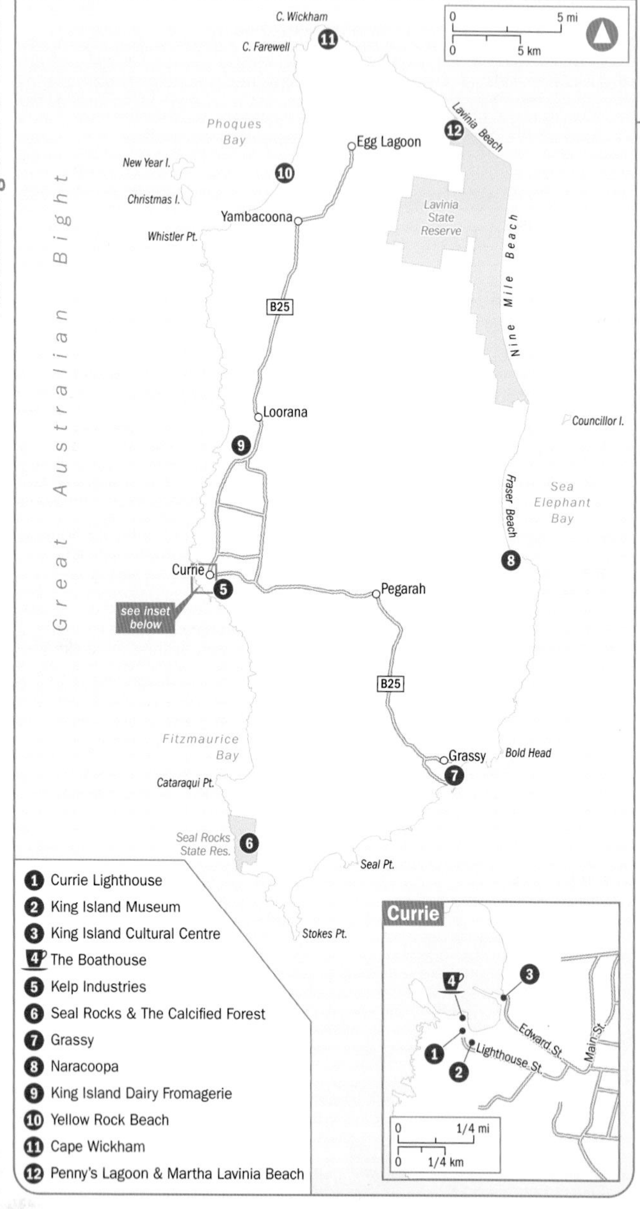
C. Wickham
C. Farewell
Phoques Bay
New Year I.
Christmas I.
Whistler Pt.
Egg Lagoon
Yambacoona
Lavinia Beach
Lavinia State Reserve
Nine Mile Beach
B25
Great Australian Bight
Loorana
Councillor I.
Fraser Beach
Sea Elephant Bay
Currie
Pegarah
see inset below
Fitzmaurice Bay
Grassy
Bold Head
Cataraqui Pt.
Seal Rocks State Res.
Seal Pt.
Stokes Pt.
0 5 mi
0 5 km
Currie
Edward St.
Main St.
Lighthouse St.
0 1/4 mi
0 1/4 km
1 Currie Lighthouse
2 King Island Museum
3 King Island Cultural Centre
4 The Boathouse
5 Kelp Industries
6 Seal Rocks & The Calcified Forest
7 Grassy
8 Naracoopa
9 King Island Dairy Fromagerie
10 Yellow Rock Beach
11 Cape Wickham
12 Penny's Lagoon & Martha Lavinia Beach

When most people think of King Island, they think of its gourmet produce. But there's much more to this windswept and sometimes storm-lashed island in the western waters of Bass Strait. Beautiful beaches, towering lighthouses and a fascinating history of shipwrecks are just some of its attractions. You could see the island in 2 days, but you'd be rushing—allow at least 4. START: **Currie.**

Travel tip

There are few stores or cafes outside of Currie, so if you're heading off to explore the farther reaches of the island, Currie is the best place to pick up supplies for a picnic lunch—try one of the two supermarkets (see below) or the bakery.

1 ★★ Currie Lighthouse. Currie's lighthouse is one of the few lighthouses in Australia that was turned off (in 1989) only to be recommissioned in 1995. Made of wrought and cast iron, it was shipped over from England in 312 prefabricated bits and was first lit in 1880. The views from the point overlooking the harbour and coastline stretch forever on a good day, and you can climb the 20m (65-ft.) spiral staircase on a 1-hour guided tour. *1 hr. Lighthouse St., Currie. ☎ 0439/705-610. www.lighthouse.net.au. Adults $15, children 12 and under $7.50. Tours Wed & Sat 3:30pm.*

2 ★★ King Island Museum. Housed in a former lighthouse keeper's cottage, this fascinating little museum has displays on the island's history and shipwreck relics. *30 min. Lighthouse St., Currie. No phone. Adults $6, children 11 and under free. Daily 2–4pm, closed July and Aug.*

3 King Island Cultural Centre. High-quality local art and crafts for sale with new exhibitions every few months. *15 min. Wharf Rd., Currie. ☎ 03/6462-1924. www.kingislandculturalcentre.blogspot.com. Free admission. Wed–Mon 1–4pm, closed Tues.*

4 ★★★ The Boathouse. Crack a crayfish (order them a day ahead from the Foodworks (☎ 03/6462-1144) supermarket in Currie if they are in season; hampers of local produce are also available), open up the King Island Dairy cheese or barbecue your own King Island beef (Russell's King Island Butchery in Currie is open Mon–Fri 8am–5:30pm) and wash it down with some King Island Cloud Juice as you enjoy the colourful art and harbour views. *See p 133.* *$–$$.*

Currie Lighthouse.

Kelp hanging out to dry.

❺ ★ **Kelp Industries.** The massive piles of stormcast bull kelp that wash up on to the island's beaches are harvested by locals and then brought to this plant in Currie, where the kelp is hung to air dry on racks before being ground up and shipped off to Scotland for processing. The basic visitor centre explains the process. *15 min. 89 Netherby Rd., Currie.* ☎ *03/6462-1340. www.kelpind.com.au. Free admission. Mon–Fri 8am–4pm.*

❻ ★★★ **Seal Rocks & The Calcified Forest.** Most of King Island is gently undulating, but down on the southern tip of the island you'll find a long line of towering cliffs. Best place to see the cliffs is the Seal Rocks lookout (keep an eye out for nesting **little penguins** underneath the boardwalk), or on the 90-minute **Copperhead Cliffs Walk.** Nearby is the **Calcified Forest,** the stumpy remains of a 7,000-year-old forest that have been preserved by the lime-laden sand. *2 hr. Seal Rocks Rd.*

❼ **Grassy.** Once a thriving scheelite mining village (the mine closed in 1990), Grassy is now little more than a sleepy collection of holiday cottages with sea-forever views, although it does have the island's only deep-water shipping port; this is where the island's supplies are brought in every Sunday morning, weather permitting. If you're staying here, head out to the breakwall on the harbour at dusk to watch the **little penguins** return to their burrows after a day at sea. Visit

Getting There & Getting Around

To get to King Island you need to fly into the airport at Currie. **TasAir** (☎ **03/6248-5088;** www.tasair.com.au) flies into King Island from Devonport and Burnie; **Regional Express** (REX: ☎ **13 17 13;** www.regionalexpress.com.au) operates daily flights from Melbourne to King Island. There is no public transport on King Island, so you will need to hire a car if you want to explore the 480km (298 miles) of roads that crisscross the island. Arrange this before you arrive, as cars are limited. Contact **King Island Car Rentals** on ☎ **1800/777-282** or see www.kingisland.org.au.

For more information, visit the King Island Visitor Information Centre, KIRDO Building, 5 George Street, Currie. ☎ **1800 645 014** or ☎ **03/6462-1355.** www.kingisland.org.au. It's open Monday, Wednesday and Thursday from 10:30am to 5pm, Friday 10:30am to 9pm, Saturday 10am to 12 noon. Closed Tuesdays, Sundays and public holidays.

Calcified Forest.

Kelp Craft (p 103) to see a range of crafty items made from bull kelp. 15 min.

8 Naracoopa. King Island's third 'village' is just a few houses strung out along a rocky beach, perfect for beachcombing. At the wharf, drop a fishing line into the sea to see what you can catch. *30 min.*

9 ★★★ King Island Dairy Fromagerie. The rich pastures of King Island (said to be the result of straw mattresses containing dried grass seeds that were washed ashore from French and English shipwrecks in the 1800s) produce some of the richest and sweetest milk in the world, which in turn produces the most sinfully indulgent range of soft cheeses, yoghurts and creams, all made here in the King Island Dairy. Watch a 20-minute video on the history of the 100-year-old dairy and cheese-making process, taste the range of cheeses, throw your diet to the wind and stock up on picnic and breakfast supplies. *45 min. North Rd., Loorana.* ☎ *03/6462-0947. www.kidairy.com.au. Mon–Sun noon–4:30pm (closed Wed May–Sept).*

10 ★★★ Yellow Rock Beach. There have been more than 60 known shipwrecks in the waters around the island, but the only one you can see without getting wet is the wreck of the ***Shannon***, a paddle steamer that was driven ashore in 1906. It's a 20-minute walk from the car park over the hill and along the usually deserted white-sand beach. *1 hr.*

11 ★★★ Cape Wickham. At 48m (157 ft.) high, the lighthouse on the northernmost point of the island is the tallest in the southern hemisphere. It was built in 1861 and marks the western entrance of the Bass Strait. Soak in the views at the lighthouse then wander across the point to Victoria Cove, a lovely little curve of white-sand beach. *40 min. www.lighthouse.net.au.*

12 ★★★ Penny's Lagoon & Martha Lavinia Beach. One of the most beautiful spots on the island, Penny's Lagoon is an unusual perched freshwater lake (a perched lake is one that is above the groundwater table). It's a good place for a swim, a walk around the lake and a picnic (there are free barbecues here). Nearby is Martha Lavinia Beach, a popular surfing and shell-hunting spot. *1 hr.*

The Shannon shipwreck off Yellow Rock Beach.

Flinders Island

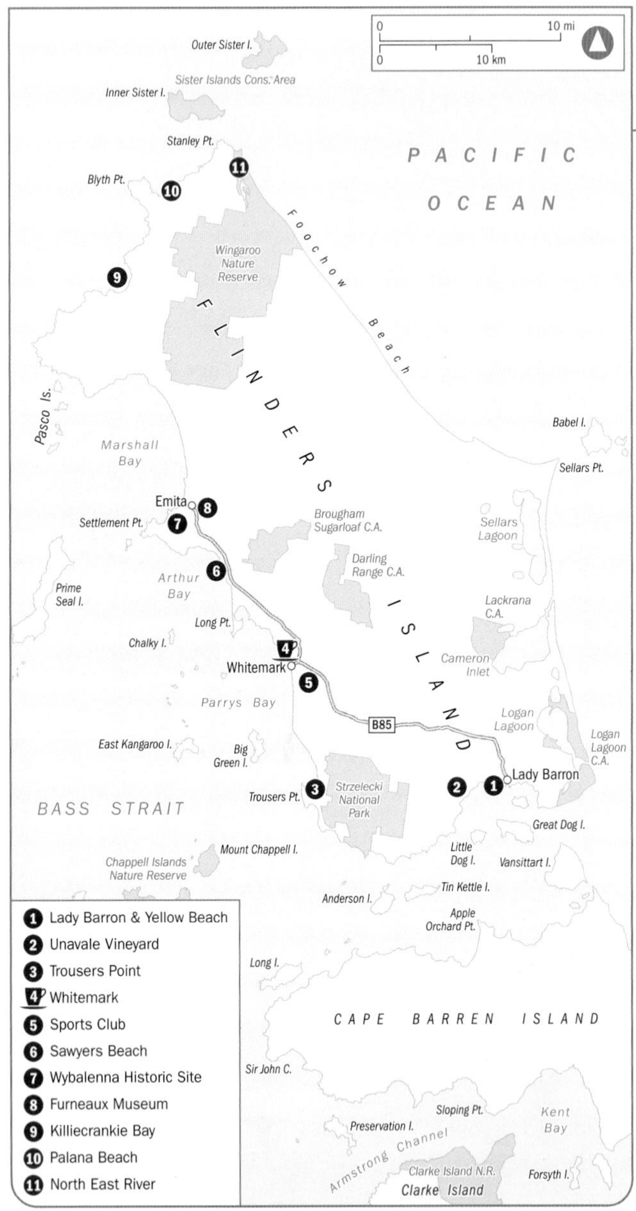

If you find a beach with someone on it, head to another—that's the advice from locals on Flinders Island. And with more than 100 beaches for fewer than 800 people, you're almost guaranteed to find an empty one. With its spine of steep granite mountains and necklace of glorious white-sand beaches, Flinders is all about getting back to nature and loving it. **START: Lady Barron.**

Travel Tip

If you're arriving on the island on a Sunday, you'll find most shops and restaurants are closed, so arrange for your accommodation to have some provisions bought in for you in advance.

1 ★ Lady Barron & Yellow Beach. Whitemark may be the commercial capital of Flinders Island, but most people live in Lady Barron, which is also the island's main port. There's no town centre to speak of, but the Shearwater Restaurant (p 138) at the Furneaux Tavern pub offers good food with knockout water views. Yellow Beach is great for walking and has ultra-clean barbecues. *20 min.*

2 Unavale Vineyard. You have to look for the vines in this little boutique winery—they are hidden away in the bush behind windbreaks of gum trees, but they do produce some great-tasting wine, which is made here on the island. One of the favourite tipples here is the sauvignon blanc. *15 min. 10 Badger Corner Rd. ☎ 03/6359-3632. www.unavale.com.au. Free admission. Open most days; call ahead to make sure.*

3 ★★★ Trousers Point. There's a bit of a mystery as to how this dazzling beach acquired its name: legend has it that a shipwrecked and trouserless Richard Burgess washed up here in the 1870s; another tale ascribes the name to the discovery on the beach of a box of trousers washed up from the wreck of the *Cambridgeshire* in 1875. Either way, it's one of the most photographed spots on the island. Have a swim, fire up the barbecue, and do the 1-hour walk along the rocky coastline to **Fotheringate Beach**—it's one of the best walks on the island. *90 min. Trousers Point Rd., Strzelecki National Park. National Park entry fee applies; see box National Parks Pass, p 115.*

Getting There & Getting Around

To get to Flinders Island you need to fly from Launceston or Melbourne with **Sharp Airlines** (☎ **1300 556 694;** www.sharpairlines.com.au). There is no public transport on Flinders Island, so you'll need to hire a car if you want to explore the island. Arrange this before you arrive, as cars are limited. Contact **Flinders Island Car Rentals** on ☎ **03/6359-2168** or see www.ficr.com.au.

For more information, visit the **Flinders Island Visitor Information Centre** at 4 Davies Street. ☎ **03/6259-5001.** www.visitflindersisland.com.au. It's open Monday to Friday from 9am to 4:30pm.

Sawyers Beach boulders.

4 Whitemark. This is the place to stock up on fuel or supplies. Flinders Island Bakery (4 Lagoon Rd. ☎ 03/6359-2105) makes fresh sandwiches and rolls and opposite, Freckles Cafe (7 Lagoon Rd. ☎ 03/6359-2138) serves good coffee, light lunches and a wicked chocolate slice. $.

5 ★ Sports Club. The nine-hole golf course has only ever been parred once in its 40-year history. It could have something to do with the distracting ocean views—or maybe it's those challenging sea breezes. *2–4 hr. Esplanade, Whitemark. ☎ 03/6359-2117. Green fees $15.*

6 ★★★ kids Sawyers Beach. White sand, gin-clear water, shady picnic areas, lots of boulders to clamber over and snorkel around, and rarely another soul in sight. With so many stunning beaches on the island, it's virtually impossible to single one out as being better than the rest, but this one is often cited as being people's favourite. It is drop-dead gorgeous and offers rock pools to explore and paddling for little kids in the many sheltered sections near the northern end. *1 hr. Around a 10-min drive north of Whitemark towards Emita.*

7 ★ Wybalenna Historic Site. In 1834, 135 Tasmanian Aborigines, many the last of their tribes, were settled on Flinders Island to be 'Civilised and Christianised'. Almost all died. All that is left of the ill-fated settlement that lasted less than 15 years is the chapel and a few graves—the Aborigines were buried in unmarked graves. For more on Aboriginal history, visit Furneaux Museum (below). *15 min. Free admission. Port Davies Rd.*

8 ★★★ Furneaux Museum. You could spend hours in this excellent museum that focuses solely on the history of the Furneaux group of islands, of which Flinders is the largest. Exhibits include the anchor of the *Sydney Cove*, wrecked on Preservation Island in 1797 more than 12

Wybalenna Chapel.

Killiecrankie Bay.

months before Bass Strait was even discovered. The story of the epic journey of some of the survivors by sea and land back to Sydney to mount a rescue mission is fascinating, as is the subsequent settlement of the islands by sealers. Other exhibitions focus on muttonbirding, an important traditional industry in the islands that is still carried on today; the Aboriginal history at nearby Wybalenna; local history preserved in hundreds of photo albums; and extensive displays of natural history specimens. The collection of exquisite Aboriginal shell necklaces, many donated by the owner of Bowman's General Store in Whitemark, where they had been traded for supplies over the years, is outstanding. *2 hr. Fowlers Rd., Emita. 03/6359-8434. Adults $4, children 15 and under free. Sat–Thurs 1–4pm Christmas to Easter; other times weekends only.*

9 ★★★ **Killiecrankie Bay.** A close-to-perfect crescent of white sand lapped by clear turquoise water. In summer, you'll often see crayboats tethered to the rocks and wooden holding pens full of crayfish bobbing in the water. *20 min.*

10 ★ **Palana Beach.** There's not much to Palana at the very northern tip of the island, except a collection of beach houses and an empty beach that's perfect for long, solitary strolls. *1 hr.*

11 ★★ **North East River.** Tidal estuaries, rock pools, granite bluffs, lichen-covered rock, raging surf and views that stretch forever. There's a little bit of everything here where the river meets the sea on the eastern side of the northern tip of the island. It's a tranquil spot for fishing and bird-watching. *1 hr.*

Killiecrankie Diamonds

They might look and feel like diamonds, but they are in fact topaz, although you'd have to be an expert to tell the difference. If you want to find them, ask a local at Killiecrankie Bay to point you in the direction of **Diamond Beach**—you'll need a shovel and sieve. If you want to buy some, head to **The Gem Shop** (p 104) in Whitemark on Flinders Island.

Central Highlands

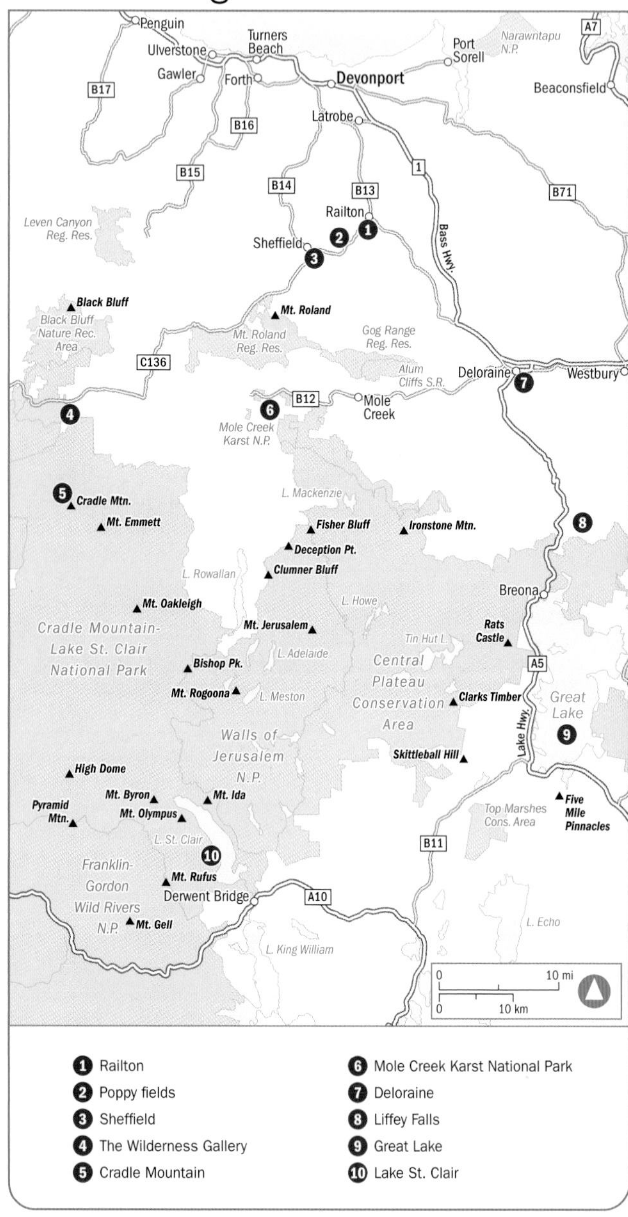

1. Railton
2. Poppy fields
3. Sheffield
4. The Wilderness Gallery
5. Cradle Mountain
6. Mole Creek Karst National Park
7. Deloraine
8. Liffey Falls
9. Great Lake
10. Lake St. Clair

Tasmania's rugged central highlands are like no other place on Earth, home to some of the most magnificent scenery you can imagine. The jagged wilderness of Cradle Mountain–Lake St. Clair is a major draw for bushwalkers and the central lakes and rivers attract anglers from all around the world who fish for trout in the pristine waters. START: **Devonport.**

Poppy Fields.

1 Railton Whilst driving through Railton keep an eye out for the quirky topiary sculptures in many of the front yards and gardens—you'll see everything from elephants and oversized bunnies and koalas to saluting soldiers.

2 Poppy fields Tasmania is the only state in Australia permitted to grow opium poppies as a crop and is one of the world's largest producers of pharmaceutical opium. You'll see vast fields of white poppies on either side of the road in the area between and Railton and Sheffield. They are very pretty when they flower in December.

3 Sheffield This enterprising town managed to put itself on the tourist map by wearing its history on its sleeve—or on its walls in this case. Almost every blank wall in the village is covered with bright and colourful murals. *10 min. Kentish Visitor Information Centre, 5 Pioneer Cres., ☎ 30/6491-1036. www.sheffieldcradleinfo.com.au.*

4 ★★★ The Wilderness Gallery One of the best landscape photography galleries you're likely to see, the 250 photos on show in this 10-roomed Wilderness Gallery will transport you to deep into the wilderness and show you parts of Tasmania that you would otherwise never get to see. While many of the

Sheffield murals.

Cradle Mountain.

images focus on Tasmanian landscapes, there is also a program of changing exhibitions from around the world, as well as a permanent one on the Tasmanian Tiger (see p 41, 8). *1–2 hr. 3718 Cradle Mt Rd. ☎ 03/6492-1404. www.wildernessgallery.com.au. Adults $7, free children 15 and under. Daily 10am-5pm.*

5 ★★★ Cradle Mountain A highlight of most people's visit to Tasmania, this wilderness area is every bit as spectacular as the tourist posters promise. The craggy peaks of Cradle Mountain are among the most well-photographed in the country and the starting point for the famous 6-day Overland track (p 113) walk to **Lake St. Clair.** There is a range of shorter walks. Favourites include the easy 2-hour walk around **Dove Lake;** a charming wheelchair-accessible 10-minute rainforest walk to **Pencil Pine Falls** near the visitor information centre; **Weindorfers Forest Walk** through a forest of King Billy pines, celery-top pines and myrtles and the delightfully named **Enchanted Walk** past waterfalls, pools, across moors and through rainforest. There are a couple of hotels (p 155) and picnic shelters with electric barbecues next to the visitor centre, which has excellent displays on the ecology and landscape, not to mention a roaring log fire, which seems to be in use all year round. There's also a range of activities, from helicopter rides to horseback trails and guided one-day walks. The weather is not always kind, so come prepared for just about anything Mother Nature can throw at you—even summer-time snow. How long you spend here is up to you, but try and spend at least a full day. *1–3 days. ☎ 03/6492-1110. www.parks.tas.gov.au. National Park entry fee applies, see box National Parks Pass, p 115. Visitor centre: daily 8:30am-4:30pm.*

Dove Lake.

6 ★★ Mole Creek Karst National Park There are more than 300 caves and sink holes in the Mole Creek area, but two of the most stunning are **Marakoopa,**

with its underground river, glow worms and 'great cathedral' cavern, and the richly decorated but smaller **King Solomon's Cave.** Guided 45-minute tours leave at regular times throughout the day. *1–2 hr. Mayberry Rd. 03/6363-5182. www.parks.tas.gov.au. Adults (per cave tour) $19, children 4–17 $9.50, family $47.50. First tour departs 10am, last tour 3:30pm.*

7 Deloraine Lying in the shadow of the **Great Western Tiers,** this pretty town on the banks of the Meander River is full of graceful historic buildings, many of which now house art galleries and boutiques. It's a crafty sort of place: in November the town is host to the 4-day **Tasmanian Craft Fair,** the biggest in the country with more than 200 exhibitors. The **Folk Museum** is worth a peek—local exhibits are housed in a collection of historic buildings. It also includes the Yarns Artwork in Silk exhibition—a four-panel tapestry telling the story of the Great Western Tiers area. More than 300 people from the region helped create the artwork that took more than 10,000 hours to complete. *30 min. 100 Emu Bay Rd. 03/6362-5280. www.yarnsartworkinsilk.com.*

King Solomon's Cave.

Liffey Falls.

Adults $8, children 5–16 $2. Daily 9:30am–4pm.

8 ★ Liffey Falls This pretty waterfall is in a forest of tree ferns, old growth myrtles and eucalypts. The 45-minute walk from the picnic area near the car park takes you past four cascades: Liffey (officially called Victoria Falls) is at the end of the track. *45 min. Access is signposted via Liffey Rd (C513), but is gravel, and has several sharp bends, so take care.*

9 Great Lake Tasmania is the wild trout capital of Australia and the remote lakes of the central highlands offer some the country's best **fly fishing.** Best time to fish is January and February. Even if you don't fish, it's a very scenic drive. The section of highway from the top of the lake to the junction of the Lyell Highway is unsealed, but in good condition and fine for normal 2WD vehicles. *2–3 hr.*

10 Lake St. Clair Carved out by glaciers over the last 2 million years, Lake St. Clair is the deepest lake in Australia and the headwaters of the Derwent River. It's the end of the trail for Overland Track walkers, but you don't have to slog it out on foot to get there; it's a few minutes' drive from the township of Derwent Bridge.

The Wild West

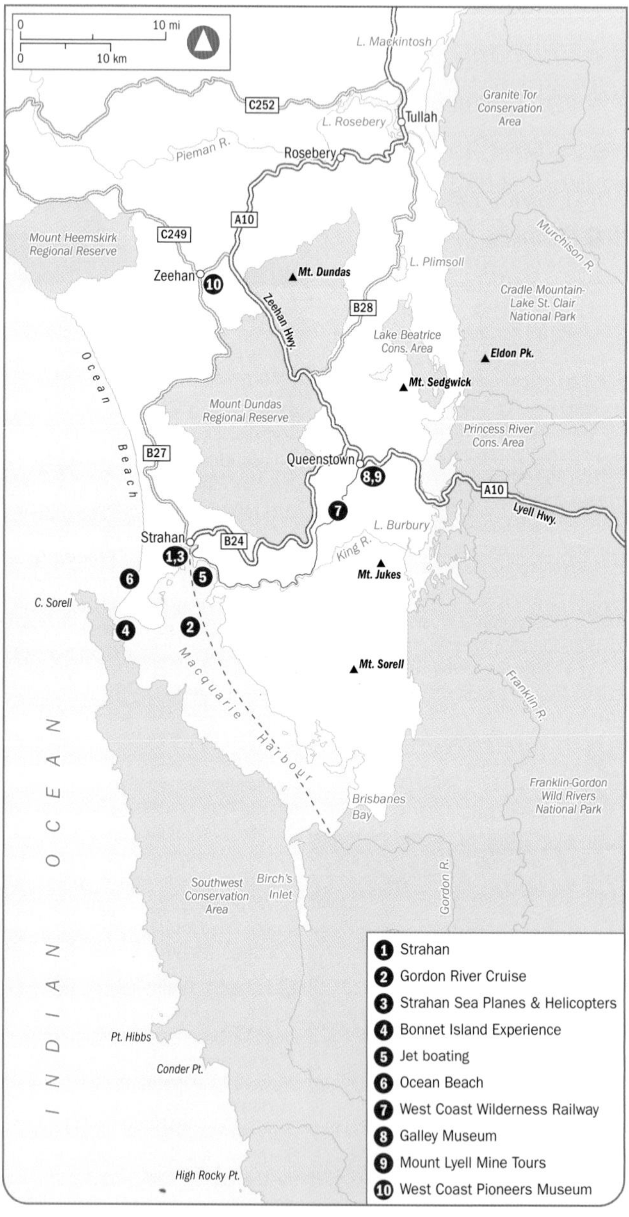

0
10 mi
0
10 km
L. Mackintosh
C252
L. Rosebery
Tullah
Granite Tor Conservation Area
Pieman R.
Rosebery
A10
C249
Mount Heemskirk Regional Reserve
Zeehan
10
Mt. Dundas
Zeehan Hwy.
B28
L. Plimsoll
Murchison R.
Cradle Mountain-Lake St. Clair National Park
Lake Beatrice Cons. Area
Eldon Pk.
Mt. Sedgwick
Ocean Beach
Mount Dundas Regional Reserve
Princess River Cons. Area
B27
Queenstown
8,9
A10
Lyell Hwy.
7
L. Burbury
Strahan
B24
1,3
King R.
Mt. Jukes
6
5
C. Sorell
4
2
Macquarie Harbour
Mt. Sorell
Franklin R.
INDIAN OCEAN
Franklin-Gordon Wild Rivers National Park
Brisbanes Bay
Southwest Conservation Area
Birch's Inlet
Gordon R.
Pt. Hibbs
Conder Pt.
High Rocky Pt.
1 Strahan
2 Gordon River Cruise
3 Strahan Sea Planes & Helicopters
4 Bonnet Island Experience
5 Jet boating
6 Ocean Beach
7 West Coast Wilderness Railway
8 Galley Museum
9 Mount Lyell Mine Tours
10 West Coast Pioneers Museum

Tasmania's west coast is one of the world's wildest places, a sparsely inhabited region with a rich mining history. In many ways, the legacies of environmental protest and the impact of mining can be seen as a snapshot of the issues that divide Tasmanians: protection of wilderness versus industry and jobs. Bring your raincoat: the west coast is notoriously wet. **START: Strahan.**

❶ **Strahan.** Use Strahan (pronounced 'Strawn') as your base, a pretty little village beside the sea at the mouth of Macquarie Harbour, the second-biggest natural harbour in Australia. There is a pleasant footpath walk that loops around the edge of Strahan Harbour to Risby Cove (from where the West Coast Wilderness Railway (p 45) departs). Detour along the way to take the 40-minute walk through the rainforest to Hogarth Falls in People's Park. ⌚ *1–2 hr. West Coast Visitor Centre, The Esplanade.* ☎ *03/6472-6800. www.tasmaniawesternwilderness.com.au. Daily Oct–Feb 10am–7pm, May–Sept 10am–12:30pm & 1:30–6pm.*

❷ ★★★ **Gordon River Cruise.** If you do only one thing in Strahan, make sure it is a cruise up the Gordon River. This ruggedly beautiful place is largely untouched and is inaccessible except by air, on foot or by the river. A highlight of the cruise is stopping to take in a short boardwalk through ancient rainforest at **Heritage Landing.** Most cruises also include a stop at the former convict settlement of **Sarah Island** (p 33, ❾). ⌚ *6 hr. World Heritage Cruises:* ☎ *03/6471-7174. www.worldheritagecruises.com.au. Adults $99–$145, children 5–16 $50–$75. Daily 8:30am (& 2:45pm summer).* ⌚ *5½ hr. Lady Jane Franklin II:* ☎ *1800/420-155. www.gordonrivercruises.com.au. Adults $99–$210, children 3–14 $45–$210. Daily 8:30am (& 2:45pm summer).*

❸ ★★ **Strahan Sea Planes & Helicopters.** The best way to get to grips with the immensity of the southwest wilderness area is to book the Gordon River scenic flight from Strahan in a seaplane that circles above the harbour and Ocean Beach before following the Gordon and

Strahan.

Gordon River Cruise.

Franklin rivers way beyond the reach of the cruise boats to land on a steep-sided section of the Gordon River at **Warners Landing.** After a 5-minute boardwalk into the rainforest to view the very pretty **Sir John Falls** and some ancient Huon pines, the tiny seaplane taxis upriver to take off again, following the Gordon River back to Strahan. *80 min. The Esplanade, Strahan. ☎ 03/6471-7718. www.adventureflights.com.au. Adults $210 pp (if 4 adults), $335 pp (if 2 adults), children 3–11 $140.*

4 Bonnet Island Experience. They don't call it Hells Gates for nothing. Take a twilight Bonnet Island Experience tour out to tiny Bonnet Island at the mouth of Macquarie Harbour and learn about what it's like to live in one of the wildest, wettest and stormiest places on earth. The highlight is watching the little penguins and muttonbirds return to their burrows at dusk. *2½ hr. ☎ 1800/420-155. www.bonnetisland.com.au. Adults $95, children 8–15 $40 (no children 8 and under allowed). Departure times vary.*

Wilderness Worth Fighting For

In the early 1980s, Strahan became the headquarters of Australia's largest ever conservation battle—known as the Franklin River Blockade. The State government accepted a proposal in 1979 to build a hydroelectric dam that would inundate around 37km (23 miles) of the middle reaches of the Gordon River, and 33km (20½ miles) of the Franklin River valley, both areas that had been nominated for World Heritage status. Over 3 months in the summer of 1982/83 about 6,000 protesters blockaded the construction roads, most at Warners Landing 6km (3½ miles) from the junction of the Franklin and Gordon rivers. So passionate were the protesters, and so aggressive were the police, that a total of 1,272 people were arrested, including current Australian Greens leader Bob Brown, who was elected as a member of parliament the day after he was released from gaol. The protest saved two of the world's most beautiful rivers and kick-started the green movement in Australia.

❺ kids **Jet boating.** You're guaranteed plenty of thrills on a jet boat ride across Macquarie Harbour and up the King River. *1 hr.* *See p 121, ❸.*

❻ **Ocean Beach.** Giant windswept sand dunes, roaring surf and ocean sunsets on Tasmania's longest beach. *1 hr.* *See p 126, ❿.*

❼ ★★ **West Coast Wilderness Railway.** Strahan's second-most popular day-trip is a ride on the restored ABT rack-and-pinion steam train that runs through the rainforest between Strahan and Queenstown. The historic 35km (22-mile) railway once serviced the Queenstown mines, hauling the copper to the port of Strahan. The 4½-hour journey features tight curves and spectacular bridges through the rugged wilderness, dense rainforest and steep gorges. Food is provided on board, and there's a 40-minute stop at Queenstown before the 1-hour return coach trip to Strahan (or vice versa if you're travelling from Queenstown). *5½–6 hr. ☎ 1800/420-155. www.westcoastwildernessrailway.com.au. Premier class: $210 per person, second class: adults $111 single, $129 return, children 3–14 $30 single, $40 return, including lunch. Trains run daily in both directions, 10am (Queenstown), 10:15am (Strahan).*

❽ **Galley Museum.** The copper-, gold- and silver-mining town of **Queenstown** is infamous for its moonscape of treeless, eroded hills, the vegetation killed off by almost 100 years of tree felling, sulphurous pollution from smelters and bushfires, although recent revegetation means it's not as barren as it once was. This museum in the original Imperial Hotel, built in 1898, has more than 900 photographs covering the history of the west coast as well as historical items. *20 min.*

West Coast Wilderness Railway.

Corner of Driffield St. & Sticht St., Queenstown. ☎ 03/6471-1483. Adults $5, children 5–15 $3. Mon–Fri (Oct–Apr) 9:30am–5:30pm.

❾ **Mount Lyell Mine Tours.** The Mount Lyell Mine, which first began operation in 1883, may not be the boom mine it once was, but it is one of the few working copper mines in the world that offers underground tours. Travel by 4WD station wagon approximately 9km (5½ miles) underground to see the dump trucks hauling the ore-laden rock and view the crusher, pump station and main headframe. Dress sensibly: covered shoes are a must. *3 hr. 2 Orr St., Queenstown. ☎ 0407/049-612. Adults $100. Not recommended for children 13 and under. Daily 10am & 2pm.*

❿ **West Coast Pioneers Museum.** Fourteen galleries chronicle the life and history of the west coast at this private museum of local and mining history. It's a bit on the old-fashioned side but if you like looking at old engines, locomotives, mining relics and photographs, you'll find it fascinating. *2 hr. 114 Main St., Zeehan. ☎ 03/6471-6225. www.westcoastheritagecentrezeehan.com.au. Adults $15, children 6–18 $12.50, family $35. Daily 9am–5pm.*

Hobart

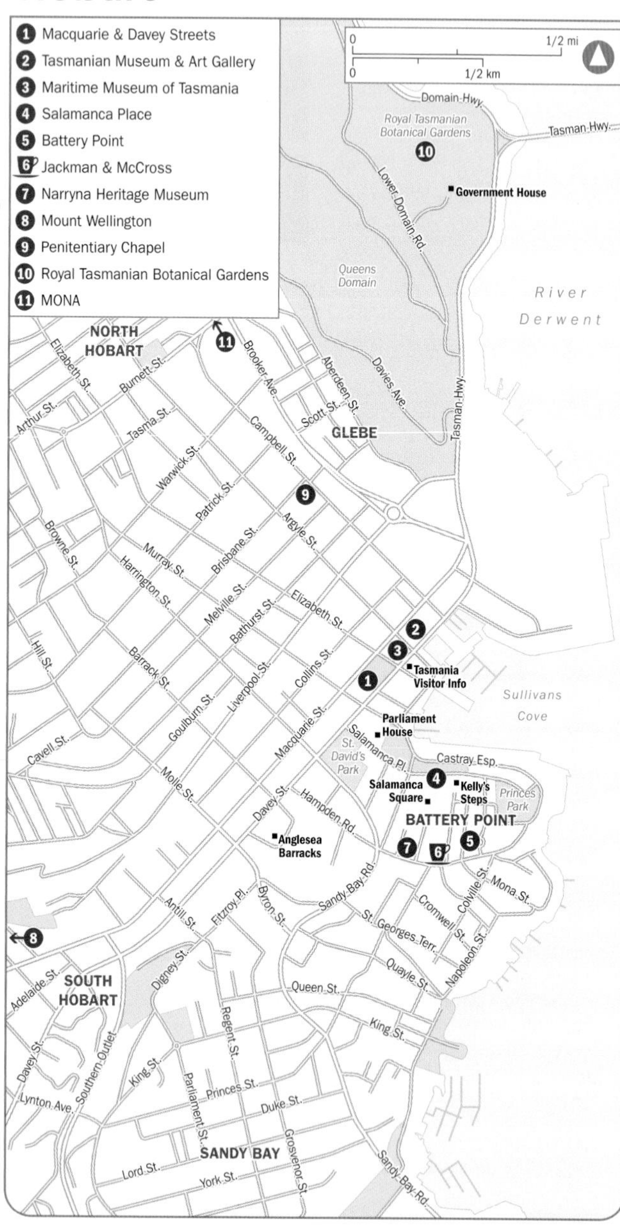

1 Macquarie & Davey Streets
2 Tasmanian Museum & Art Gallery
3 Maritime Museum of Tasmania
4 Salamanca Place
5 Battery Point
6 Jackman & McCross
7 Narryna Heritage Museum
8 Mount Wellington
9 Penitentiary Chapel
10 Royal Tasmanian Botanical Gardens
11 MONA
0
1/2 mi
1/2 km
Domain Hwy.
Royal Tasmanian Botanical Gardens
Tasman Hwy.
Government House
Lower Domain Rd.
Queens Domain
River Derwent
NORTH HOBART
GLEBE
Davies Ave.
Tasman Hwy.
Brooker Ave.
Aberdeen St.
Scott St.
Elizabeth St.
Burnett St.
Arthur St.
Tasma St.
Campbell St.
Warwick St.
Patrick St.
Argyle St.
Browne St.
Murray St.
Harrington St.
Brisbane St.
Melville St.
Elizabeth St.
Bathurst St.
Hill St.
Barrack St.
Liverpool St.
Collins St.
Tasmania Visitor Info
Sullivans Cove
Goulburn St.
Macquarie St.
Parliament House
Cavell St.
Salamanca Pl.
St. David's Park
Castray Esp.
Molle St.
Salamanca Square
Kelly's Steps
Princes Park
Davey St.
Hampden Rd.
BATTERY POINT
Anglesea Barracks
Sandy Bay Rd.
Colville St.
Mona St.
Antill St.
Fitzroy Pl.
Byron St.
Cromwell St.
St. Georges Terr.
Napoleon St.
Quayle St.
Adelaide St.
SOUTH HOBART
Digney St.
Queen St.
King St.
Regent St.
Southern Outlet
Davey St.
King St.
Parliament St.
Princes St.
Lynton Ave.
Duke St.
Grosvenor St.
SANDY BAY
Lord St.
York St.
Sandy Bay Rd.

Hobart may be Australia's smallest capital city, but it is also one of its most charming. Huddled under the shadow of the often snow-capped peak of Mount Wellington, Hobart is first and foremost a maritime city. Full of beautiful, honey-coloured Georgian and Victorian architecture, its history is all around you. START: **Macquarie & Davey Streets.**

Salamanca Place.

1 Macquarie & Davey Streets. Founded in 1804 by Colonel David Collins, Hobart is the second-oldest city in Australia, and that sense of history permeates almost every corner. Hobart's two main streets, Macquarie and Davey, run parallel to the waterfront and have more than 60 buildings classified by the National Trust. But, unlike many cities, where the historical enclaves have been transformed into tacky tourist haunts, the original buildings are still used for the same purposes they were built for—as homes, warehouses and offices. *30 min.*

2 ★ Tasmanian Museum & Art Gallery. Giant squid, Tasmanian tigers, rare colonial furniture and iconic colonial art—there's something for everyone at Tasmania's state museum and art gallery, known as T-MAG, which was

Hobart Walking Tour

Sometimes it's what you can't see that makes the past come alive. The **Henry Jones Art Hotel** (p 156) runs an excellent 1-hour walking history tour of the waterfront and city centre. You'll learn just how much Hobart has changed in the past 200 years, and be surprised at how much it hasn't. The tour runs on Tuesdays, Wednesdays, Thursdays and Saturdays. Booking is essential. The price is $25 (not really recommended for children). 25 Hunter Street, Hobart. ☎ **03/6210-7700.**

Battery Point.

established in the 1840s as the museum of the Royal Society of Tasmania and is one of the oldest in the country. The collections include natural and applied science, arts, social history, indigenous cultures, a library and the Tasmanian Herbarium. But the main attraction for most visitors is the display on the thylacine (Tasmanian tiger), although the 7m (23-ft.) long 150kg (330 lb.) giant squid that washed up on Ocean Beach (p 126, ⑩) on Tasmania's west coast is hard to beat. *90 min. 5 Argyle St., Hobart. ☎ 03/6211-4114. www.tmag.tas.gov.au. Free admission. Daily 10am–5pm, free 50-min tour 2:30pm Wed–Sun.*

View from Mount Wellington.

③ Maritime Museum of Tasmania. Hobart's seafaring heritage is brought alive through this collection of historical artefacts, paintings, ships models, and displays telling stories of the exploits of early explorers, whalers, sailors and ferrymen. *1 hr. Corner of Davey St. & Argyle St., Hobart. ☎ 03/6234-1427. www.maritimetas.org. Adults $7, children 13–18 $4, 12 and under free. Daily 9am–5pm.*

④ ★★ Salamanca Place. The most popular historical cranny of the city is undoubtedly Salamanca Place, a terrace of warehouses dating back to the whaling days of the 1830s, now mostly filled with boutiques and galleries. It comes alive on Saturday mornings with a huge outdoor local produce and craft market of more than 300 stalls selling everything from handcrafted wooden sushi trays and hand-spun woollen jumpers to organic vegetables. *1 hr. See p 80.*

⑤ ★★★ Battery Point. Battery Point was the original seamen's quarters of the city; the best way to explore the area is to simply walk up Kelly's Steps from Salamanca Place and start wandering through the winding streets and around Arthur's Circus. Neat, tiny cottages owned by working people stand next to mansions in streets that wind around the point, punctuated with 'village greens' designed to mimic the streets of rural and urban England. *30 min.*

6 All-day breakfast, brunch, pies, coffee and cake; no matter what you fancy **Jackman & McCross** (57 Hampden Rd. ☎ 03/6223-3186) is the place to refuel in Battery Point. The pastries, cooked on the premises, are superb and the service both speedy and friendly. *$.*

7 ★ **Narryna Heritage Museum.** Step inside the past in this gracious merchant's home that dates from the early days of the colony. *30 min.* *See p 37, 11.*

8 **Mount Wellington.** Wherever you are in Hobart you can see Mount Wellington—often covered in snow, even in summer. Standing sentinel 1,271m (4,170 ft.) over Hobart and its harbour, the summit is just a 20-minute (very winding) drive from the centre of the city. On a clear day, you can see across to the D'Entrecasteaux Channel and the Tasman Peninsula. There are a number of walking tracks crisscrossing the mountain, but be warned: the wind is often cold, so coats and warm weather gear are always needed. *30 min.*

9 **Penitentiary Chapel.** All that's left of the once sprawling Old Hobart Gaol, which was closed in 1961, is the chapel, built by convicts in the 1830s. After the closure of the gaol, the chapel became a courthouse, in use until the 1980s. The most interesting part of this tour, however, is the murky underground solitary confinement cells and the rather gruesome execution yard, complete with hangman's noose and trapdoor. *75 min. Corner of Brisbane St. & Campbell St., Hobart. ☎ 03/6231-0911. www.penitentiarychapel.com. Adults $10, children 5–16 $8. Tours Sun–Fri 10, 11:30am, 1 & 2:30pm, Sat 1 & 2:30pm.*

Royal Tasmanian Botanical Gardens.

10 ★ **Royal Tasmanian Botanical Gardens.** Set amidst sprawling lawns with expansive views of the Derwent, the famous gardens have more than 6,000 exotic and native plant species and are renowned for magnificent spring displays. Highlights include the vegetable plot from ABC-TV's *Gardening Australia* show, an old-fashioned conservatory, a Macquarie Island Subantarctic Plant House, the best collection of conifers in the Southern Hemisphere, and a splendid rose garden. *30 min. Queens Domain, Hobart. ☎ 03/6236-3075. www.rtbg.tas.gov.au. Free admission. Daily 8am–6:30pm Oct–Mar, 8am–5pm May–Aug, 8am–5:30pm Apr & Sept.*

11 ★★★ **MONA.** The largest privately owned museum in Australia, the collection includes ancient, modern and contemporary art and really is a must-see while in Hobart. The half-hour ferry trip up the river to get there adds to the fun. *3 hr.* *See p 81, 2.*

Tasman Peninsula

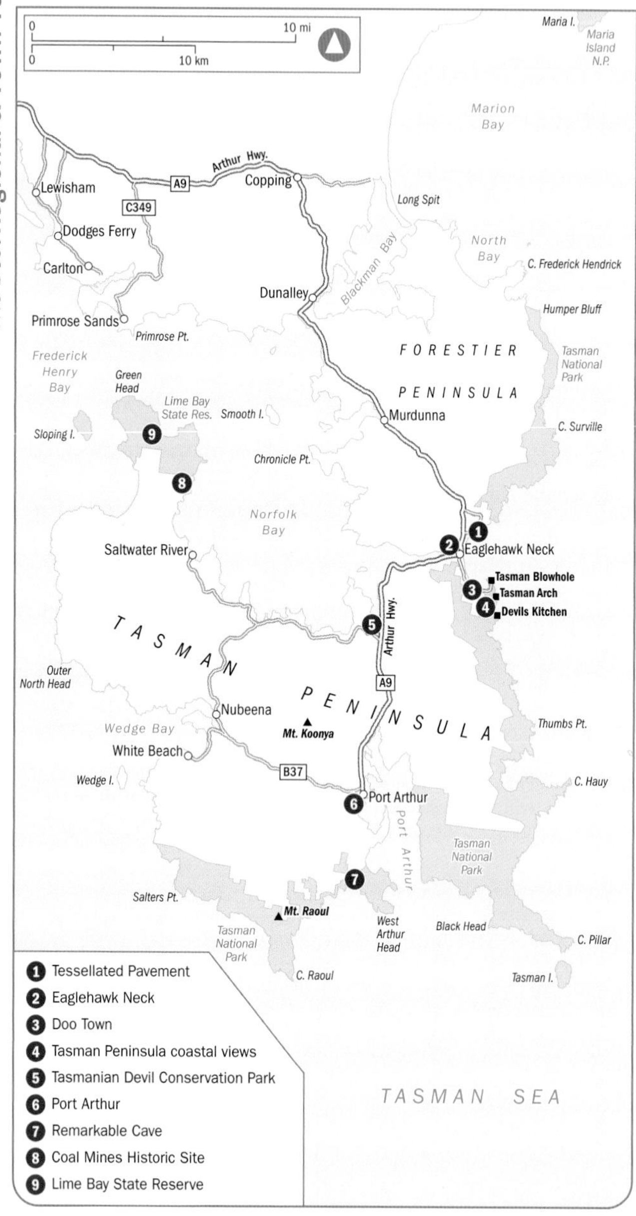

1. Tessellated Pavement
2. Eaglehawk Neck
3. Doo Town
4. Tasman Peninsula coastal views
5. Tasmanian Devil Conservation Park
6. Port Arthur
7. Remarkable Cave
8. Coal Mines Historic Site
9. Lime Bay State Reserve

The Tasman Peninsula harbours a dramatic and often tragic history. Practically cut off from mainland Tasmania by Eaglehawk Neck, a strip of land less than 100m (330 ft.) wide, the peninsula was a natural penitentiary, or so thought the colonial powers at the time. This drive can be done in a day, but there are some good evening tours, so it's worth spending the night. **START: Hobart.**

TRAVEL TIP

Much of this tour is in the Tasman National Park, so you will need to pay the $24 park entry fee (valid for 24 hours) to park in the car park or display your National Parks Pass, see box, p 115.

1 ★ Tessellated Pavement. From Hobart, head north out past the airport to Sorell and then cut across to Dunalley and wind your way down towards Eaglehawk Neck, around 75km (47 miles) from Hobart. Just before you reach the narrow isthmus, you'll see the signs to the Tessellated Pavement. A short walk leads to an unusual geological formation where the rocks were fractured by tectonic plate movements—it looks as if the coastline has been tiled by a giant. *15 min.*

2 Eaglehawk Neck. This narrow neck of land less than 100m (330 ft.) wide was the reason Port Arthur (p 31, 2) was chosen as the site for a prison in 1830: the tiny strip of land was easily patrolled, few people could swim, the surrounding bush was dense and inhospitable, and, if all else failed, a line of snarling dogs would rouse the soldiers should anyone try to get by. **The Officers' Quarters** (no entry to the building), built in 1832, is reputed to be the oldest wooden military building remaining in Australia; it's been restored and has a few displays on the front veranda relating to the history of the dog line that are worth reading. *10 min.*

Tessellated Pavement.

3 Doo Town. This unassuming small town—little more than a collection of holiday shacks—is a 'can do' type of place. Or should that be 'doo'? Almost every cottage sports a name plate, and they all end or start in doo: Thistledoo, Gunnadoo, Doo-Me, Doo-Us, Doo Come In, Just Doo It, Love Me Doo, Doodle Doo, Much-A-Doo and so on. Legend has it the tradition started in 1935, and the townspeople have been continuing it ever since. *15 min.*

4 ★★ Tasman Peninsula coastal views. The coastline of the Tasman Peninsula is riddled with dramatic rock formations, extraordinary rock pillars and sea stacks. On the southern side of Eaglehawk Neck you'll find the **Tasman Blowhole,** where you can watch the waves whoosh through the giant hole in the rocks, the ruins of once-huge sea caves at **Tasman Arch** and the **Devil's Kitchen,** a 60m (197-ft.) deep cleft in the rocks that would once have been a natural

Tasman Peninsula.

arch. There are car parks near each of the three formations; don't forget to display your National Parks Pass or entry ticket. ⌚ *30 min.*

5 ★★★ kids Tasmanian Devil Conservation Park. Learn all about the plight of Tasmania's famous carnivorous marsupial. Stay for feeding time and you'll soon see why they are called devils. ⌚ *2 hr.* *See p 43,* **4**.

6 ★★★ kids Port Arthur. You'll need a minimum of half a day, preferably a full day or even longer to explore the Port Arthur penal settlement, one of Australia's most significant historical sites. More than just the ruins of a gaol, it was, at its height in the 1850s, an entire village. ⌚ *½ day.* *See p 31,* **2**.

7 Remarkable Cave. This sea cave is around 6km (3½ miles) south of Port Arthur and is worth the drive for the coastline views alone, which live up to the remarkable name, across to Cape Raoul from the lookout above the beach. You can climb down the staircase to the sand to explore the cave at low tide, but be wary of freak waves. ⌚ *30 min.*

8 ★★ Coal Mines Historic Site. Head to the farming community of Nubeena and drive along the western edge of Norfolk Bay, where you'll find the Coal Mines Historic Site, another one of Tasmania's World Heritage convict sites. ⌚ *90 min.* *See p 32,* **4**.

9 ★★ Lime Bay State Reserve. One of the best-kept beachside

Port Arthur Memorial Garden

In 1996 Port Arthur was again the scene of great tragedy when a lone gunman killed 35 people, the worst mass murder in post-colonial Australian history. It resulted in State and Federal governments passing new gun-control laws, which are among the strictest in the world. There is a moving memorial to the victims on the site.

Tasman Peninsula Adventure Playground

The spectacular dolerite columns and cliffs along the coastline of the **Tasman National Park** are popular areas for climbing and abseiling. Divers head to **Cathedral Cave** at Waterfall Bay, a maze of caverns, passageways, narrow swim-throughs and vast underwater giant kelp forests.

From the beach at **Fortescue Bay** there is a lovely 2-hour return walk to Canoe Bay, where you can see the remains of a wrecked steel boat—it's a good walk for when you have small children in tow. Serious bushwalkers can tackle the 3- to 5-day **Tasman Coastal Trail** (p 114, ④) along the cliff tops from Waterfall Bay through to Fortescue Beach, out to Cape Hauy and on to Cape Pillar. Be aware that the Tasman Peninsula is exposed to the weather—especially Cape Pillar, where places like Tornado Ridge and Hurricane Heath often live up to their descriptive names. National Park entry fee applies (see box, p 115).

camping secrets in Australia is here at beautiful Lime Bay just a few minutes' drive farther north from the Coal Mines. Think shady campsites with million-dollar water views, although facilities are basic. Even if you're not camping, it's a great place to spread out a picnic and go for a swim. ***Camping fees: $13 per night. No bookings.***

Lime Bay camp site.

The East Coast

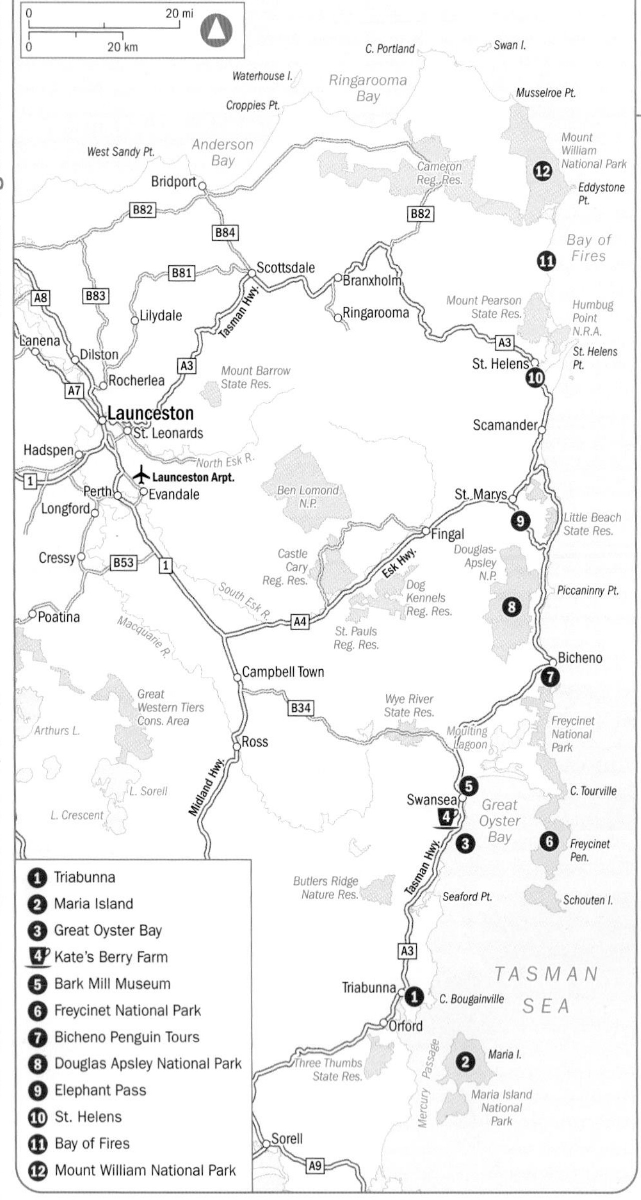

Tasmania's eastern coast is spectacularly scenic from the azure waters of Freycinet to the white sands, strewn with boulders that are covered with orange lichen, of the far north, the beaches of the east coast. It's a long, ragged strip of peninsulas, islands, channels and windswept beaches, flanked by rugged mountains and littered by gorges, waterfalls and forests. START: **Hobart.**

1 Triabunna. Head north from Hobart on the A3 towards Sorell, climbing up over descriptively named sections of road such as Break-me-gall Hill and down Break-me-neck Hill and across the valley floor, following the river to Orford, where the road, carved into the mountainside above the Prosser River, winds its way to the coast. Stretch your legs at Triabunna and watch the crew of the fishing boats unload their catch or tend to their deckside chores. *10 min.*

2 ★★★ Maria Island. No cars are allowed on Maria Island, which makes it the perfect place to explore on foot. Spend a day exploring the ruins of the convict settlement at Darlington, or 4 days walking the length of the island. Ferries depart twice daily in summer from Triabunna, less frequently during winter (June–Aug). *1–2 days.* *See p 39 for the full tour.*

3 Great Oyster Bay. Between Triabunna and Swansea, the cliff-hugging road meanders beside deserted beaches and offers magnificent coastal views across Great Oyster Bay and the rocky peaks of the Freycinet Peninsula. *30 min.*

4 Kate's Berry Farm. Tassie, with its cool climate, is famous for its berries, with many small producers making delicious jams, spreads, sauces and even wines from the fruit. Call into Kate's Berry Farm on the southern outskirts of Swansea for a tea and scones smothered with one of her thick homemade jams of strawberry, raspberry, Himalayan wild berries, youngberries or wild blackberry. *12 Addison St. (3km/2 miles south of Swansea). 03/6257-8428. www.katesberryfarm.com. Daily 9:30am–4:30pm. $.*

5 Bark Mill Museum. Built in 1885, this bark mill is the only working one of its kind in Australia. Learn how bark from local black wattle trees was used to tan leather. There's also a good display focusing

Great Oyster Bay.

Fairy penguin.

on the local history and particularly the early French exploration of the area. Engine buffs will love the working steam engines; foodies will enjoy the shop selling local produce; and there's a bakery and tavern on site. ◷ *30 min. 96 Tasman Hwy., Swansea.* ☎ *03/6257-8094. www.barkmilltavern.com.au. Adults $10, children 5–15 $6, family $23. Daily 9am–4pm.*

From Swansea, continue north to Cranbrook and take the turn-off to Coles Bay and Freycinet National Park.

6 ★★★ Freycinet National Park. The distinctive pink granite peaks of the Hazards dominate the scenery as you drive along the edge of the bay to the tiny town of **Coles Bay,** a collection of holiday homes clinging to the shoreline. There are many secluded beaches in the park, with beautiful **Wineglass Bay** (p 114, **2**) the most popular of them all. Take a drive up to the **Cape Tourville Lighthouse** for sunset views and whale and dolphin-watching in season, or spend a few hours on one of several longer walks in the park, such as the 3-hour climb to the summit of Mount Amos or the 5-hour Wineglass Bay/Hazards Beach circuit which features some of the park's best scenery. ◷ *1 day. National Park entry fee applies; see box National Parks Pass, p 115.*

7 Bicheno Penguin Tours. The east coast is home to many of Tasmania's commercial fishing fleet, and seaside towns like Bicheno are low-key holiday-cum-fishing towns. It has seemingly endless stretches of pristine white beaches close to town where you can often see penguins come ashore in the evenings. Wear covered shoes: penguins have been known to bite toes. No cameras allowed. ◷ *1 hr. Bicheno.* ☎ *03/6375-1333. www.bichenopenguintours.com.au. Adults $25, children 4–15 $15. Daily at dusk.*

8 Douglas Apsley National Park. For a change of scenery (if you can tear yourself away from the beautiful coastal views), head inland to this riverside national park just north of Bicheno. Highlights include deep river gorges, waterfalls, swimming holes and a dolerite-capped plateau with lots of walking tracks. My favourite spot is **Apsley Waterhole,** a 10-minute walk from the car park off Rosedale Road. ◷ *1 hr. National Park entry fee applies; see box National Parks Pass, p 115.*

9 Elephant Pass. The very pretty but steep winding A4 road up the range to St. Marys is popular with motorcyclists, but can be slow if you get stuck behind a caravan. ◷ *20 min.*

10 St. Helens. Unless you have a burning need to visit St. Marys or to tackle the Elephant Pass, take the A3 coast road instead to St. Helens. It's right beside the sea almost all the way and offers amazing views—and no traffic, as the cars are all on the Elephant Pass. St. Helens is a pretty fishing town on the edge of the narrow Georges Bay. It's known as the 'game-fishing capital of

Fishing boat at Georges Bay.

Tasmania', but you don't have to catch your own: all the cafes and pubs here do delicious seafood. Try the Bayside Inn (p 132). ⌚ *30 min.*

⓫ ★★★ **Bay of Fires.** The section of coastline known collectively as the Bay of Fires is not only heart-achingly beautiful, it's also, for the most part, completely deserted. Only in Tasmania can you find somewhere this close to paradise and have it all to yourself. The best spot is a beach reserve known as **The Gardens,** named by Lady Jane Franklin, the wife of Governor John Franklin, who spent some time in the region in the 1840s and thought the landscape as pretty as a garden. There are good (unpatrolled) swimming beaches, lots of rock pools to explore, and, of course, the ubiquitous orange-lichen-covered boulders to climb over and around and paddle between. Within the Bay of Fires Conservation Park are several free camping areas, most in the middle and southern sections overlooking the beach, and because it's a conservation park, rather than a national park, you can even bring your dog. ⌚ *3 hr. Free admission to the Conservation Park.*

⓬ ★★★ **Mount William National Park.** Adjoining the Bay of Fires Conservation Park, Mount William boasts exactly the same type of scenery, but with more established campgrounds and toilet facilities. From the northern tip at Musselroe Bay, you can see across to the Bass Strait islands. The shady banksia grove picnic area of **Stumpys Bay** is beside a very pretty coastal lagoon and offers easy access to the beach. At the southern end is the **Eddystone Point Lighthouse,** a striking, pink-granite tower on a point that juts out into the sea. ⌚ *3 hr. National Park entry fee applies; see box National Parks Pass, p 115.*

Eddystone Point Lighthouse.

Down South: Huon Valley & beyond

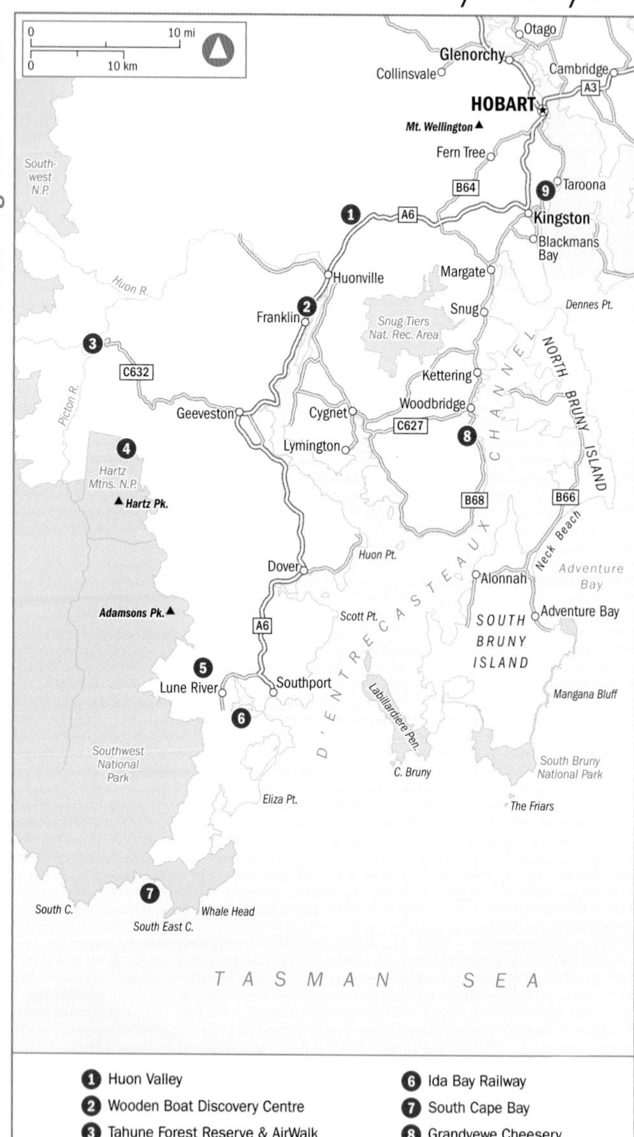

1. Huon Valley
2. Wooden Boat Discovery Centre
3. Tahune Forest Reserve & AirWalk
4. Waratah Lookout
5. Hastings Caves & Thermal Springs
6. Ida Bay Railway
7. South Cape Bay
8. Grandvewe Cheesery
9. Shot Tower

The best way to explore the beautiful countryside south of Hobart is via the Huon Trail, a signposted route that travels along the Huon River and out into the forests, before circling the coastline back to Hobart. Farther south are the tall southern forests and the wild Hastings Caves and South Cape Bay, closer to the Antarctic ice shelf than it is to Cairns. START: **Hobart.**

Huon Valley Apple Museum.

1 Huon Valley. From Hobart take the Southern Expressway and follow the signs to Huonville, through apple orchards that in early spring blanket the slopes in white and pink blossoms. Stop at one of the many farm gate stalls to buy fresh fruit in season, or call into the **Huon Valley Apple Museum** (p 27, 1). *Huon Valley Visitor Centre, 2273 Huon Hwy., Huonville. ☎ 03/6264-0326. www.huontrail.org.au.*

2 ★ Wooden Boat Discovery Centre. This is a showcase for traditional boat-building skills, and you can watch students and master craftsmen at work. You can learn everything you've ever wanted to know about wooden boats (their history, construction and use, the tools that shape them, and all the peculiar names and terms that describe them). *30 min. Main Rd., Franklin. ☎ 03/6266-3586. www.woodenboatcentre.com. Adults $8, children 16 & under $2. Daily 9:30am–5pm Sept–May, 10am–4pm June–Aug.*

3 ★★★ Tahune Forest Reserve & AirWalk. This forest reserve is home to the Tahune Forest AirWalk, a 600m (1,969-ft.) elevated treetop walk that leads out over the canopy of the wet eucalypt forest to a cantilevered platform 50m (164 ft.) above the ground that looks out over the Huon and Picton rivers. Apart from the elevated walkway, there are several lookouts and short walks leading off the Arve Forest Drive. The 10-minute riverside loop at the **Arve River Streamside Reserve** is one of our favourite short walks, as is the 20-minute **Huon Pine boardwalk** underneath the AirWalk. *3 hr. Arve Rd., Tahune. ☎ 03/6295-7170. www.adventureforests.com.au. Adults $25, children 5–16 $12.50, family $50. Daily 9am–5pm Sept–May, 10am–4pm June–Aug.*

4 Waratah Lookout. Just west of Geeveston and part of the World Heritage Wilderness Area, the Hartz

Peppermint Bay Cruises

Peppermint Bay (p 136) is the perfect place to linger over a long lunch and even longer views, but the journey almost beats being there. If you take the 2-hour catamaran trip from Hobart down the Derwent River past the spectacular cliffs and coastline of the channel district, you've a good chance of seeing dolphins, seabirds, seals, penguins and the occasional whale. The underwater 'spy ball' cameras provide you with a close-up view of sea life and the colourful kelp and coral gardens where parrotfish and leafy sea dragons are often seen. Cruises depart Hobart (Brooke Street Pier, Sullivans Cove) daily at 11am, arriving back at 4pm, and cost $98 to $168 per adult and $58 to $68 for children aged 4 to 14, and include an onboard lunch prepared by the chefs at Peppermint Bay. ☎ **1800/751-229;** www.peppermintbay.com.au.

Mountains National Park features a range of walking tracks through subalpine woodlands to ice-carved crags, lakes and alpine moorlands. On a clear day, **Hartz Peak** (1,255m/4,117 ft.) provides panoramic views into the heart of the southwest, but it's a fairly strenuous 3- to 5-hour climb and you need to keep in mind that blizzard weather conditions can occur with little warning, in any month. An easier option with similar views is the drive up to Waratah Lookout, although the road is unsealed and is subject to snow during bad weather. 🕘 *3–5 hr. National Park entry fee applies; see box National Parks Pass, p 115.*

5 ★★ Hastings Caves & Thermal Springs. Newdegate Cave is one of the largest tourist caves in Australia, and features large and quite spectacular formations, including flowstone, stalactites, columns, shawls, straws and stalagmites. It is one of the few caves in Australia to have formed in dolomite, which is harder and heavier than limestone. You can join a 45-minute guided tour, but be warned: there are 240 metal stairs to climb. If you prefer to stay above ground, you can soak in the thermal pool surrounded by forest and ferns. It's fed from a spring that supplies water at a delightfully warm 28°C (82°F) all year round.

Tahune AirWalk.

Hastings Caves.

There are changing rooms with showers and barbecue and picnic facilities at the pool. Take the time to do the 15-minute wheelchair-accessible walk through the nearby forest that starts near the pool. ⏱ *2 hr. 54 Hastings Caves Rd., Hastings.* ☎ *03/6298-3209. www.parks.tas.gov.au. Cave tours: adult $24, children 5–17 $12, family $60, and include pool entry. Pool only: adult $5, children 5–17 $2.50, family $12. Daily 9am–5pm, 10am–4pm May–Sept. Cave tours depart on the hour, 1 hr after opening.*

6 Ida Bay Railway. Australia's southernmost railway, the Ida Bay Railway, is the last remaining original narrow-gauge bush tramway left in Tasmania. Built in 1922 to haul limestone to the (now disused) wharf at Southport, the track is 7km (4.34 miles) long and terminates at Deep Hole Bay, a long beach accessible only by rail. It's a very picturesque trip. ⏱ *2 hr. Lune River.* ☎ *03/6298-3110. www.idabayrailway.com.au. Adults $25, children 3–16 $12, family $60. Daily except Fri; May–Sept Wed, Sat & Sun; check website for timetable.*

7 South Cape Bay. The 4-hour South Cape Bay walk starts from the end of Australia's most southerly road and is the eastern end of the popular 7-day South Coast Track to Port Davey. ⏱ *4 hr.* *See p 113, 2.*

8 ★★ Grandvewe Cheesery. Tasmania's only organic sheep dairy. ⏱ *30 min.* *See p 27, 2.*

9 Shot Tower. Ever wondered how they made those old-fashioned bullets so perfectly round? Easy, they dropped them from a great height and let natural forces do the rest. Climb the 259 steps to the top of the 48m (157-ft.) high shot tower to see how the lead was dropped to form spherical lead shot. Erected in 1870, this is Australia's oldest, and tallest, circular sandstone shot tower. There are good views of the River Derwent Estuary from the top. ⏱ *40 min. Channel Hwy., Taroona.* ☎ *03/6227-8885. Adults $7, children 5–17 $3, family $20. Daily, 9am–5pm.*

Shot Tower.

Bruny Island

1 Dennes Point
2 The Neck
3 Bruny Island Cruise
4 Adventure Bay
5 Fluted Cape
6 Cape Bruny Lighthouse
Margate
South Arm
C. Direction
Snug
Dennes Pt.
Dennes Point
B68
C625
One Tree Pt.
NORTH
Kettering
Yellow Bluff
C626
Trumpeter Bay
BRUNY
Cygnet
Woodbridge
C627
Channel Hwy.
CHANNEL
B66
Stallards Pt.
Great Bay
Variety Bay
ISLAND
Cheverton Pt.
Middleton
B68
Huon River
Simpsons Pt.
Isthmus Bay
C. Queen Elizabeth
Verona Sands
Neck Beach
Huon Pt.
Huon I.
D'ENTRECASTEAUX
Alonnah
Satellite I.
Adventure Bay
Esperance Pt.
B66
Ventenat Pt.
Little Taylors Bay
Adventure Bay
Lunawanna
S.B.N.P.
SOUTH BRUNY ISLAND
C. Connella
Partridge I.
Tinpot Pt.
Hopwood Pt.
Bay of Islands
Great Taylors Bay
Labillardiere Pen.
Mangana Bluff
South Bruny National Park
Cloudy Bay
South Bruny National Park
C. Bruny
West Cloudy Head
East Cloudy Head
Boreel Head
Tasman Head
The Friars
0 5 mi
0 5 km
TASMAN SEA

Bruny is an island clinging to the edge of an island clinging to the edge of the world. Practically cut in half by a narrow sandy isthmus called The Neck, the south features dense forests, national park, and spectacular cliffs; the north, rolling farmlands. It's wild, beautiful and remote, and home to some of the best artisan food producers in Tasmania. **START: Kettering.**

The Neck.

❶ ★ **Dennes Point.** The ferry arrives at Roberts Point, and most of the island's attractions lie to the south, but turn left rather than right on to Bruny Island Main Road and follow it to the northern tip of the island and take the lovely little circular drive around the coast from Dennes Point to Killara. ◷ *1 hr.*

❷ ★★★ **The Neck.** Climb the 180 or so steps to the top of the dune

Getting There & Getting Around

Access to Bruny Island is by vehicle ferry from Kettering, around a 40-minute drive south of Hobart. The **Bruny Island Ferry** (☎ **03/6273-6725;** www.brunyislandferry.com.au) takes 20 minutes to cross the D'Entrecasteaux Channel to Roberts Point on North Bruny Island. Ferries depart regularly between 6:35am and 7pm, but if you want to do this tour in a day, try to catch the 7:45am ferry in the morning, returning on the 5:30pm from Bruny Island. Return fares for a standard car cost $28 during the week, $33 on public holidays and long weekends. Caravans cost extra. Most of the roads are unsealed, but are fine for conventional cars. However, some car-hire companies will not allow you to drive their vehicles on Bruny, so check when hiring.

For more information, visit the Bruny D'Entrecasteaux Visitor Centre at the Ferry Terminal in Kettering. It's open daily from 9am to 5pm. ☎ **03/6267-4494;** www.brunyisland.org.au.

Well Fed

Apart from a general store in Adventure Bay that sells just the basics, there's no supermarket on Bruny, so you'll need to forage for your supper by visiting producers direct. Buy delicious smoked trout, salmon and quail from the **Bruny Island Smokehouse,** otherwise known as **BISH** (360 Lennon Rd., Roberts Point, daily 11am until late), sensational handmade cheese from **Bruny Island Cheese** (1807 Bruny Island Main Rd., daily 10am–5pm), freshly shucked oysters from the delightfully named oyster farm **Get Shucked** (1650 Bruny Island Main Rd., daily 10am–5pm, 4pm in winter), and island-made chocolate fudge from **Bruny Chocolate Factory Outlet** (53 Adventure Bay Rd., daily 10am–4pm).

for sweeping views of the isthmus and the long curve of white-sand beaches stretching south on both sides. There's a viewing platform at the bottom of the steps where you can see little penguins come back to their burrows at dusk. There's also a memorial to **Truganini** here; generations of Australians were taught that she was the last full-blooded Tasmanian Aborigine, although it has subsequently been proven that a handful of tribal Aborigines in remote areas did manage to survive her. Either way, the story of her violent life as told at the memorial is heartbreaking. ⌚ *30 min.*

3 ★★★ Bruny Island Cruise. Much of southern Bruny is state forest or national park, and the only way you can really see the dramatic coastline with its towering cliffs is by water, so join a 3-hour wildlife-spotting cruise that loops south from Adventure Bay to Cape Bruny and back. ⌚ *3 hr. Adventure Bay, Bruny Island. ☎ 03/6293-1465. www.brunycruises.com.au. Adults $100, children 3–16 $55, family $300. Daily, 11am.*

4 Adventure Bay. It would be a stretch to call Adventure Bay a town, or even a village, but it is the main settlement on the island and the place to go if you need to stock up on supplies. It's in a gorgeous spot, opposite the beach, and has been host to some illustrious visitors in its time, including Abel Tasman, Captain Cook and William Bligh in the *Bounty*. Learn all about them at the rather old-fashioned but fascinating **Bligh Museum of Pacific Exploration.** ⌚ *30 min. 876 Main Rd., Adventure Bay. ☎ 03/6293-1117. Adults $4, children 4–16 $2. Daily 10am–5pm Dec–Apr, 10am–4pm May–Nov.*

5 ★★★ Fluted Cape. You'll be afforded coastal views from the cliff tops on this 10.8km (6.7-mile) circuit walk from the southern end of Adventure Bay in **South Bruny National Park**. Be careful if you have children, as cliff edges are unfenced. ⌚ *2½ hr. National Park entry fee applies;* *see box National Parks Pass, p 115.*

6 ★ Cape Bruny Lighthouse. Drive down to the southernmost point of the island and climb the hill to the lighthouse for views across the cliffs to the southern edge of Australia. Built in 1838, it's the third-oldest in Australia. ⌚ *20 min. National Park entry fee applies;* *see box National Parks Pass, p 115.* ●

5 The Best **Shopping**

Shopping Best Bets

Best for **Antiques**
The Drill Hall Emporium *17 Stephen St., New Norfolk (p 101)*

Best **Books on Tasmania**
★★★ The Hobart Book Shop *22 Salamanca Sq., Hobart (p 101)*

Best if you're **Caught in the Rain**
Old Umbrella Shop *60 George St., Launceston (p 105)*

Best **Contemporary Jewellery**
McLachlan Studio *Highland Lakes Rd., nr Deloraine (p 104)*

Best **Diamonds**
★★★ The Gem Shop *Patrick St., Whitemark, Flinders Island (p 104)*

Best for **Everything**
★★★ Reliquaire *139 Gilbert St., Latrobe (p 103)*

Best **Huon Pine Designs**
★★★ Wilderness Woodworks *12 Esplanade, Strahan (p 106)*

Best **Market**
★★★ Salamanca market *Salamanca Place, Hobart (p 105)*

Best **Handmade Paper**
★★ Makers' Workshop *2 Bass Hwy., Burnie (p 105)*

Best **Photos of Tasmania**
★★★ Wilderness Gallery *3718 Cradle Mountain Rd. (p 104)*

Best **Scented Souvenir**
Bridestowe Lavender Farm *296 Gillespies Rd., Nabowla (p 103)*

Best **Seaweed Souvenir**
Kelp Craft *6 Currie Rd., Grassy, King Island (p 103)*

Best for a **Sweet Tooth**
Honey Tasmania *22 Quadrant Mall, Launceston (p 102)*

Best **Winter Woollies**
★ The Tasmanian Wool Centre *Church St., Ross (p 102)*

Salamanca market. Previous page: Salamanca market.

Hobart Shopping

Handmark Gallery 7
The Hobart Book Shop 3
Love & Clutter 1
Salamanca market 6
The Salmon Shop 4
Tasmania Shop & Gallery 5
Wursthaus Kitchen 2

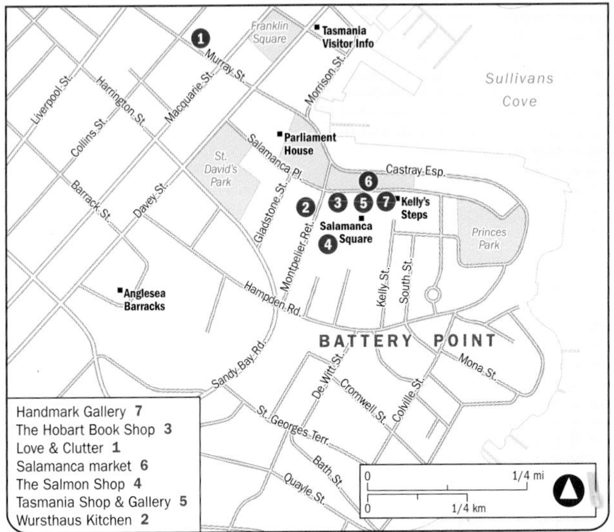

Launceston Shopping

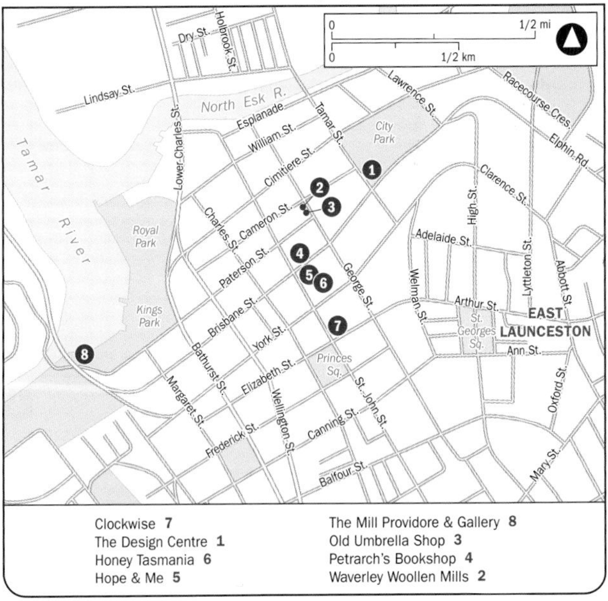

Clockwise 7
The Design Centre 1
Honey Tasmania 6
Hope & Me 5
The Mill Providore & Gallery 8
Old Umbrella Shop 3
Petrarch's Bookshop 4
Waverley Woollen Mills 2

Tasmania Shopping

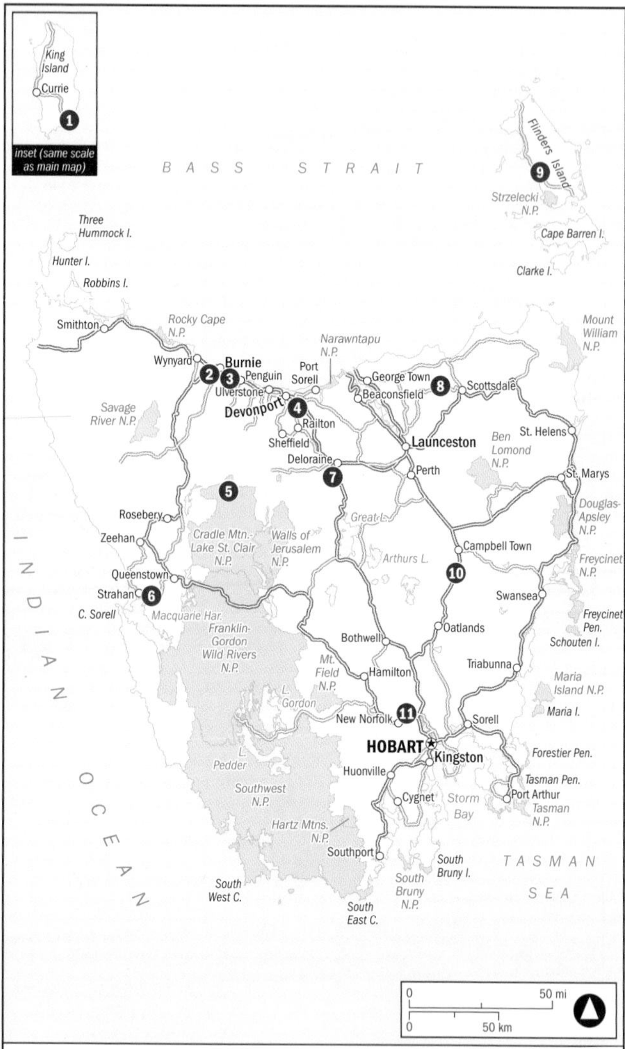

Bridestowe Lavender Farm **8**
The Drill Hall Emporium **11**
Furneaux Gallery **9**
The Gem Shop **9**
Kelp Craft **1**
Makers Workshop **2**
McLachlan Studio **7**
New Norfolk Antiques **11**
Penguin Markets **3**
Reliquaire **4**
Ring Road Antique Centre **11**
Tasmanian Special Timbers **6**
The Tasmanian Wool Centre **10**
The Wilderness Gallery **5**
Wilderness Woodworks **6**

Tasmania Shopping A to Z

Antiques

Clockwise LAUNCESTON If you've ever wondered what a horologist does, you'll find out in this quirky little store. Although they specialise in the restoration and repair of antique and old clocks, you'll find more old (and weird) clocks and pocket watches for sale than you can count. Closed weekends. *143 St John St. ☎ 03/6334-7211. MC, V. Map p 99.*

The Drill Hall Emporium NEW NORFOLK There are eight antiques stores in town, where you can find anything from Australian colonial furniture and Georgian silver to retro deco items. This one, housed in a former Army Drill Hall, has a great range of antique furniture and decorative items. *17 Stephen St. ☎ 03/6261-3651. MC, V. Map p 100.*

New Norfolk Antiques NEW NORFOLK This shop specialises in 20th-century glass and ceramics as well as art deco furniture. It's closed midweek. *15 Stephen St. ☎ 03/6261-1636. MC, V. Map p 100.*

Ring Road Antique Centre NEW NORFOLK Home to four antiques dealers, this antique centre stocks a wide range of furniture, glassware, china, bric-a-brac and vintage toys. *99 Ring Rd. ☎ 03/6261-5880. MC, V. Map p 100.*

Art & Design

Furneaux Gallery WHITEMARK This gallery showcases hundreds of watercolours of local scenes around Flinders Island by local artist Dawn Zelman. There's also a small collection of pottery and jewellery and some lovely hand-painted postcards. *Corner of Robert St. & The Esplanade. ☎ 03/6359-2125. No credit cards. Map p 100.*

★★★ Handmark Gallery HOBART If you're interested in Tasmanian art and craft, you'll find a wide range of the best here. Exhibits change regularly, but there's always a good collection of ceramics, glass, jewellery, wood and textiles, together with paintings, works on paper and sculpture. *77 Salamanca Place. ☎ 03/6223-7895. www.handmarkgallery.com. AE, MC, V. Map p 99.*

Blankets & Rugs

★ Waverley Woollen Mills LAUNCESTON Waverley is Australia's oldest weaving mill and it still operates from its original site in Launceston. They make a beautiful range of fine-wool blankets and rugs from super-fine merino, mohair and alpaca, as well as scarves and shawls. *58 George St. ☎ 03/6331-8881. www.waverleyaustralia.com.au. AE, MC. V. Map p 99.*

Books

★★★ The Hobart Book Shop HOBART This bookshop has the best range of books on Tasmania, many written by Tasmanians. Whether you're after detailed walking guides, fiction set in Tasmania, or Tasmanian history and poetry, you'll find it here. There's also a large second-hand and antiquarian section. *22 Salamanca Square. ☎ 03/6223-1803. www.hobartbookshop.com.au. AE, MC, V. Map p 99.*

Petrarch's Bookshop LAUNCESTON Petrarch's prides itself on reading the books it sells and has a huge range of recommended non-fiction titles. It also has a large selection of books on Tasmania. *89 Brisbane St. ☎ 03/6331-8088. MC, V. Map p 99.*

Books on Tasmania

Tasmania's wild landscape and colourful, often tragic, history have inspired many great novels. Marcus Clarke's *For the Term of his Natural Life* was first published in 1874 and has been called 'the classic convict tale of Australia'. The story follows the fortunes of Rufus Dawes, transported for a murder that he did not commit; much of the novel is set at Port Arthur. Novelist Richard Flanagan is probably Tasmania's best-known contemporary writer. Two of his best books are *Death of a River Guide*, set on the Franklin River, and *Gould's Book of Fish*, based on the life of convict artist William Buelow Gould on Sarah Island. Carmel Bird's *Cape Grimm* is a dark mythical tale about an apocalyptic cult set in the northwest wilderness. Nicholas Shakespeare's *In Tasmania* makes the past come alive as he traces the life and times of some of his colourful ancestors and Peter Timms delves into the fabric of Hobart in his non-fictional account *In Search of Hobart*.

Clothing & Accessories

Hope & Me LAUNCESTON This very girly shop stocks a great range of sleepwear as well as stylish housewares, cushions, ceramics, toiletries and jewellery. *27 Quadrant Mall. ☎ 03/6331-0166. www.hopeandme.com.au. MC, V. Map p 99.*

Love & Clutter HOBART This shop sells locally designed and handmade clothing, jewellery, hair accessories, stuffed toys, cards and more. *31 Murray St. ☎ 03/6224-2222. www. loveandclutterhobart.wordpress.com. MC, V. Map p 99.*

★ **The Tasmanian Wool Centre** ROSS This showroom and museum in Ross offers a great range of clothing—everything from jumpers and jackets, scarves and gloves to woollen underwear and knitting yarns—all made from superfine merino wool. A good place to shop if the weather is cooler than you anticipated. *Church St. ☎ 03/6381-5466. www.taswoolcentre.com.au. MC, V. Map p 100.*

Food & Drink

Honey Tasmania LAUNCESTON This store in the heart of Launceston is the place to go if you like honey. It offers free tastings, and stocks all sorts of honey products, from dried pollen pellets to spiced mead, and 40 varieties of Tasmanian honey. *22 Quadrant Mall. ☎ 03/6331-9300. www.honeytasmania.com. MC. V. Map p 99.*

★★ **The Mill Providore & Gallery** LAUNCESTON This food store in Ritchies Mill above one of Tassie's best restaurants, Stillwater (p 138), is one of the best places to buy Tasmanian produce. The ready-packed hampers make ideal gifts or souvenirs. *2 Bridge Rd. ☎ 03/6331-0777. MC, V. Map p 99.*

★ **The Salmon Shop** HOBART You can't leave Tassie without feasting at least once on its famous Tasmanian Salmon, and Tassal's Salmon Shop in Salamanca is the place to buy it. The range includes everything from fresh to smoked salmon, and the large deli section has just about everything you need (fishy and non-fishy) to put together the perfect picnic lunch. *2 Salamanca Square.* ☎ *03/6224-9025. MC, V. Map p 99.*

★★ **Wursthaus Kitchen** HOBART If you're self-catering, looking for a one-stop shop full of Tasmanian produce, or just enjoy fine food, you'll love this food store in Battery Point. It's a deli, a butcher-cum charcuterie, wine and cheese shop and cooking school all rolled into one. *1 Montpelier Retreat.* ☎ *03/6224-0644. www.wursthauskitchen.com.au. MC, V. Map p 99.*

Gifts & Souvenirs

Bridestowe Lavender Farm NABOWLA Tasmania is one of Australia's largest producers of commercial lavender, and a fragrant sachet or a bottle of essential oil makes a charming gift. You'll often see it for sale at the roadside and on market stalls in late summer but the best place to buy it is straight from the farm. Bridestowe is Australia's largest lavender farm, and the gift shop has a staggering array of oils and other lavender-scented and lavender-themed products. *296 Gillespies Rd., Nabowla, around a 45-min drive east of Launceston.* ☎ *03/6352-8182. www.bridestowelavender.com.au. MC, V. Map p 100.*

Bridestowe Lavender Farm.

Kelp Craft.

Kelp Craft GRASSY Most kelp is collected by islanders and is eventually processed for use in a range of food and cosmetic items, but some of it is cleverly made into a range of quirky souvenirs, such as seahorses to hang on your wall. It's not as weird, or smelly, as it sounds—when dried it becomes as hard as burnished leather. *6 Currie Rd., Grassy, King Island.* ☎ *03/6461-1464. No cards. Map p 100.*

★★★ **Reliquaire** LATROBE There's so much stuffed into this shop that you are offered a map as well as a piece of chocolate fudge when you walk through the door. There are 20 rooms of everything, including (but not limited to) life-size Betty Boop dolls and court jesters, fairy dresses, games, jewellery, exotic teas, olive oils, soaps, lotions, potions, cupids, cookbooks, gumboots, door knobs and hinges. There's even a glow-in-the-dark room and a mirror-lined 'Tardis' complete with flashing disco lights and thumping techno music. *139 Gilbert St., Latrobe.* ☎ *03/6426-2599. www.reliquaire.com. MC. V. Map p 100.*

Tasmania Shop & Gallery HOBART A cross between an upmarket souvenir shop and gallery, you can find some nice Tasmanian-made art and craft items here.

Reliquaire.

Some of the glassware is truly covetable, and there is usually a good range of wood, jewellery and textile items for sale as well. *65 Salamanca Place. ☎ 03/6223-5022. AE, MC, V. Map p 99.*

★★★ The Wilderness Gallery CRADLE MOUNTAIN Take home a fantastic photographic print of some of Tasmania's stunning wilderness from this gallery. The large gift shop at the Wilderness Gallery has not only prints and posters for sale but also a wide range of Tasmanian souvenirs. *3718 Cradle Mt Rd. ☎ 03/6492-1404. www.wildernessgallery.com.au. AE, MC, V. Map p 100.*

Jewellery

★★★ The Gem Shop WHITEMARK Technically a white topaz, Killiecrankie diamonds look and feel just like real diamonds, but at a fraction of the price. There's a small range of jewellery at The Gem Shop—at the end of the veranda of the Interstate Hotel—but a better bet is to buy just the stone and get it made into jewellery when you get home. You can also buy here the beautiful paper nautilus shells that are blown on to the local beaches in May. *Patrick St., Whitemark. ☎ 03/6359-2160. No cards. Map p 100.*

Killiecrankie Diamonds.

McLachlan Studio DELORAINE You'll love the elegant jewellery handmade in this little garden studio beside the Meander River by husband-and-wife team, Hugh McLachlan and Mary Phillips-McLachlan. Designs are bold and contemporary in gold, silver and pearls. Each piece is unique. Call to make an appointment before heading to the studio. *Highland Lakes Rd. (A5), 6km (3.7 miles) from Deloraine. ☎ 03/6362-2171. www.mclachlanstudio.com.au. AE, MC, V. Map p 100.*

Markets

Penguin Markets PENGUIN Every Sunday morning (9am–noon) between 100 and 200 stalls offer fresh produce, arts, crafts, gifts, housewares, woodwork and jewellery for sale at this undercover market. *Corner of Arnold St. & King Edward St. Map p 100.*

★★★ Salamanca market HOBART These lively Saturday-morning markets are some of the best in Australia and a shopping experience not to miss while you are in Tasmania. Start with breakfast at one of the food and coffee stalls, pick up some fresh fruit and vegetables, then browse the 300 or so stalls selling Tasmanian art and craft. There are also antiques, collectibles, books, curios, trash and treasure. Roving buskers keep you entertained. The markets are on every Saturday, come rain, hail or shine, from around 8:30am until 3pm. It can get crowded, so go earlier rather than later, and not all stallholders accept credit cards, so take cash. *Salamanca Place. www.salamanca.com.au. Map p 99.*

Paper

★★ Makers' Workshop BURNIE If it's made with paper then you'll find it at the gift shop at the Makers Workshop, which stocks beautiful art cards, prints, handmade paper and papier-mâché sculptures. There's also a range of fabric art,

Paper nautilus shell.

Tasmanian Devils at Salamanca market.

textiles, glass and hand-woven baskets. *2 Bass Hwy.* ☎ *03/6430-5831. www.discoverburnie.net. MC, V. Map p 100.*

Umbrellas

Old Umbrella Shop LAUNCESTON More of a museum than a shop, and you have to fight your way through the souvenirs, but it is a good place to pop into if you've been caught short without a brolly because this old shop still stocks tons of umbrellas. *60 George St., Launceston.* ☎ *03/6331-9248. MC, V. Map p 99.*

Woodwork

★★★ The Design Centre LAUNCESTON It can be hard to tell the difference between the museum displays and the retail area in this gallery of wood design because the quality is so good. If you are looking for a unique piece of functional wooden art to take home, this is the place to go. *City Park, corner of Brisbane St. & Tamar St.* ☎ *03/6331-5505. www.designcentre.com.au. AE, MC, V. Map p 99.*

★★★ Tasmanian Special Timbers STRAHAN This timber shop next to Morrison's Huon Pine Sawmill is worth visiting just for the smell

The Design Centre.

alone. If you've been looking for the perfect piece of timber to turn into an 18-seat dining table, look no further. Make your own furniture (or breadboard) or get a craftsman to do it for you. They will ship to anywhere in Australia. ***12 Esplanade. ☎ 03/6471-7190. www.tasmanianspecialtimbers.com.au. No cards. Map p 100.***

★★★ Wilderness Woodworks

STRAHAN A great place to pick up a gorgeous piece of finely crafted Huon pine to take home: think bowls, platters, breadboards, frames, furniture and sculptures. ***12 Esplanade. ☎ 03/6471-7244. MC, V. Map p 100.*** ●

Wilderness Woodworks.

Huon Pine

Huon pine is not only the slowest-growing and longest-living plant in the world (it can grow to an age of 3,000 years or more). It is also one of the toughest—go to the cemetery in Strahan and you'll see 100-year-old headstones carved from wood that look as if they were made yesterday. The timber is protected these days, and only wood found on the forest floor or buried in riverbeds can be used. Its rich honey colour and fresh scent make beautiful furniture and other items, and the wood here is sold in its natural state.

6 The Great Outdoors

Maria Island

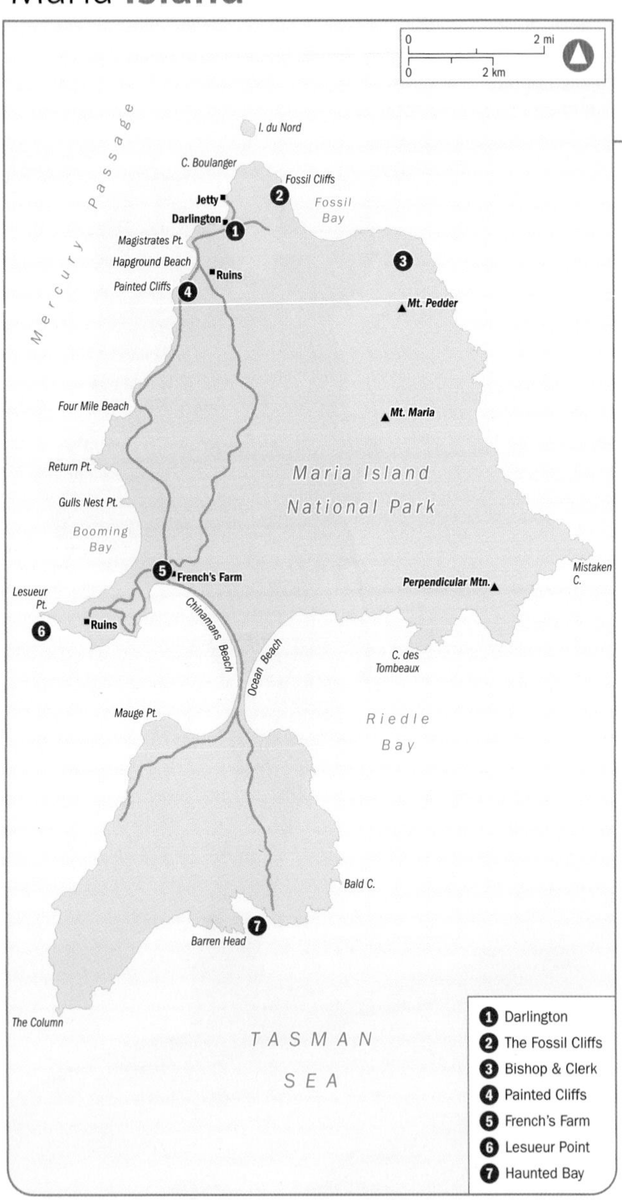
0
2 mi
0
2 km
I. du Nord
C. Boulanger
Fossil Cliffs
Fossil Bay
Jetty
Darlington
Magistrates Pt.
Hapground Beach
Ruins
Painted Cliffs
Mercury Passage
Mt. Pedder
Four Mile Beach
Mt. Maria
Return Pt.
Maria Island National Park
Gulls Nest Pt.
Booming Bay
French's Farm
Mistaken C.
Lesueur Pt.
Perpendicular Mtn.
Ruins
Chinamans Beach
Ocean Beach
C. des Tombeaux
Mauge Pt.
Riedle Bay
Bald C.
Barren Head
The Column
TASMAN SEA
1 Darlington
2 The Fossil Cliffs
3 Bishop & Clerk
4 Painted Cliffs
5 French's Farm
6 Lesueur Point
7 Haunted Bay

Lake St. Clair.

Maria Island is essentially two smaller islands joined by a narrow sandy isthmus. It's tiny—less than 20km (12½ miles) long and 13km (8 miles) at its widest point—but it's home to a staggering array of birdlife and large populations of possums, wallabies, pademelons, echidnas, kangaroos and wombats. With no cars allowed, and no shops, it's the perfect back-to-nature escape. **START: Triabunna.**

Darlington.

❶ ★★★ **Darlington.** Originally settled by whalers and sealers, the island became a penal colony in 1825. You can wander around the extensive convict settlement ruins at Darlington, which are one of the five Tasmanian World Heritage convict sites. By 1832, the convict settlement was abandoned in favour of Port Arthur (p 14) to the south. After a second incarnation as a convict probation station between 1842 and 1850, it was taken over by flamboyant Italian entrepreneur Diego Bernacchi, who planted grapes, cultivated silk worms, built a hotel and restaurant, and established a cement works—none of which survived the Great Depression. By the 1930s, the island was home to just a

Getting to Maria Island

You can catch the 9:30am ferry over and return on the 4:30pm one, but consider staying overnight to explore more. The **Maria Island Ferry** (☎ **0419/746-668;** www.mariaislandferry.com.au) makes a twice-daily 40-minute ferry crossing from December to April between Triabunna (88km/55 miles north of Hobart) and Darlington—less frequent crossings in winter. Return fares cost $37 per adult, $27 for children aged 5 to 10, under 5s go free. Daily National Park fees apply (see box, p 115). No cars are allowed on the island—there's a free car park near the wharf at Triabunna—but you can hire bikes for $20 a day at Triabunna ferry terminal and from **Triabunna Visitor Centre,** Esplanade, ☎ **03/6257-4772;** www.tasmaniaseastcoast.com.au.

Where to Stay

There is very basic accommodation on Maria Island: you can either stay at the Maria Island Camping Ground close to the creek at Darlington (www.parks.tas.gov.au; $13 per site for two people) or bunk down in the dorms of the **Old Penitentiary** ($15 per adult, $7.50 children 5–17, under 5s free, $50 per family; bookings essential, ☎ 03/6257-1420). All fees can be paid at the visitor centre in the old Commissariat Store, 150m (490 ft.) from the jetty. Free campsites are also available at **French's Farm** (❺) and **Encampment Cove** (3–4 hr walk from Darlington).

handful of farmers. There's a small museum in the rather grandly named Coffee Palace, a visitor centre in the convict-built stone Commissariat Store, and you can wander inside most of the other intact buildings, including the barracks, cottages, mill house and penitentiary. Bernacchi's former home is not open to the public, although if you do the privately run Maria Island Walk (see below) you stay in the house overnight. 🕘 *3–4 hr.*

❷ ★★ **The Fossil Cliffs.** It's an easy stroll from Darlington to the northern shores of the island and the spectacular cliffs that contain thousands of fossils in the limestone. Keep your eyes peeled for little-penguin (fairy penguin) burrows in the rocks beneath the cliffs. 🕘 *2 hr.*

❸ ★★★ **Bishop & Clerk.** It's a strenuous climb to the summit of Bishop and Clerk mountain, with lots of rock hopping and scrambling over large boulders, but the views from the top stretch forever. It's not a climb recommended if you're scared of heights. 🕘 *4–5 hr.*

❹ ★ **Painted Cliffs.** Time your visit to these beautifully patterned sandstone cliffs to coincide with low tide. The patterns are caused by groundwater percolating down through the sandstone and leaving traces of iron oxides. 🕘 *45-min walk from Darlington.*

Maria Island.

Painted Cliffs.

❺ **French's Farm.** There are always a few inquisitive Bennett's wallabies hanging around the old farmhouse, which is also one of the island's public camping spots. *3- to 4-hr walk from Darlington.*

❻ **Lesueur Point.** Take the time to amble around the melancholy ruins of the convict punishment cells. *45-min walk from French's Farm.*

❼ ★★★ **Haunted Bay.** You'll find spectacular views and a colony of little penguins that lives in the gaps between the granite boulders high on the cliff top. How they manage to scale the granite cliffs with those tiny legs as they return from the sea each night defies explanation. *2- to 3-hr walk from French's Farm.*

Haunted Bay.

Maria Island in Style

One of the best experiences you can have in Tasmania is the 4-day fully guided ★★★ **Maria Island Walk** (www.mariaislandwalk.com.au). The walk includes luxury safari tent accommodation and a stay at Bernacchi House at Darlington. It operates from November to April and costs $2,150 per person, inclusive of return transport to Hobart, park entry fees, gourmet meals, wine and twin-share accommodation (if travelling on your own you may have to share; guides team you up with someone of the same sex, but it's not guaranteed; single supplements are not available).

Best Bushwalks

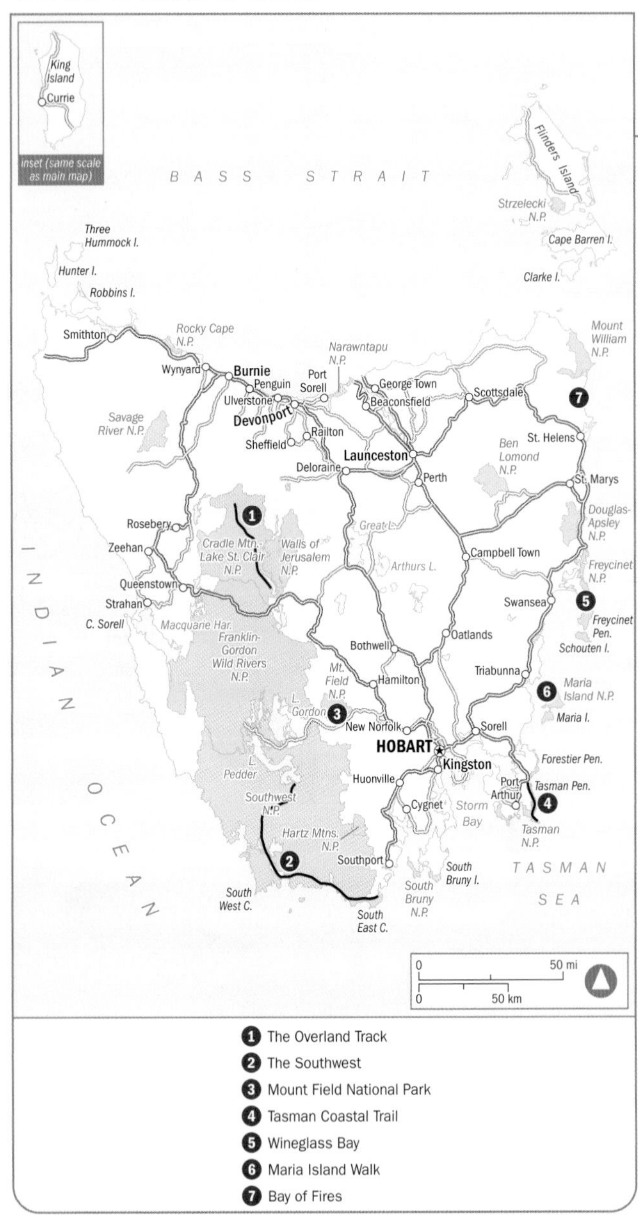

1. The Overland Track
2. The Southwest
3. Mount Field National Park
4. Tasman Coastal Trail
5. Wineglass Bay
6. Maria Island Walk
7. Bay of Fires

If Tasmania were to have a national sport, it would be bushwalking. More than one third of the island is protected in national parks and World Heritage areas. With so much pristine wilderness, it's a hiker's version of heaven on earth, with thousands of kilometres of walking trails—everything from tough week-long wilderness treks to beautiful 3-hour rainforest rambles.

❶ ★★★ **The Overland Track.** Tasmania's most famous walk, from Cradle Mountain to Lake St. Clair, attracts hikers from all around the world. But there are also plenty of good short walks. The 2-hour **Dove Lake Loop Track** takes you under the shadow of Cradle Mountain through the tranquil **Ballroom Forest** and back along the western shore of the lake. Time your visit for autumn (late Apr and May) when the deciduous beech (also known as fagus) cloak the lower slopes in a brilliant fiery red. *2 hr–6 days.* *For the full tour, see p 116.*

Dove Lake.

❷ ★★ **The Southwest.** Two of the country's most challenging wilderness walks are in the rugged **Southwest National Park.** Both are extremely demanding walks and for experienced and self-sufficient walkers only. The 70km (43-mile) **Port Davey Track** links Scotts Peak Road and Melaleuca, while the 85km (53-mile) **South Coast Track** traces the magnificent coastline between Melaleuca and Cockle Creek. There are no roads to Melaleuca, so you must fly, sail or walk in and out. (You can organise a flight from or to Hobart with **Par Avion** for around $400 return; see www.paravion.com.au). The Port Davey track takes 4 to 5 days, but be warned: it can be steep and muddy in places. You can

Walk Safe

Wherever you go walking in Tasmania, the weather can, and does, change unexpectedly and rapidly—a warm sunny day can quickly turn to a day of high winds, hail, sleet and snow, even in summer—so always be prepared with a warm jacket and good rain gear. Even on cold days, you'll need to take and drink plenty of water, and don't forget the sunscreen. Don't walk alone and always advise someone of your plans. Best months for walking are September through to late May: many mountain tracks are snowbound during winter (June to Aug). For more safety tips, see p 10, ❽.

either fly out at Melaleuca or continue along the South Coast Track—most people take about 6 to 8 days to complete this section. There is no accommodation on either track so you will need to carry a tent and all your provisions. ⌚ *4–12 days. National Park entry fee applies;* *see box National Parks Pass, p 115.*

❸ ★★ **Mount Field National Park.** The 25-minute, wheelchair-accessible circuit of the three-tiered **Russell Falls** takes you through a forest of the tallest flowering plant on Earth—the swamp gum—and lush rainforest full of stunning tree ferns. The 1¾-hour **Lady Barron Falls Circuit** features the best of the Mount Field National Park's lower-altitude tracks and includes Russell Falls, Horseshoe Falls, Lady Barron Falls and the Tall Trees Walk. The **Pandani Grove** walk (40 min) circles Lake Dobson and, as the name suggests, features many of the unique pandani (not to be mistaken with pandanus) plants. Keep an eye out for platypuses in the lake, especially at dusk and dawn. ⌚ *3–6 hr. Take the A1 from Hobart then A10 and B61. National Park entry fee applies;* *see box National Parks Pass, p 115.*

❹ ★★ **Tasman Coastal Trail.** This 3- to 5-day walk on the Tasman Peninsula in the **Tasman National Park** follows the coastal cliffs from Waterfall Bay through to Fortescue Beach, out to Cape Hauy, and on to Cape Pillar. Highlights include some of the highest sea cliffs in Australia, **Waterfall Bay** with its spectacular view across the cliff-lined bay to a waterfall that, after rain, spills straight into the sea, the squeaky white sands of **Fortescue Bay,** and spectacular dolerite columns and cliffs at **Cape Hauy.** You'll need to organise transport, or a car shuffle, at either end or you can break the walk into shorter sections if you don't want to do the whole thing. ⌚ *3–5 days. National Park entry fee applies;* *see box National Parks Pass, p 115.*

Cape Hauy.

❺ ★★★ **Wineglass Bay.** Often cited as one of the world's top 10 beaches, Wineglass Bay is a stunning wineglass-shaped curve of fine white sand lapped by the blue of the Tasman Sea. The 1-hour climb up to the lookout over Wineglass Bay in **Freycinet National Park** is one of the best short walks in Australia and the breathtaking view is worth the steep climb. What's more, while you'll see a few people on the trek up to the lookout, if you continue down to the beach (2 hr return), you're more than likely to have it to yourself, as the walk unjustly deters most day-trippers, who seem happy enough to snap a picture of this almost perfect beach and continue on their way. ⌚ *1–3 hr. Take the C302 (Coles Bay Rd.) from the A3 to Wineglass Bay car park. National Park entry fee applies;* *see box National Parks Pass, p 115.*

❻ ★★★ **Maria Island Walk.** It's not cheap, but if you can afford it,

National Parks Pass

Entry fees apply to all national parks in Tasmania—$24 per vehicle per day for up to eight people, or $12 per adult, $6 per child aged 5–17 per day if you're on foot, while Cradle Mountain alone costs adults $16.50, children 5–17 $8.25 per day on foot. The fee includes parking but does not cover camping, which, depending on the park, may carry an additional fee. If you're planning on spending more than 1 or 2 days in national parks throughout the state, consider buying a **National Parks Pass.** For most travellers, the **Holiday Vehicle Parks Pass,** which lasts for 8 weeks and covers all parks, offers the best value, costing less than the price of 3 days' entry ($60 per vehicle or $30 per person). There are also 8-week Backpackers passes for travellers on foot. You can buy a pass at National Park visitor centres, most Tasmanian visitor centres or online at the Parks and Wildlife Service website: www.parks.tas.gov.au.

the 4-day guided walk across Maria Island is an unforgettable way to explore one of the most beautiful parts of Tasmania in luxury. Alternatively, pack a tent and do it on the cheap: it will still be a walk you'll never forget. 🕘 *4 days. See box Maria Island in Style, p 111.*

7 ★★★ **Bay of Fires.** Like the Maria Island Walk above, the 4-day **Bay of Fires Walk** (☎ 03/6392-2211; www.bayoffires.com.au) is a commercially run guided walk, largely along the coastline and beaches, with accommodation in a luxury lodge and gourmet food and wine each night. It costs $2,150 per person, including accommodation, meals, wine and return transfers to Launceston. Those on a budget can walk on almost identical beaches in neighbouring **Mount William National Park,** and camp for free overlooking the beach in the southern section of the Bay of Fires Conservation Park. 🕘 *4 days. National Park entry fee applies; see box National Parks Pass, above.*

Wineglass Bay.

The Overland Track

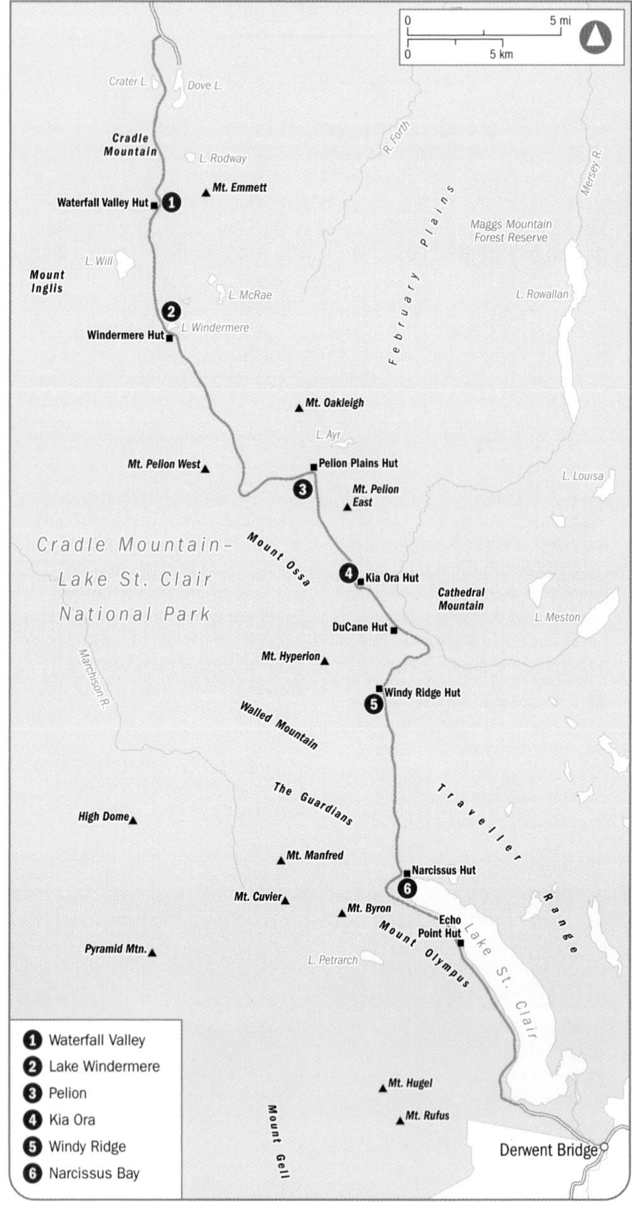

Every day is a surprise on the 6-day Overland Track, including the weather. The scenery on Tasmania's most famous long-distance hiking trail is nothing short of majestic, and each day will take you through a different landscape, from mountains to myrtle forests and button grass plains. The 65km (40-mile) trail can be challenging, but it's a walk that you will never forget. START: **Waldheim.**

Overland Track.

❶ ★★★ **Waterfall Valley.** The first day is the hardest as you hit the trail on a very steep climb to the top of **Marion's Lookout** (1,223m/4,012 ft.) at the base of Cradle Mountain. The views from the top over Crater and Dove lakes are superb. The track then skirts the western flank of

The Overland Track—When to Go

All walkers must follow the track from north to south from November 1 to April 30. To prevent overcrowding and degradation of the track, a maximum of 60 walkers are allowed to start the walk on any given day. You must book ahead from July onwards with the **Parks & Wildlife Service** (☎ **03/6233-6047;** www.parks.tas.gov.au). The track fee is $180 per person ($144 for seniors and children 17 and under), which is in addition to the park entry fee of $16.50 per day ($8.25 for children 17 and under). If you have a National Parks Pass (see box, p 115), you will still need to pay the track fee but you won't have to pay the park entry fee.

If you're brave enough to face the weather outside of the peak season (when days are short and deep snow can make the track impassable for days), you do not need to book. At this time, you can start the walk from Lake St. Clair and you need only to pay the daily park entry fee or use your National Parks pass.

See www.parks.tas.gov.au for details of bus companies that service Cradle Mountain and Lake St. Clair.

Cradle Mountain.

Cradle's craggy dolerite peaks, cuts across exposed alpine plains and descends into Waterfall Valley. *5–6 hr. Distance 10km (6.2 miles).*

2 ★★★ **Lake Windermere.** Day 2 is thankfully a lot easier than yesterday as you make your way across the glacier-carved valley, walking mostly on raised boardwalks that protect the fragile environment. Highlights include **Lake Wills** and dramatic views of Barn Bluff before reaching Lake Windermere, a great spot for an invigorating swim if the weather is kind. It's a relatively short day, and some walkers continue on to the hut at Pelion, where they stay for 2 days and take their time climbing **Mount Ossa** (p 119, **4**). *2–3 hr. Distance 7.75km (4.8 miles).*

3 ★★★ **Pelion.** It's mostly downhill on day 3, but don't let that lull you into a false sense of security: going down can sometimes be tougher on the knees and muscles than going up. After leaving Windermere, the trail descends to **Frog Flats** beside the **Forth River** (a favourite spot for leeches and mosquitoes), the lowest point on the track. Along the way you'll be treated to spectacular mountain views, before climbing back up through the aptly named **Enchanted Forest,** a beautiful forest of myrtle, sassafras and pandani. *7–8 hr. Distance 16.75km (10.4 miles).*

4 ★★★ **Kia Ora.** If day 3 was downhill, day 4 is definitely uphill, all the way. After climbing to the top of

The Overland in Comfort

If you're keen on walking the track but don't feel like roughing it, then look at booking **Cradle Mountain Huts** (☎ 03/6392-2211; www.cradlehuts.com.au). Accompanied by two guides, you walk the track just like everyone else, but come the end of the day your home for the night is a privately owned hut, complete with hot showers, soft beds in private twin rooms, and, best of all, a three-course dinner cooked by the guides accompanied by Tasmanian wines. Bliss! This luxury doesn't come cheap, at $2,600 to $2,800 per person, but it does cover everything, including the Overland Track Fee and use of a backpack and raincoat for the trip. For an extra $1,200 per person, they'll even carry your backpack for you.

The Overland Track—What to Pack

The Cradle Mountain–Lake St. Clair National Park is a fuel stove only area—campfires are not permitted. You should also carry a tent; there are six public huts along the track, but even with the booking system there is no guarantee there will be room at the hut when you arrive, so you may need to camp. You may also need to camp if the weather turns bad during the day. The huts do not provide food, cooking utensils, cooking stoves, toilet paper, mattresses or bedding, so you'll need to bring what you want. Untreated water is available from water tanks at the huts and from deep-flowing streams along the track. See www.parks.tas.gov.au for an essential gear list.

Pelion Gap (1,126m/3,694 ft.) you have the option of climbing **Mount Ossa** (p 118, ❷), Tasmania's highest peak (1,617m/5,305 ft.), which you should definitely do if you have good weather (as a rule of thumb, if it's raining or snowing at Pelion Gap there's no point in climbing Ossa). It's a tough 3- to 5-hour return trip with a lot of scrambling over large rocks, and a bit scary if you don't have a head for heights, but the view from the summit on a good day takes in almost one-quarter of the state. At the very least, climb **Mount Doris** (around a third of the way to Mount Ossa's summit) for lunch with a view in a garden of ancient cushion plants. 🕘 *3–4 hr, 7–9 hr including Mount Ossa. Distance 9km (5.6 miles).*

❺ ★★ **Windy Ridge.** Today can be a challenge if your knees are screaming after yesterday's hike to the top of Mount Ossa, but it is beautiful, with side trips to three waterfalls and a long stretch of silent rainforest as you climb up and over the **Ducane Gap** (1,060m/3,478 ft.), the last big climb of the trip. The trail underfoot is largely exposed tree roots, so you need to watch where you put your feet. 🕘 *6–7 hr, including side trips to D'Alton, Fergusson and Hartnett Falls. Distance 10km (6.2 miles).*

❻ **Narcissus Bay.** The last day is an easy one, a long gradual downhill run through sclerophyll forests and across button grass plains to the shore of **Lake St. Clair,** Australia's deepest lake and the headwaters of the Derwent River. 🕘 *3–4 hr, plus 30-min ferry ride to Cynthia Bay. Distance 9km (5.6 miles).*

Climbing Mount Ossa.

Tasmania for **Thrill Seekers**

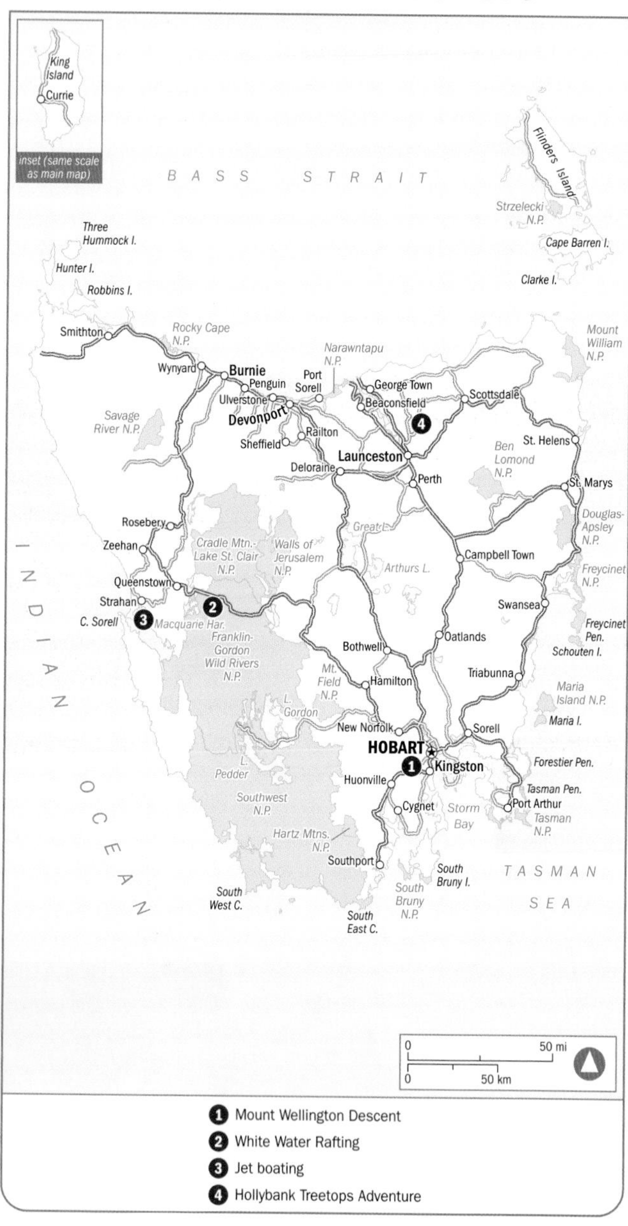

Tassie is Australia's adventure capital. Whether you're shooting rapids on one of the world's wildest rivers, tackling mountain trails on two wheels or skimming the tree tops on a 'flying fox', this special-interest tour is perfect for anyone who likes their holidays to be active and adventurous. Pump it up! **START: Hobart.**

1 Mount Wellington Descent. Mount Wellington is the undisputed king of mountain biking in Hobart with a thrilling 21km (14-mile) downhill ride. If you don't fancy the 2½-hour ride up the mountain from the city, Mount Wellington Descent operates a tour that includes not only hiring the bike but also a lift up the mountain. ⌚ ***2½ hr. Tours depart from Brooke St. Pier, Hobart. ☎ 03/6274-1880. www.mtwellingtondescent.com.au. Tour: adults $75, children 8–16 $65. Daily 9:30am & 1pm (& 4pm Jan–Feb).***

2 ★★★ White Water Rafting. The Franklin River, one of the world's last major wild rivers, is Australia's best white water rafting destination. Rafting this river is challenging, with rapidly fluctuating water levels, unpredictable weather and demanding portages, but it is a magnificent wilderness adventure through deep gorges, superb rapids and awesome scenery. The river is in a remote area with no roads in and is a serious undertaking so it's not for first timers or the unfit (it has claimed several lives). ⌚ ***5–10 days. www.raftingtasmania.com & www.tas-ex.com. Adults $1,750–$2,700. Not for children or non-swimmers.***

Hollybank Treetops Adventure.

3 kids Jet boating. Take an exhilarating jet boat ride for up to 10 people across Macquarie Harbour and through the rain-forested gorges of the King River. Along the way you'll be treated to a number of adrenalin-pumping, high-speed spins; it feels dangerous but it's safe, although you should be able to swim, just in case. ⌚ ***1 hr. Strahan Wharf. ☎ 03/6471-7396. www.wildriversjet.com.au. Adults $75, children 4–16 $45. Daily; bookings essential.***

4 ★★ kids Hollybank Treetops Adventure. The only one of its kind in Australia, this 730m (2,400-ft.) long 'flying fox' (a gravity-compelled cable ride, like a zip line) above the forest canopy reaches speeds of up to 40kmh (25 mph). Broken up into sections, some are as short as 15m (50 ft.); the longest is a breathtaking 372m (1,220 ft.) and includes crossing 50m (164 ft.) above the Pipers River. Open for all ages but you'll need a head for heights. ⌚ ***3 hr. 66 Hollybank Rd., Underwood. ☎ 03/6395-1390. www.treetopsadventure.com.au. Adults $100, children 3–16 $80. Tours daily 9am and 2pm, night-time tours 8:30pm; bookings essential.***

The Best Beaches

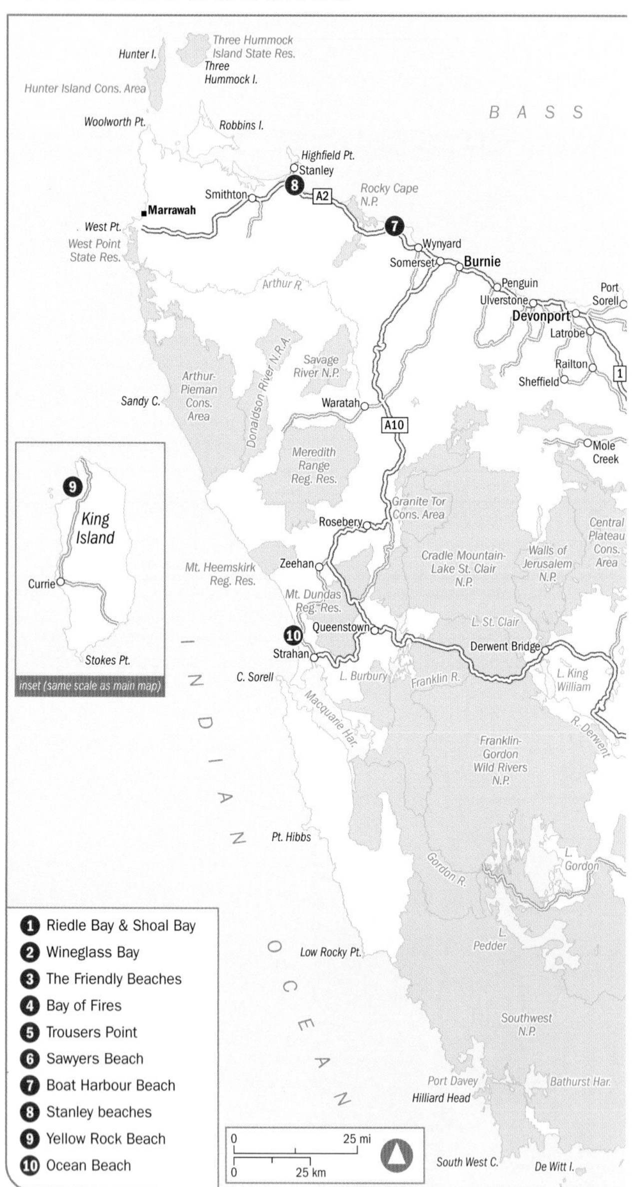

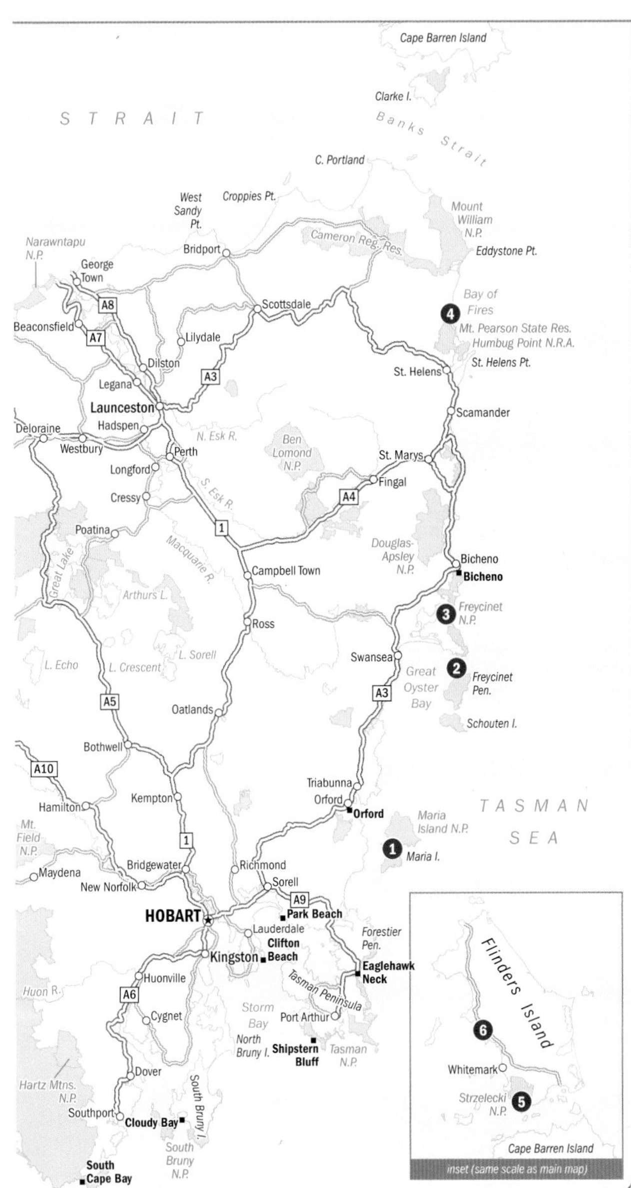
Cape Barren Island
Clarke I.
STRAIT
Banks Strait
C. Portland
West Sandy Pt.
Croppies Pt.
Mount William N.P.
Eddystone Pt.
Narawntapu N.P.
Bridport
Cameron Reg. Res.
George Town
A8
Scottsdale
Bay of Fires
4
Mt. Pearson State Res.
Humbug Point N.R.A.
Beaconsfield
A7
Lilydale
St. Helens Pt.
Dilston
St. Helens
A3
Legana
Launceston
Scamander
Deloraine
Hadspen
N. Esk R.
Ben Lomond N.P.
Westbury
Perth
St. Marys
Longford
Fingal
Cressy
S. Esk R.
A4
1
Poatina
Macquarie R.
Douglas-Apsley N.P.
Bicheno
Bicheno
Great Lake
Campbell Town
Arthurs L.
Freycinet N.P.
3
Ross
L. Sorell
Swansea
L. Echo
L. Crescent
Great Oyster Bay
2
Freycinet Pen.
A5
A3
Oatlands
Schouten I.
Bothwell
A10
Triabunna
Kempton
Orford
Orford
TASMAN SEA
Hamilton
Maria Island N.P.
Mt. Field N.P.
1
1
Maria I.
Bridgewater
Richmond
Maydena
New Norfolk
Sorell
A9
HOBART
Park Beach
Lauderdale
Forestier Pen.
Clifton Beach
Kingston
Eaglehawk Neck
Huonville
Tasman Peninsula
Huon R.
A6
Storm Bay
Cygnet
Port Arthur
North Bruny I.
Shipstern Bluff
Tasman N.P.
Flinders Island
6
Dover
South Bruny I.
Whitemark
Hartz Mtns. N.P.
Strzelecki N.P.
5
Southport
Cloudy Bay
South Bruny N.P.
Cape Barren Island
South Cape Bay
inset (same scale as main map)

Like most islands, Tasmania is encircled by beautiful beaches. But don't expect palm-fringed stretches of sand flanked by ritzy resorts: beaches in Tasmania are wild, windswept and more often than not deserted. The rugged seas and cool currents don't always produce the ideal swimming conditions, but the white sands are always perfect for strolling along and beachcombing.

❶ ★★★ **Riedle Bay & Shoal Bay.** There are dozens of beaches on Maria Island worthy to be included in this list of Tasmania's best, but Riedle Bay and Shoal Bay, that wash either side of a sandy isthmus, together offer a bit of everything. **Shoal Bay,** on the eastern side, is calm and protected; **Riedle Bay** faces the ocean, and so has some swell, but still offers good swimming, especially after the long walk to get there. The southern reaches of the ocean beach, known as **Trigonia Corner,** are a beachcomber's delight, with piles of shells and starfish and seahorses banked up between rocks. *For more information about Maria Island, see p 108.*

❷ ★★★ **Wineglass Bay.** Widely celebrated by travel guides and magazines as one of the top 10 beaches in the world, Wineglass Bay is spectacular—a wineglass-shaped curve of fine white sand lapped by crystal-clear blue water—but it's just one of many almost-too-good-to-be-true beaches you'll find along the eastern coast of Tasmania. *See p 114,* ❺.

❸ **The Friendly Beaches.** Freycinet National Park is Tassie's most popular coastal park, but most people don't realise that there are plenty of beautiful beaches with squeaky white sand, crystal-clear water, and views that stretch forever in the northern section of the park. For that reason, more often than not you have The Friendly Beaches all to yourself. *20km (12½ miles) south of Bicheno on the Coles Bay road (C302). National Park entry fee applies; see box National Parks Pass, p 115.*

❹ ★★★ **Bay of Fires.** Almost as famous as Wineglass Bay, the Bay of Fires is much easier to get to (you can drive), and has less than half the

Wineglass Bay.

Sawyers Beach.

crowds. It's a stretch of coastline, rather than one individual beach, so even in peak season you can usually find a deserted boulder-strewn bay to call your own. You can spend days exploring the coastline on foot—which is exactly what many people do. *See p 89,* **11**.

5 ★★★ **Trousers Point.** Despite the odd name, Trousers Point is one of Australia's most beautiful beaches. *See p 67,* **3**.

6 ★★★ kids **Sawyers Beach.** There's no shortage of stunning beaches on Flinders Island, but this one is very special. *See p 68,* **6**.

7 ★★ **Boat Harbour Beach.** If you like your beaches low-key, you'll love Boat Harbour. Flanked by a collection of beach houses that march up the dune behind the white-sand beach, it's one of the best spots for a back-to-basics beach holiday. The water's always cold, but that doesn't seem to deter the locals from diving in. You can also spend time picking through the driftwood and shells along the high-water mark, before walking up along the sand. *15-min drive west of Wynyard.*

8 **Stanley beaches.** Most people come to Stanley to visit **The Nut** (p 60, **10**), but some of the best views of the circular headland are from the two beaches that fan out from either side. Both beaches are within walking distance of the town centre. *Follow either Green Hills Rd. or Wharf Rd.*

9 ★★★ **Yellow Rock Beach.** The rusting remains of the *Shannon*, a paddle steamer that was driven ashore by wild weather in 1906, are exposed at low tide just metres

Tassie's Best Surf Breaks

Surfing in Tasmania is not for the faint-hearted. Waves are wild, out of the way and the water is cold (bring your wetsuit), but at least the beaches are uncrowded. The famous monster wave of **Shipstern Bluff,** considered one of the world's heaviest waves, is off the coast of Port Arthur. There are less brutal breaks along the east coast: top spots include **Eaglehawk Neck** on the Tasman Peninsula and all up the east coast from **Orford to Bicheno;** close to Hobart, **Park Beach,** and **Clifton Beach** are the popular spots, along with Bruny Island's **Cloudy Bay,** where huge waves roll in from the Southern Ocean. If you don't mind hauling your board on a 7km (4-mile) bushwalk, **South Cape Bay** also gets really big breaks. Over on the west coast the legendary Roaring Forties winds whip up swells around **Marrawah** that are for experienced surfers only. You'll need your own board; Tassie has very few surf shops. For more information, see www.surfingaustralia.com/tas/.

Stanley beaches by The Nut.

from the shore at this beautiful beach on King Island. *See p 65,* .

⑩ ★ **Ocean Beach.** The longest beach in Tasmania, Ocean beach stretches for more than 30km (18½ miles) from Macquarie Heads in the south to Trial Harbour in the north. Thousands of **muttonbirds** (short-tailed shearwaters) breed here during summer and provide an amazing wildlife spectacle each night at dusk as they return from their feeding forays over the ocean. There is a walkway over the dunes to a viewing platform. It was here that a 7m (23- ft.) long 150kg (330 lb.) giant squid was washed ashore (now in the Tasmanian Museum & Art Gallery, p 79, ❷). *Drive out of Strahan towards Zeehan and turn left at the first intersection past the caravan park. Follow this road for 4km (2½ miles) and park behind the dunes.*

Staying Safe in Tasmania's Waters

Tasmania's beaches are beautiful, but they can also be dangerous, and very few are patrolled by surf lifesavers. Never swim alone, and always supervise children at the beach. Even the strongest swimmers can be swept out to sea if they get caught in a rip (a current of water that usually starts close to shore and moves away from the beach). Rips don't always move fast, so sometimes you may not even realise you are in one until you notice that you are a long way from the beach. If you do get caught, swim across the rip (parallel to the beach) as most are quite narrow. Before you take the plunge, try to identify any potential undercurrents, rips or sandbars—things to watch out for are patches of dark water, an area of relatively calm surf surrounded by larger waves or a channel of choppy water.

7 The Best Dining

Dining Best Bets

Barilla Bay oysters.

Best Breakfast
★ House of Anvers *9025 Bass Hwy., Latrobe (p 135)*

Best Bring Your Own (BYO)
★★★ The Boathouse *Currie, King Island (p 133)*

Best Dessert
★ Raspberry Farm Cafe *9 Christmas Hills Rd., Elizabethtown (p 137)*

Best Fish & Chips
★★★ Fish Frenzy *Elizabeth St. Pier, Hobart (p 134)*

Best Log Fire
The Gorge Restaurant *Cataract Gorge Cliff Grounds, Launceston (p 135)*

Best Local Produce
★ Bold Head Brasserie *Grassy Club, Currie Rd., Grassy (p 133)*

Best Long Lunch
★★★ Peppermint Bay *3435 Channel Hwy., Woodbridge (p 136)*

Previous page: Stillwater.

Best Oysters
★★ Barilla Bay *1388 Tasman Hwy., Cambridge (p 132)*

Best for People Watching
Maldini *47 Salamanca Place, Hobart. (p 136)*

Best for Sharing
★★★ Garagistes *103 Murray St., Hobart (p 135)*

Best Splurge
★★★ Stillwater *Ritchies Mill, Paterson St. (p 138)*

Best Steak
Black Cow Bistro *Ritchies Mill, Paterson St. (p 133)*

Best View
★ View 42° Restaurant & Bar *The Esplanade, Strahan (p 138)*

Best Winery Restaurant
★★ Josef Chromy *370 Relbia Rd., Relbia (p 135)*

Launceston Dining

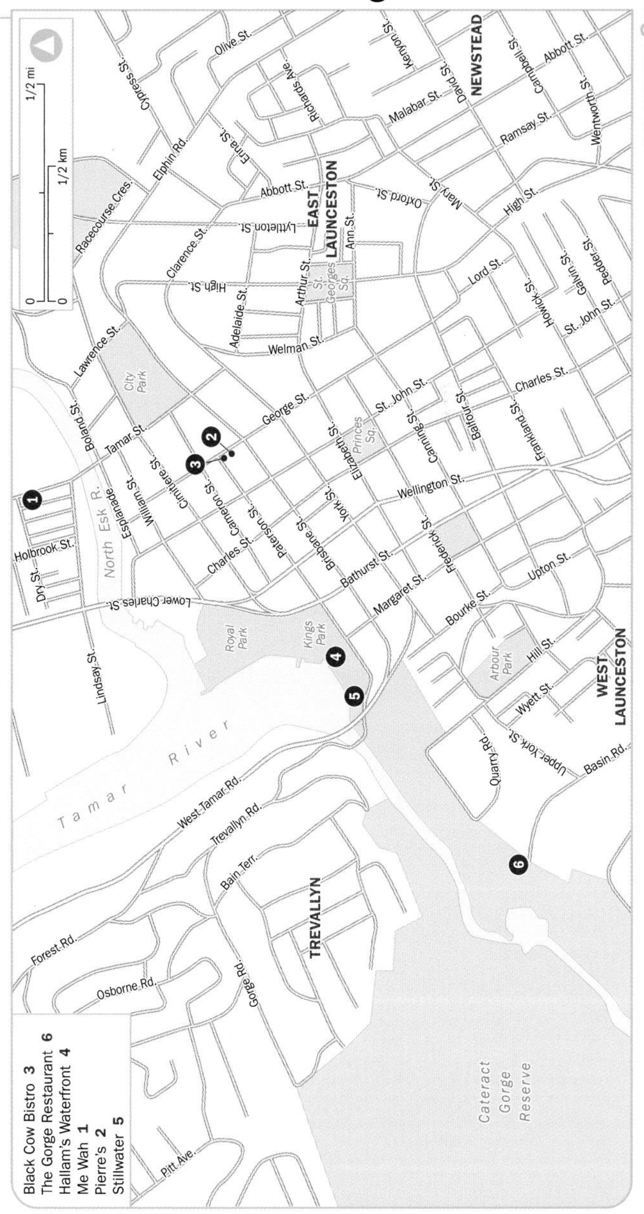

Tasmania Dining

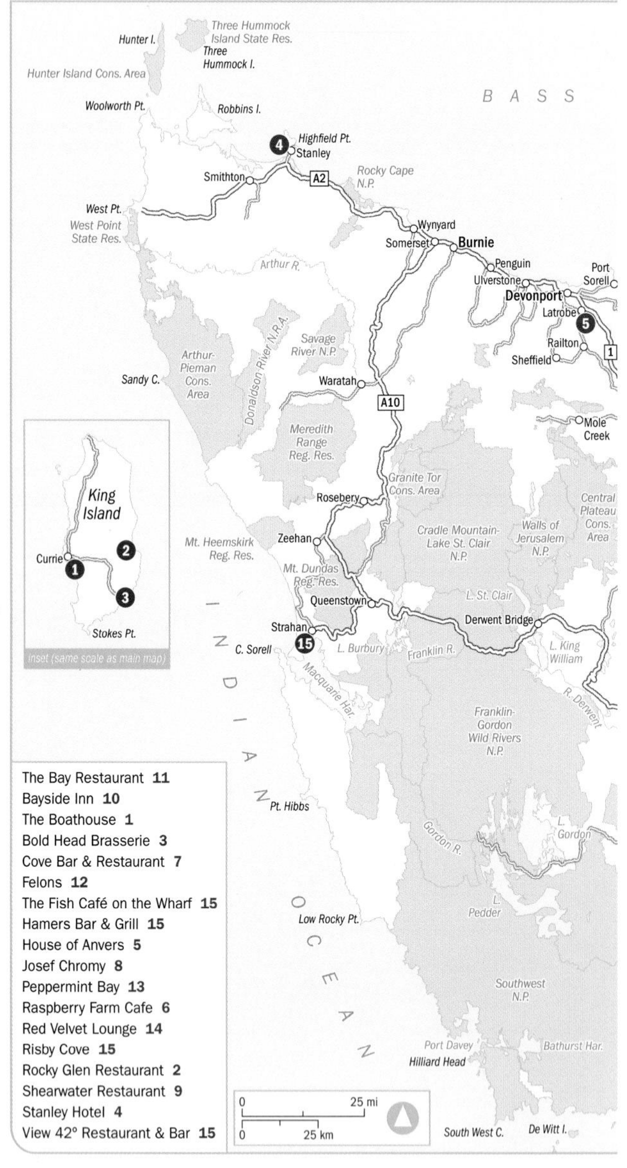

The Bay Restaurant **11**
Bayside Inn **10**
The Boathouse **1**
Bold Head Brasserie **3**
Cove Bar & Restaurant **7**
Felons **12**
The Fish Café on the Wharf **15**
Hamers Bar & Grill **15**
House of Anvers **5**
Josef Chromy **8**
Peppermint Bay **13**
Raspberry Farm Cafe **6**
Red Velvet Lounge **14**
Risby Cove **15**
Rocky Glen Restaurant **2**
Shearwater Restaurant **9**
Stanley Hotel **4**
View 42° Restaurant & Bar **15**

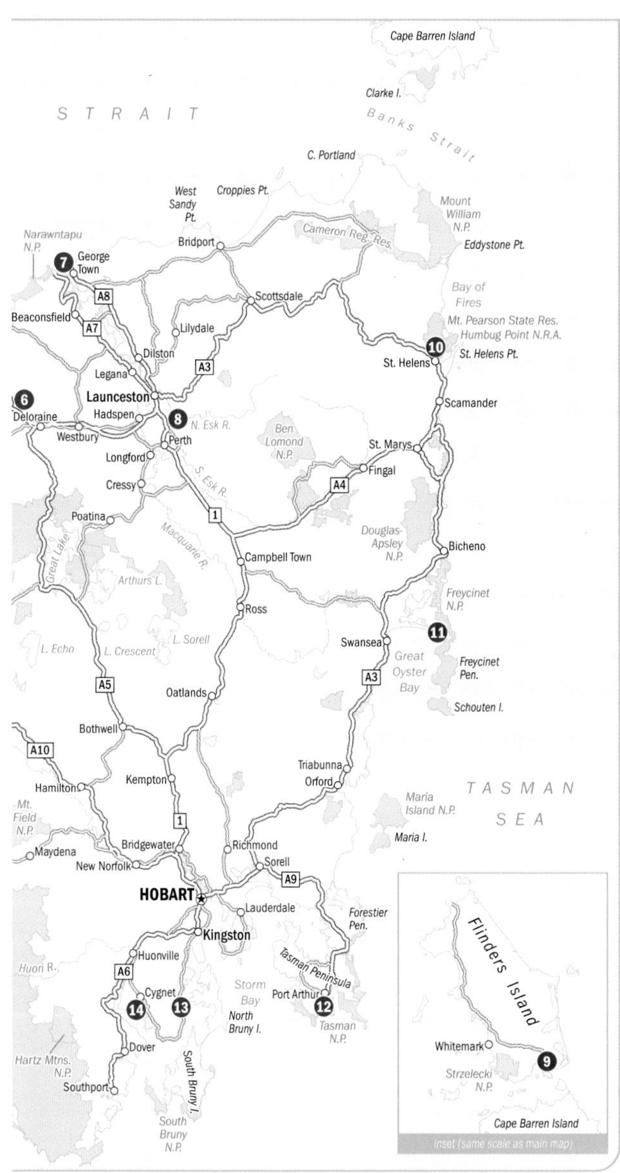
Cape Barren Island
Clarke I.
STRAIT
Banks Strait
C. Portland
West Sandy Pt.
Croppies Pt.
Mount William N.P.
Narawntapu N.P.
Bridport
Cameron Reg. Res.
Eddystone Pt.
7
George Town
A8
Scottsdale
Bay of Fires
Beaconsfield
A7
Lilydale
Mt. Pearson State Res.
Humbug Point N.R.A.
Dilston
10
St. Helens Pt.
St. Helens
A3
Legana
6
Launceston
Scamander
Deloraine
Hadspen
8
N. Esk R.
Ben Lomond N.P.
Westbury
Perth
St. Marys
Longford
Fingal
S. Esk R.
Cressy
A4
1
Poatina
Macquarie R.
Douglas-Apsley N.P.
Bicheno
Great Lake
Campbell Town
Arthurs L.
Freycinet N.P.
Ross
11
Swansea
L. Echo
L. Crescent
L. Sorell
Great Oyster Bay
Freycinet Pen.
A5
A3
Oatlands
Schouten I.
Bothwell
A10
Triabunna
Orford
TASMAN SEA
Hamilton
Kempton
Maria Island N.P.
Mt. Field N.P.
1
Maria I.
Bridgewater
Richmond
Maydena
New Norfolk
Sorell
A9
HOBART
Lauderdale
Forestier Pen.
Kingston
Flinders Island
Huonville
Huon R.
A6
Tasman Peninsula
Storm Bay
Cygnet
Port Arthur
14
13
12
North Bruny I.
Tasman N.P.
Whitemark
9
Dover
Hartz Mtns. N.P.
South Bruny I.
Strzelecki N.P.
Southport
South Bruny N.P.
Cape Barren Island
inset (same scale as main map)

Hobart Dining

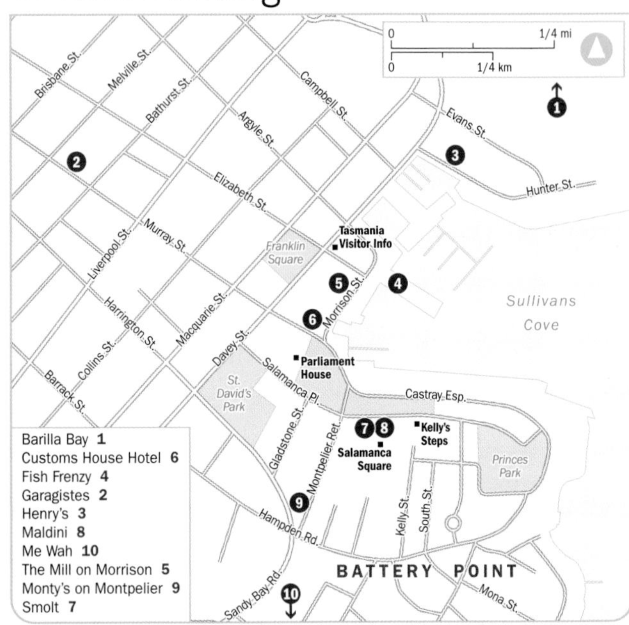

Tasmania Dining A to Z

★★ **Barilla Bay** CAMBRIDGE *SEAFOOD* Oysters are the main drawcard at this restaurant overlooking Barilla Bay's oyster farm, and you can have them just about any way you can think of, especially if you order the 'shucking awesome' platter of 30 oysters. There are plenty of non-bivalve dishes on the menu for those that dislike them. *1388 Tasman Hwy. ☎ 03/6248-5458. www.barillabay.com.au. Mains $27–$33. MC, V. Lunch & dinner daily, Wed–Sat July & Aug. Map p 132.*

★★★ **The Bay Restaurant** COLES BAY *CONTEMPORARY AUSTRALIAN* You'll need to book at this restaurant at Freycinet Lodge because it's just as popular with locals and people staying at nearby resorts or camping in the national park as it is with the lodge's guests. And it's easy to see why, with its combination of great views and superb food. The seafood platter, which apart from the prawns is sourced locally, is enormous. *Freycinet National Park. ☎ 03/6256-7016. www.freycinetlodge.com.au. Mains $32–$38. AE, DC, MC, V. Map p 130.*

Bayside Inn ST. HELENS *PUB BISTRO* The menu in this friendly pub has all your standard pub favourites, with good steaks and fresh seafood, including crayfish in season. The large dining room may lack some style but this is amply compensated for by the amazing views over

Georges Bay. *2 Cecilia St.* ☎ *03/6376-1466. www.baysideinn.com.au. Mains $17–$25. MC, V. Lunch & dinner daily. Map p 130.*

★★ **Black Cow Bistro** LAUNCESTON *STEAKHOUSE* All the meat served in this upmarket steakhouse in an old butcher's shop is dry aged, free range, grass fed, hormone free, Tasmanian (naturally) and very, very good. There are a few non-bovine dishes on offer, and the dark Belgian chocolate mousse will make you swoon, but really, it's all about the beef. *70 George St. (corner of Paterson St.).* ☎ *03/6331-9333. www.blackcowbistro.com.au. Mains $31–$40. MC, V. Dinner daily. Map p 129.*

★★★ **The Boathouse** KING ISLAND *BYO* It's strictly BYO (bring your own)—that's both food and drink—at The Boathouse tucked under the shadow of the lighthouse on the southern side of Currie Harbour on King Island. Set up by local artist Caroline Kininmonth, it's a fantastic place for a long lunch or romantic dinner. There's a barbecue, outdoor tables and chairs, and several tables inside the colourful art-filled room with floor-to-ceiling harbour views. Anyone is free to use the space and cooking facilities, so long as you clean up after yourself—and pop a few dollars in the donation box. *At the end of Lighthouse Rd., Currie. Donations welcome. Daily; if locked, call Caroline on* ☎ *0429/621-180. Map p 130.*

★ **Bold Head Brasserie** KING ISLAND *CONTEMPORARY* There's always something different on the menu here because it changes daily according to what's been plucked from the sea or been picked. The focus is very much on local King Island produce, so try the sea elephant oysters if they are in season or the wonderfully tender beef. Stick to the restaurant—the bar meals can be a bit hit and miss—and go early as the club shuts around 8pm. *Grassy Club, Currie Rd., Grassy.* ☎ *03/6461-1003. www.kingscuisine.com.au. Mains $24–$27. MC, V. Lunch Fri–Sun & dinner Wed–Mon. Map p 130.*

The Bay Restaurant.

★ **Cove Bar & Restaurant** GEORGE TOWN *CONTEMPORARY AUSTRALIAN* Perched on the water's edge at York Cove opposite the historic township of George Town at the mouth of the Tamar River this modern restaurant is the place to go to soak in the water views as you dine on Tasmanian produce such as oysters, Tasmanian salmon fish cakes, Longford lamb and Cape Grim beef. Sunsets can be spectacular. *2 Ferry Blvd.* ☎ *03/6382-9900. www.yorkcove.com.au. Mains $19–$31. AE, MC, V. Lunch Tues–Sun, dinner Mon–Sat. Map p 130.*

Customs House Hotel HOBART *PUB BISTRO* This restaurant in one of Hobart's oldest hotels serves up succulent steak and pasta, but it's best known for its super-fresh local seafood (especially the scallops) sourced straight from the fishing boats on the dock opposite. *1 Murray St.* ☎ *03/6234-6645. www.customshousehotel.com. Mains $23–$33. MC, V. Lunch & dinner daily. Map p 132.*

Dining on the High Seas

You don't have to wait until you've made it across Bass Strait to try out some of Tasmania's famed beef, seafood, cheese and wine. The *Spirit of Tasmania*'s (www.spiritoftasmania.com.au) fine-dining restaurant, **Leatherwood,** offers a great-value set menu of local produce, and each dish is matched with a Tasmanian wine. Two courses cost $56, three courses $64. It's popular though, given the other food options (a buffet) on board the ferry are pretty uninspiring, so book a table when you first board the ship as bookings cannot be made beforehand. AE, DC, MC, V.

Felons PORT ARTHUR *CONTEMPORARY AUSTRALIAN* Most restaurants inside major tourist attractions are usually pretty ordinary, but this licensed bistro inside the grounds of Port Arthur Historic Site is better than most. Focus is on local produce with local salmon, Tasmanian scallops, venison and even wallaby featuring on the menu. ***Port Arthur Visitor Centre. ☎ 1800/659-101. www.portarthur.org.au. Mains $21–$32. MC, V. Dinner daily. Map p 130.***

The Fish Café on the Wharf STRAHAN *SEAFOOD* This restaurant serves up the freshest fish in town; after all, it's right where the fishing boats unload. The local salmon is fantastic and the wine list features mainly Tasmanian wines. Leave room for some Tasmanian ice cream. ***The Esplanade. ☎ 03/6471-4332. Mains $14–$27. MC, V. Lunch & dinner daily. Map p 130.***

★★★ **Fish Frenzy** HOBART *SEAFOOD* For a few dollars you'll get big paper cones of excellent fish 'n' chips with a choice of batters, mountainous seafood platters and a few more adventurous seafood things. They even serve beer and wine. Where better to watch the world go by than outside on Elizabeth Street Pier? ***Elizabeth St. Pier.***

Calamari at Fish Frenzy.

☎ 03/6231-2134. www.fishfrenzy.com.au. Mains $12–$28. AE, MC, V. Lunch & dinner daily. Map p 132.

★★★ **Garagistes** HOBART *CONTEMPORARY AUSTRALIAN* Hobart's hottest restaurant right now is Garagistes, housed in an old motor garage. The food is very modern, and while the focus, like many Tasmanian restaurants, is on local produce, the food is given a very innovative treatment (think tartare of wallaby with fresh wasabi or grilled calamari with pickled zucchini and raisin purée) and designed to share, so you can graze the entire menu quite happily. You'll probably need to queue to get a seat at the communal table, but it's worth the wait. *103 Murray St.* ☎ *03/6231-0588. www.garagistes.com.au. Mains $15–$36. MC, V. Dinner Wed–Sat, 4-course lunch Sun ($75). No bookings except for lunch Sun. Map p 132.*

The Gorge Restaurant LAUNCESTON *CONTEMPORARY AUSTRALIAN* Most of the dishes tend to be a bit on the heavy side (think steaks, roasts, venison and duck), so this rather old-fashioned restaurant in the equally (but delightfully) old-fashioned pleasure gardens of Cataract Gorge is a better option for winter, when you can enjoy the roaring log fire. There are some outdoor tables that are used in summer, but be prepared to do battle with the resident peacocks. *Cataract Gorge Cliff Grounds.* ☎ *03/6331-3330. www.launcestoncataractgorge.com.au. Mains $30–$33. MC, V. Lunch Tues–Sun, dinner Tues–Sat. Map p 129.*

Hallam's Waterfront LAUNCESTON *SEAFOOD* Overlooking the Tamar Yacht Basin, Hallam's boasts superb fresh seafood. Opt for the chilli scallops and seafood platter with the Tasmanian crayfish—it's their speciality. *13 Park St.* ☎ *03/6334-0554. www.hallamswaterfront.com.au. Mains $28–$34. AE, MC, V. Lunch & dinner daily. Map p 129.*

Hamers Bar & Grill STRAHAN *PUB BISTRO* While away the afternoon sitting by the fire with a bowl of soup and watch the boats dock at the wharf. *The Esplanade.* ☎ *03/6471-7191. Mains $22–$32. MC, V. Lunch & dinner daily. Map p 130.*

★★★ **Henry's** HOBART *CONTEMPORARY AUSTRALIAN* The food here is excellent. Opt for one of the classics (grass-fed Cape Grim beef or pan-roasted salmon) or try one of the more innovative dishes from the 'evolution' section of the menu: you won't be disappointed. *25 Hunter St.* ☎ *03/6210-7700. www.thehenryjones.com. Mains $29–$40. AE, MC, V. Dinner daily. Map p 132.*

★ **House of Anvers** LATROBE *EUROPEAN* Spice up your day with one of the sweetest breakfasts around at this cute little chocolate factory near the turnoff to Devonport airport. The pain au chocolat will transport you straight to Paris, and the Aztec chilli hot chocolate is divine—just what you need if you're heading east or south after an overnight ferry trip. *9025 Bass Hwy.* ☎ *03/6326-2958. www.anvers-chocolate.com.au. Mains $18–$27. MC, V. Breakfast & lunch daily. Map p 130.*

★★ **Josef Chromy** RELBIA *CONTEMPORARY AUSTRALIAN* Soak in the sunshine and the vineyard views on the cafe deck at the cellar door of the Josef Chromy winery, 15 minutes from Launceston. Choose from gourmet antipasto platters, light meals or more substantial dishes, like oven-roasted spatchcock and Cape Grim scotch fillets. *370 Relbia Rd.* ☎ *03/6335-8700. www.josefchromy.com.au. Mains $28–$35. MC, V. Lunch daily. Map p 130.*

Stackings at Peppermint Bay.

Maldini HOBART *ITALIAN* During the day, the outside tables on the footpath in buzzy Salamanca Place are one of the city's best people-watching posts; at night the place to be is inside the stone-fronted warehouse tucking into delicious Italian classics like oh-so-tender veal scallopini, prosciutto-wrapped chicken and risotto alla pescatore. *47 Salamanca Place.* ☎ *03/6223-4460. www.maldinirestaurant.com.au. Mains $20–$37. AE, DC, MC, V. Breakfast, lunch & dinner daily. Map p 132.*

★★ **Me Wah** HOBART & LAUNCESTON *CHINESE* Consistently lauded as the best Chinese food in Tasmania, Me Wah has restaurants in both Hobart and Launceston. If you've never tried greenlip abalone before, this is a good place to do it: the Me Wah chefs marinate it for a whole day then braise it for 12 hours. At $95 a dish, you can be pretty sure it will be one you won't forget in a hurry. *Suite 16 Magnet Court, Sandy Bay Rd, Hobart.* ☎ *03/6223-3688 & 39-41 Invermay Rd, Launceston.* ☎ *03/6331-1308. Mains $24-$40. AE, MC, V. Lunch & dinner daily. Map p 132 & p 129.*

★ **The Mill on Morrison** HOBART *MODERN AUSTRALIAN* If you've ever wondered what you get if you mix together a tapas bar, wine bar, oyster bar and steakhouse, then go to the Mill on Morrison. From a shared lunch to after-work wine and tapas or a leisurely meal, this brand new stylishly casual waterfront eatery does it all really well. Love the sundae bar! *11 Morrison St.* ☎ *03/6234-3490. Mains $10-$15. MC, V. Lunch & dinner daily. Map p 132.*

Monty's on Montpelier HOBART *MODERN EUROPEAN* Cosy up beside the fire in this sweet little cottage in Battery Point. The menu changes seasonally and features local produce, prepared with a slightly French twist. *37 Montpelier Rd., Battery Point.* ☎ *03/6223-2511. www.montys.com.au. Mains $35. MC, V. Dinner Thurs–Tues. Map p 132.*

★★★ **Peppermint Bay** WOODBRIDGE *CONTEMPORARY AUSTRALIAN* A spectacularly sited restaurant complex on the shores of the D'Entrecasteaux Channel with magnificent water views, Peppermint Bay offers good-value bistro food in the bar at night (mains $18–$35), and superb a la carte lunch in the main restaurant, **Stackings,** with an exclusively Tasmanian wine list. The complex includes a providore selling handmade foods from local produce. Drive, or take a cruise from Hobart to make a day of it. *3435 Channel Hwy.* ☎ *03/6267-4088. www.peppermintbay.com.au. 3 courses $65, 5 courses $85. AE,*

DC, MC, V. Lunch daily (Stackings: Thurs–Mon), dinner Thurs–Sat. Map p 130.

Pierre's LAUNCESTON *FRENCH* Pierre's likes to boast that it is Tasmania's oldest brasserie, and given that it's been going strong since 1956, it probably is. It's a long, narrow, dark and moody space, which makes it just as inviting for a drink as it is for a meal. The menu has all the bistro classics, such as steak with *Cafe de Paris* butter, steak tartare and escargot. *88 George St. ☎ 03/6331-6835. www.pierres.net.au. Mains $26–$40. AE, MC, V. Lunch Mon–Sat, dinner Tues–Sat. Map p 129.*

★ **Raspberry Farm Cafe** ELIZABETHTOWN *CONTEMPORARY AUSTRALIAN* If you have a sweet tooth, you'll love the range of raspberry-flavoured desserts on offer at this busy riverside restaurant midway between Launceston and Devonport, but they also serve up lots of savoury light meals (think pastas, savoury crepes, veggie wraps, salads and gourmet burgers) as well. See also p 29. *9 Christmas Hills Rd. ☎ 03/6362-2186. www.raspberryfarmcafe.com. Mains $14–$19. MC, V. Breakfast & lunch daily. Map p 130.*

★★★ **Red Velvet Lounge** CYGNET *CONTEMPORARY AUSTRALIAN* Housed in an old general store, this little restaurant serves up excellent food in a friendly and casual atmosphere. It's worth the drive from Hobart for the crab cakes with saffron mayo alone, but if that doesn't convince you, the slow-cooked lamb or the potato gnocchi with Huon Valley mushrooms will. *24 Mary St. ☎ 03/6295-0466. www.theredvelvetlounge.com.au. Mains $20–$29. MC, V. Lunch daily, dinner (bookings essential) Fri & Sat. Map p 130.*

Risby Cove STRAHAN *CONTEMPORARY AUSTRALIAN* This is fine dining in a lovely quiet waterfront setting. The menu is predominately local and very seasonal, with lots of local fish and seafood. *The Esplanade. ☎ 03/6471-7572. www.risby.com.au. Mains $23–$36. AE, MC, V. Breakfast & dinner daily. Bookings essential. Map p 130.*

Rocky Glen Restaurant KING ISLAND *EUROPEAN* It's all about the spectacular views at this family-run restaurant opposite the beach at Naracoopa on what the locals like to call the sunny side of King Island (the eastern side). Servings are huge, and tend to be smothered in heavy European-style sauces. As always, the local King Island beef and seafood is a good choice. *1 Lovers Lane, Naracoopa. ☎ 03/6461-1103. www.rockyglen.com.au. Mains $28–$38. AE, DC,*

Stillwater.

MC, V. Lunch Sat, dinner Thurs–Sun. Map p 130.

Shearwater Restaurant FLINDERS ISLAND *PUB BISTRO* The menu features all your favourite pub classics, like steak and fish and chips—if you give them 24 hours' notice they'll organise a crayfish for you (mid-Nov to Sept)—but the real reason you should eat here is for the amazing views across the Franklin Sound. It is also the only restaurant on Flinders Island that is open every day. ***Furneaux Tavern, 11 Franklin Pde., Lady Barron. ☎ 03/6359-3521. www.furneauxtavern.com.au. Mains $16–$33. MC, V. Lunch & dinner daily. Map p 130.***

★★ Smolt HOBART *MEDITERRANEAN* A smolt is a baby salmon, and while you'll always find a couple of Tasmanian salmon dishes on the menu, there's not as much seafood on the menu as the name implies. Focus is on Italian and Spanish dishes, including pizza and pasta and dishes to share. ***2 Salamanca Square. ☎ 03/6224-2554. www.smolt.com.au. Mains $19–$36. AE, DC, MC, V. Lunch & dinner daily. Map p 132.***

Stanley Hotel STANLEY *PUB BISTRO* This bistro serves good-value lunch and dinner with a focus on local produce and Tasmanian wines. Try the octopus, caught fresh at Stanley wharf, or the local handcrafted venison and cranberry sausages. ***19–21 Church St. ☎ 03/6458-1161. www.stanleyhotel.com. Mains $18–$34. MC, V. Lunch & dinner daily. Map p 130.***

★★★ Stillwater LAUNCESTON *CONTEMPORARY AUSTRALIAN* During the day this elegant restaurant in a restored riverside mill has a casual cafe atmosphere with extensive outdoor dining overlooking the Tamar River and the yachts moored in its Basin. At night, it's fine dining with plenty of fresh Tasmanian seafood and local produce. Each dish is matched with the best local wine. ***Ritchie's Mill, Paterson St. ☎ 03/6331-4153. www.stillwater.net.au. Mains $40–$42. 6 courses $120. AE, DC, MC, V. Breakfast & lunch daily, dinner Mon–Sat. Map p 129.***

★ View 42° Restaurant & Bar STRAHAN *CONTEMPORARY AUSTRALIAN* It's a bit of a steep walk up to the top of the hill but the view of the township and harbour from this bar and restaurant is worth it. The nightly seafood buffet is hard to resist, but it also serves tapas from 2:30 to 8:30pm every day. ***The Esplanade. ☎ 03/6471-4200. Buffet $47.50, tapas $3.50–$12.50. AE, DC, MC, V. Dinner daily. Map p 130.***

View from View 42.

8 The Best Nightlife

Nightlife Best Bets

Mud Bar at Peppers Seaport Hotel.

Best for Alfresco Wines
Mud Bar *Seaport Blvd., Launceston (p 143)*

Best Art House Movies
★★★ State Cinema *375 Elizabeth St., Hobart (p 145)*

Best Blues & Jazz
★★★ Republic Bar & Café *299 Elizabeth St., Hobart (p 145)*

Best Classical Music
Tasmanian Symphony Orchestra, *Federation Concert Hall, 1 Davey St., Hobart (p 146)*

Best Cocktails
Observatory Bar *Murray St. Pier, Hobart (p 143)*

Most Historic Theatre
★★ Theatre Royal *29 Campbell St., Hobart (p 146)*

Best Music Festival
★★★ The Falls Festival *Marion Bay (p 145)*

Best Night Cap
★★★ IXL Long Bar *25 Hunter St., Hobart (p 143)*

Best Rock
★★★ Brisbane Hotel *3 Brisbane St., Hobart (p 144)*

Best Rooftop Bar
★★★ The Rooftop *112 Murray St., Hobart (p 143)*

Best View
Onyx Bar *Wrest Point Casino, Hobart (p 143)*

Previous page: Theatre Royal.

Hobart Nightlife

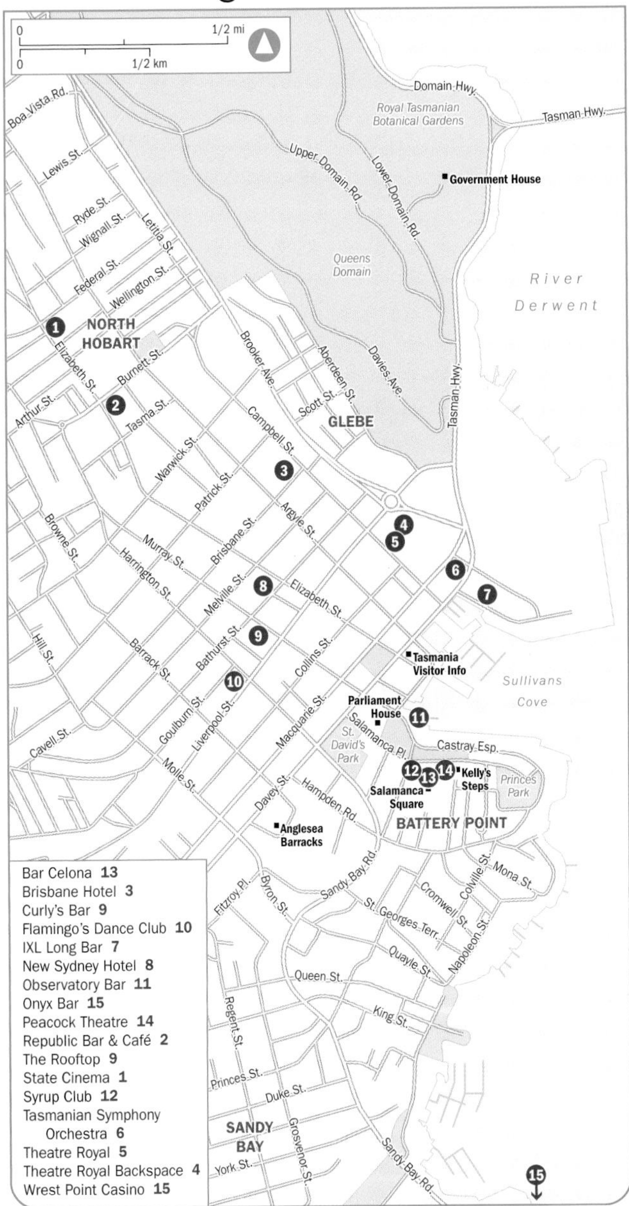

Launceston Nightlife

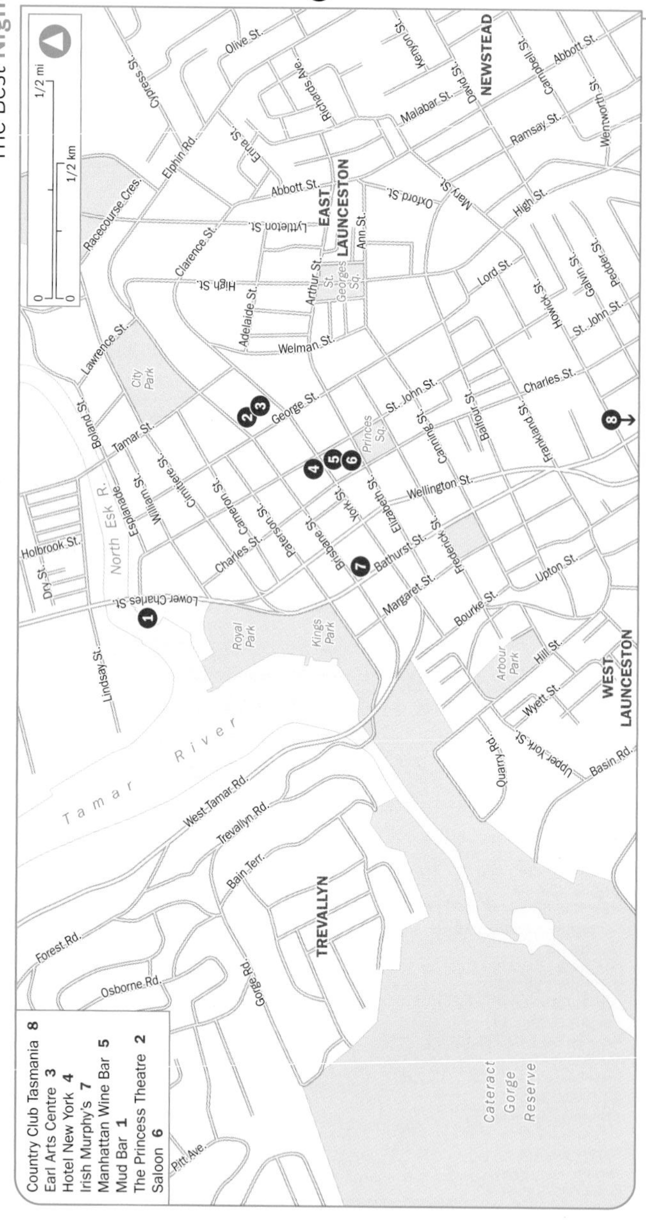

Tasmania Nightlife A to Z

Bars & Lounges

Bar Celona HOBART By day it's a cafe but come sundown this tiny little place in Salamanca Square becomes a popular bar, particularly in summer, when you can sip your drinks out in the courtyard in the balmy twilight. *23 Salamanca Place. ☎ 03/6224-7557. www.barcelonahobart.com. Map p 141.*

★★★ **IXL Long Bar** HOBART Part of the Henry Jones Art Hotel, this moody bar is the place for a martini. The red-leather stools, exposed brick wall and the live jazz on Thursday, Friday and Saturday nights all add to the atmosphere. In winter, don't go home until you've had a warm nightcap cocktail. *25 Hunter St. ☎ 03/6210-7700. www.thehenryjones.com. Map p 141.*

Manhattan Wine Bar LAUNCESTON Classic cocktails are the go here, and, not surprisingly, there are plenty of twists on the classic Manhattan, usually made with whisky, sweet vermouth and bitters. Try the Honey Vanilla version, with honey vodka, Galliano and a squeeze of lemon. Yum! *81 York St. ☎ 03/6334-2414. www.manhattanwinebar.net.au. Map p 142.*

Mud Bar LAUNCESTON A nice spot for a glass of wine or two before dinner, the bar section of this popular restaurant on the ground floor of Peppers Seaport Hotel enjoys views of the marina and North Esk River—try to nab a seat outside on the wharf. There's a good range of Tasmanian wines available by the glass. *Seaport Blvd. ☎ 03/6334-5066. www.mudbar.com.au. Map p 142.*

Observatory Bar HOBART It's only open Wednesdays through to Sunday, but it stays open late. The cocktail list is huge (there were more than 40 on there at last count), they have good snacks, and after around 10pm the dance music starts pumping. It's where the beautiful people hang out. *Lvl 1, Murray St. Pier. ☎ 03/6223-1273. www.observatorybar.com.au. Map p 141.*

Onyx Bar HOBART Most people don't usually head to casinos unless they're keen on a flutter, but this bar at Wrest Point (see below) has water views and is the perfect place for a sunset cocktail. *410 Sandy Bay Rd. ☎ 03/6221-1700. www.onyxbar.net.au. Map p 141.*

★★★ **The Rooftop** HOBART The best spot to be on those hot summer nights (yes, Hobart does have them). The Rooftop is not just a good place to drink, but every now and then they screen art movies on the massive outdoor wall. When there's no movie showing, there's usually an art exhibition of some kind and live music. Open on Friday and Saturday nights only. *Tattersalls Hotel, 112*

IXL Long Bar, Henry Jones Art Hotel.

Murray St. ☎ 03/6234-5112. www.tattersallshoteltas.com.au. Map p 141.

Casinos

Country Club Tasmania LAUNCESTON Tasmania's two casinos are more than just gambling dens. They are the main venues for interstate and international big-name live music acts and have some of the best cocktail bars in the city. In this case, the bar in question is **Tonic,** with live entertainment Thursday, Friday and Saturday nights, a good cocktail list and bar snacks. If gaming is really your thing, you'll find all the popular table games, including blackjack, Texas Hold 'Em Poker and roulette as well as a bank of pokies. *Country Club Ave., Prospect Vale. ☎ 03/6335-5777. www.countryclubtasmania.com.au. Map p 142.*

Wrest Point Casino HOBART Hobart has lots of 'Australia's oldest' and that includes, rather unexpectedly, Australia's oldest (legal) casino. It opened in 1973, nearly a quarter of a century before Sydney's. Like its sister property in Launceston (above), this is the best (often only) place to go to see big-name music, comedy and theatrical acts and it has some of the best bars in town. *410 Sandy Bay Rd. ☎ 1800/703-006. www.wrestpoint.com.au. Map p 141.*

Live Music & Dance Clubs

★★★ **Brisbane Hotel** HOBART This is the home of rock 'n' roll and indie live music in Hobart. There's nothing fancy about this pub, but if you like your beer cold and your music live and loud, you'll love the Brissie. *3 Brisbane St. ☎ 03/6234-4920. Cover price varies; often free. Map p 141.*

Curly's Bar HOBART It's in the same building as The Rooftop (p 143) but it's a world away in real life. Burn up the dance floor with live music or great DJs. It's only open on Wednesday and Saturday nights and can get crowded as the night wears on, especially on Saturdays, so be prepared to press some flesh with people you've never met—all part of the fun really. *Tattersalls Hotel, 112 Murray St. ☎ 03/6234-5112. Cover price varies. www.tattersallshoteltas.com.au. Map p 141.*

Flamingo's Dance Club HOBART One of the only gay and lesbian clubs in Tasmania, Flamingo's

Wrest Point Casino.

★★★ The Falls Festival

The ultimate New Year's Eve party is held simultaneously in Lorne on Victoria's Great Ocean Road and on a farm in Marion Bay overlooking Maria Island. Dance in the New Year with a line-up of local and international bands on two stages, or enjoy comedians, roving performers, market stalls and moonlit cinema. Camping is included in the ticket price (you can hire tents) and there is plenty of food and drink available. It's on every year from December 29 to January 1. www.fallsfestival.com.

is open Friday and Saturday nights from 10pm until late and has a huge dance floor. *Lvl 2, 251 Liverpool St. ☎ 036/6294-6173. Cover price varies; often $5 or free before midnight. www.flamingosbar.com. Map p 141.*

Hotel New York LAUNCESTON The place to go in Launceston to see touring indie bands and international DJs. *122 York St. ☎ 03/ 6334-7231. Cover price varies. www.hotelnewyork.net.au. Map p 142.*

Irish Murphy's LAUNCESTON There are so many Irish pubs in Tasmania, but they do seem to offer more entertainment than most. This one in Launceston has live bands every night. *211 Brisbane St. ☎ 03/ 6331-4440. Cover price varies. www.irishmurphys.net.au. Map p 142.*

New Sydney Hotel HOBART The New Sydney feels like an Irish pub because there's plenty of Guinness and Kilkenny on tap, and a fair bit of Paddy paraphernalia on the walls, but it manages to still feel like a real pub rather than a theme park. The line-up is more varied, with live music 6 nights a week—traditional folk, blues and jazz, rock and just a dash of Irish. *87 Bathurst St. ☎ 03/ 6234-4516. No cover. www.newsydneyhotel.com.au. Map p 141.*

★★★ Republic Bar & Café HOBART Soak up the live jazz (or blues) every night of the week in this old-style art deco pub (it's still called the Empire on the outside) in the northern suburbs. You won't find many tourists here, as it's away from the harbourside flesh pots, so it's a good place to mix with locals. The food's better than you'd expect as well. *299 Elizabeth St., North Hobart. ☎ 03/6234-6954. Cover price varies. www.republicbar.com. Map p 141.*

Saloon LAUNCESTON Popular with students, the Saloon often has live music. Tuesday night is trivia night. *191 Charles St. ☎ 03/6331-7355. No cover. www.saloon.com.au Map p 142.*

Syrup Club HOBART It used to be a brothel, then it was a pub, and now it's the 'Nightclub at the end of the world', proudly boasting that it's the 'last hotspot before you reach Antarctica'. Hit the dance floor Wednesday through to the early hours of Sunday morning; doors open at 9pm, but the real fun starts around midnight. *39 Salamanca Place. ☎ 03/ 6224-8249. Cover price varies. www.syrupclub.com.au. Map p 141.*

Movies

★★★ State Cinema HOBART Tasmania's oldest-running and only independent movie theatre was purpose built in 1913 as a 'moving picture house'. It's the place to go to see art-house, foreign-language and quality films. *375 Elizabeth St. ☎ 03/6234-6318. www.statecinema.com.au. Map p 141.*

Performing Arts

★ Peacock Theatre HOBART Catch experimental drama in this unique little theatre that has a natural rock face for a stage wall. It's part of the Salamanca Arts Centre. *77 Salamanca Place ☎ 03/6234-8414. Tickets start from $10. www.salarts.org.au. Map p 141.*

Tasmanian Symphony Orchestra HOBART If you like classical music, try to catch a performance of the Tasmanian Symphony Orchestra while in Tassie; they usually perform every couple of weeks. The TSO, as it's known, is resident in Hobart at the **Federation Concert Hall** but does tour around the state, so check the website for details of venues and concerts. *Federation Concert Hall, 1 Davey St. ☎ 1800/001-190. Tickets $21–$83. www.tso.com.au. Map p 141.*

Theatre North LAUNCESTON An eclectic line-up of local thespians and performers from mainland Australia and around the world are brought to the stage by this theatre company based in Launceston. There are two venues: **The Princess Theatre** (57 Brisbane St.) and the smaller **Earl Arts Centre** right behind it (10 Earl St.). *☎ 03/6323-3270. Ticket prices vary. www.theatrenorth.com.au. Map p 142.*

★★ Theatre Royal HOBART This grand old theatre first opened its doors in 1837, and has been entertaining the glitterati (and others) of Hobart Town ever since. The folk at the theatre say that early patrons were offered diversions ranging from music hall to cockfights, and 'prostitutes, sailors and general riffraff would enter the pit with full tankards, creating all sorts of drama of their own, much to the displeasure of the gentry in the boxes'. Today, however, all you're likely to be presented with is a programme of live theatre, contemporary music, dance, opera and comedy. *29 Campbell St. ☎ 03/6233-2299. Tickets $35–$60. www.theatreroyal.com.au. Map p 141.*

Theatre Royal Backspace HOBART Home to the Tasmanian Theatre Company, this intimate little theatre space is the place to catch local drama. *Sackville St. (off Campbell St., behind the Theatre Royal). ☎ 03/6234-8561. Tickets start from $19. www.tastheatre.com. Map p 141.* ●

Theatre Royal.

9 The Best **Hotels**

Hotel Best Bets

@VDL.

Best for **Art Lovers**
★★★ Henry Jones Art Hotel *25 Hunter St., Hobart (p 156)*

Best **for Beach Lovers**
★★★ The Harbour Houses *256 Port Rd., Boat Harbour (p 156)*

Best for **Contemporary Architecture**
MONA Pavilions *655 Main Rd., Berriedale (p 157)*

Best for **Golfers**
★ Barnbougle Dunes *Waterhouse Rd., Bridport (p 153)*

Best for **History**
★★★ @VDL *16 Wharf Rd., Stanley (p 153)*; and ★★ Cascades *533 Main Rd., Koonya (p 154)*

Previous page: Henry Jones Art Hotel.

Best **Luxury Hotel**
★★★ Saffire *2352 Coles Bay Rd., Coles Bay (p 159)*

Best **Value**
Montgomery's Private Hotel & YHA Backpackers *9 Argyle St., Hobart (p 157)*

Best **Views**
★★ Edge of the Bay *2308 Main Rd., Coles Bay (p 155)*

Best **Wilderness Getaway**
★★★ Cradle Mountain Lodge *4038 Cradle Mountain Rd., Cradle Mountain (p 155)*

Best for **Wine Lovers**
Rosevears Vineyard Retreat *1a Waldhorn Dr., Rosevears (p 159)*

Hobart Hotels

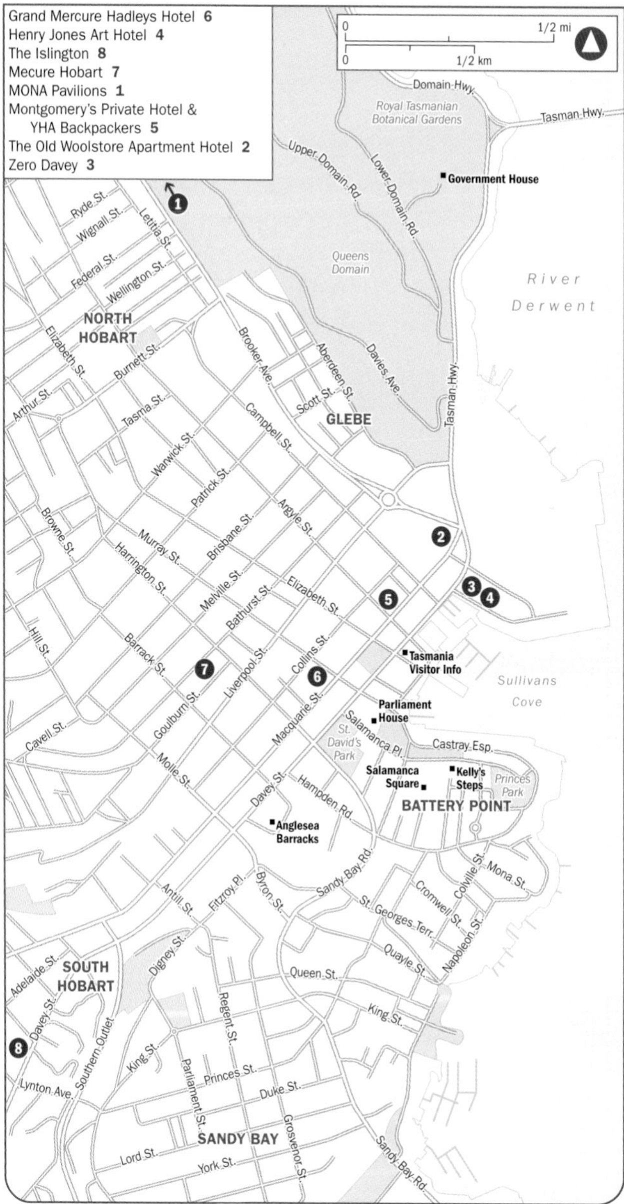

Tasmania Hotels

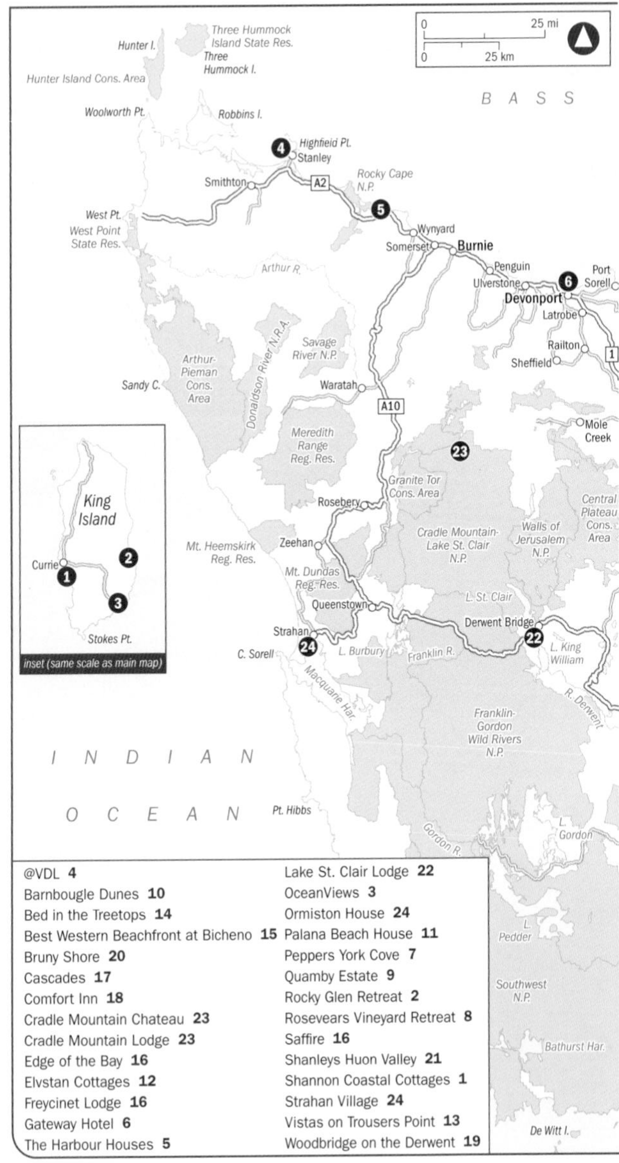

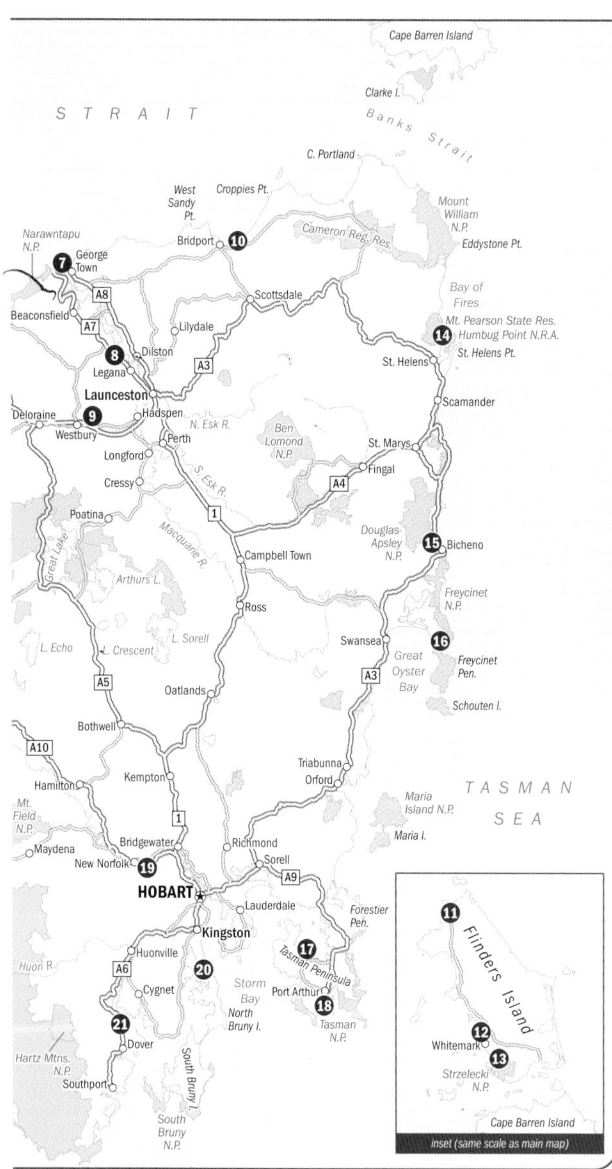
Cape Barren Island
Clarke I.
STRAIT
Banks Strait
C. Portland
West Sandy Pt.
Croppies Pt.
Mount William N.P.
Cameron Reg. Res.
Eddystone Pt.
Narawntapu N.P.
Bridport
10
7
George Town
A8
Scottsdale
Bay of Fires
Beaconsfield
A7
Lilydale
Mt. Pearson State Res.
14
Humbug Point N.R.A.
8
Dilston
St. Helens Pt.
Legana
A3
St. Helens
Launceston
Scamander
Deloraine
9
Hadspen
N. Esk R.
Westbury
Ben Lomond N.P.
Perth
St. Marys
Longford
Fingal
Cressy
S. Esk R.
A4
Poatina
1
Macquarie R.
Douglas-Apsley N.P.
15
Bicheno
Campbell Town
Great Lake
Arthurs L.
Freycinet N.P.
Ross
L. Sorell
Swansea
16
L. Echo
L. Crescent
Great Oyster Bay
Freycinet Pen.
A5
A3
Oatlands
Schouten I.
Bothwell
A10
Triabunna
Kempton
Orford
Hamilton
TASMAN SEA
Maria Island N.P.
Mt. Field N.P.
1
Maria I.
Bridgewater
Richmond
Maydena
New Norfolk
19
Sorell
A9
HOBART
Lauderdale
Forestier Pen.
Kingston
11
Flinders Island
17
Huonville
Tasman Peninsula
Huon R.
20
A6
Storm Bay
Cygnet
Port Arthur
18
North Bruny I.
Tasman N.P.
21
12
Whitemark
Dover
13
Hartz Mtns. N.P.
South Bruny I.
Strzelecki N.P.
Southport
Cape Barren Island
South Bruny N.P.
inset (same scale as main map)

Launceston Hotels

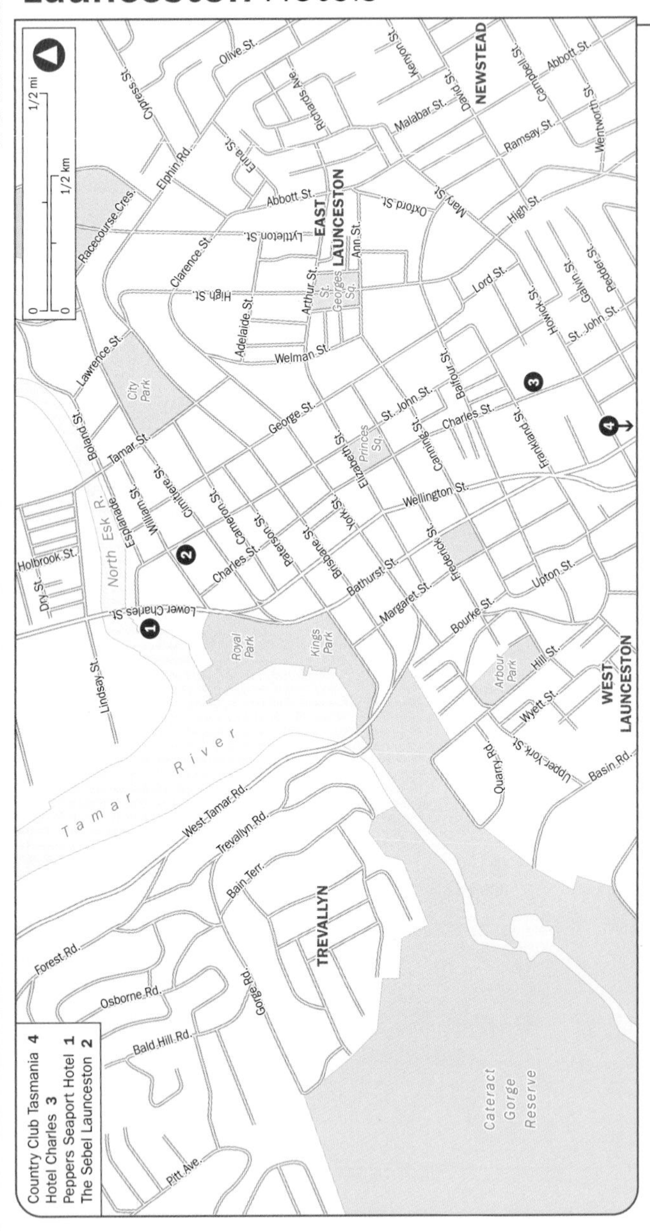

Tasmania Hotels A to Z

★★★ **@VDL** STANLEY In 1843, the Van Diemen's Land Company built a bluestone store on the waterfront in Stanley beneath the shadow of The Nut, a 152m (500- ft.) high flat-topped circular headland. Fast forward some 160 years and the company store is now one of the most stylish luxury B&Bs on the island. The three large suites are beautifully appointed, the beds sublime, there's a superb art collection and the owners are the consummate hosts. *16 Wharf Rd. ☎ 03/6458-2032. www.atvdlstanley.com.au. 3 units. Doubles $180–$350. MC, V. Map p 150.*

★ **Barnbougle Dunes** BRIDPORT There's nothing fancy about these little two-bedroom cottages, but the mad keen golfers who stay in them don't care one little bit. They overlook the first tee on Australia's top-ranking public golf course (currently ranked 35th in the world), a stunning links course that spills over the dunes on the edge of the wild Bass Strait coast. *Waterhouse Rd. ☎ 03/6356-0094. www.barnbougledunes.com.au. 22 units. Doubles $170. MC, V. Map p 150.*

Bed in the Treetops BINALONG BAY This B&B hideaway is high on a hill with views to die for just north of St. Helens near the Bay of Fires, and makes a great base from which to explore the beautiful northeast coast. No children under 12. Rates include pre-dinner drinks. *701 Binalong Bay Rd. ☎ 03/6376-1318. www.bedinthetreetops.com.au. 2 units. Doubles $270–$310 w/breakfast. MC, V. Map p 150.*

Best Western Beachfront at Bicheno BICHENO Bicheno is a good spot to base yourself if you want to spend a few days exploring the east coast, and this mid-range motel is a good option. There are

Barnbougle Dunes cottages.

Former Probation Station, Cascades.

poolside and courtyard rooms, but the only ones really worth staying in are the slightly more expensive seaview rooms which overlook the beach. *232 Tasman Hwy.* ☎ *03/6375-1111. www.beachfront.bestwestern.com.au. 50 units. Doubles $150–$170. AE, DC, MC, V. Map p 150.*

★★★ **Bruny Shore** BRUNY ISLAND Perched in the treetops 70m (230 ft.) above the beach on the very northern tip of Bruny Island, this three-bedroom timber-and-glass eyrie has fantastic ocean views: there's so much glass that it can sometimes feel as if you are in the sea, rather than overlooking it. There are large wrap-around decks, a fully equipped kitchen, absolute privacy, a fully loaded MP3 player and views from every room, including the main bathroom. *215 Bruny Island Main Rd.* ☎ *03/6294-6854. www.brunyshore.com.au. 1 unit. Double $300. MC, V. Map p 150.*

★★ **Cascades** KOONYA If these walls could talk, what stories they might tell. Cascades was built in 1841 as a Convict Probation Station and housed up to 400 convicts. The buildings have been authentically restored and offer self-catering accommodation in the former officers' quarters or luxury cottages. The added bonus of staying here is that the museum is only open to houseguests. *533 Nubeena Rd., Koonya.* ☎ *03/6250-3873. www.cascadescolonial.com.au. 5 units. Doubles $180–$230. MC, V. Map p 150.*

Comfort Inn PORT ARTHUR There's nothing flash about this three-star motel (in fact the rooms are very average given the price), but it's in a fantastic location, practically in the grounds of the Port Arthur site, which makes it very handy if you intend doing a ghost tour of the site or want to get up early to wander around the convict ruins before the crowds arrive. *29 Safety Cove Rd.* ☎ *03/6250-2101. www.portarthur-inn.com.au. 35 units. Doubles $145–$208. AE, DC, MC, V. Map p 150.*

Country Club Tasmania LAUNCESTON Located 5 minutes' drive from Launceston, the Country Club is full of genteel charm—think lots of wood panelling, overstuffed leather chairs, soft lights and subdued tones. There's an 18-hole golf course, big-name live shows, a casino, pool, tennis, squash and horse riding to keep you entertained. *Country Club Ave., Prospect Vale.* ☎ *1800/635-344. www.countryclubtasmania.com.au. 104 units. Doubles $175–$285. AE, MC, V. Map p 152.*

★ Cradle Mountain Chateau CRADLE MOUNTAIN Just minutes away from Dove Lake and Cradle Mountain, the chateau has decent motel-style rooms in two wings, and is next door to The Wilderness Gallery (entry is free for guests of the chateau; p 71, ❹). *Cradle Mountain Rd.* ☎ *1800/420-155. www.puretasmania.com.au. 60 units. Doubles $148–$198. AE, MC, V. Map p 150.*

★★★ Cradle Mountain Lodge CRADLE MOUNTAIN Upmarket accommodation is in tastefully decorated timber cabins that encircle the lodge, many with spas and most with great views. The lodge also offers a range of guided activities in and around the national park. *4038 Cradle Mountain Rd.* ☎ *03/6492-2100. www.cradlemountainlodge.com.au. 86 units. Doubles $250–$593. AE, MC, V. Map p 150.*

★★ Edge of the Bay COLES BAY This accommodation is suites and cottages set on the beachfront with dazzling views across the bay to the peaks of the pink-granite Hazards of Freycinet from your own private deck, which can be very hard to leave. There's a licensed restaurant here or you'll find cafes in Coles Bay are a 20-minute walk up the beach. *2308 Main Rd.* ☎ *03/6257-0102. www.edgeofthebay.com.au. 21 units. Doubles $270–$354. MC, V. Map p 150.*

Elvstan Cottages FLINDERS ISLAND Comfortable rather than flash, these two-bedroom, self-contained cottages are opposite the beach in the centre of Whitemark, the main (only) town on Flinders Island. They sleep five (there's a bed in the sunroom), have a well-equipped kitchen and are the ideal base from which to explore the island. *The Esplanade, Whitemark* ☎ *03/6359-2008. www.visitflindersisland.com.au. 2 units. Doubles $100–$160. No cards. Map p 150.*

★★ Freycinet Lodge COLES BAY You'll love the little balconies in these cabins just inside the

Eco-accredited Freycinet Lodge.

border of one of Tasmania's most popular national parks, especially if you have a water view (not all of them do). Freycinet is right on your doorstep and the resort has an excellent range of guided activities, so plan to spend at least a couple of days here. Rooms do not have TVs, however, so bring a book just in case the weather turns nasty. *Freycinet National Park. ☎ 03/6256-7016. www.puretasmania.com.au. 60 units. Doubles $260–$430; minimum 2-night stay. AE, DC, MC, V. Map p 150.*

Gateway Hotel DEVONPORT If you do need to stay overnight in Devonport then the Gateway is your best bet. It's in the centre of town and an easy walk to pubs, restaurants and the harbour. The brand-new deluxe rooms on the top floor have water views. *16 Fenton St. ☎ 03/6424-4922. www.batmanshill.com.au. 87 units. Doubles $170–$300. AE, DC, MC, V. Map p 150.*

Grand Mercure Hadleys Hotel HOBART The oldest continuously operating boutique hotel in Tasmania, this National Trust-listed hotel was built in 1834 and has played host to some of the most celebrated characters to have lived or visited Hobart, including Errol Flynn and Antarctic explorer Roald Amundsen. It's full of old-world charm in a great location in the centre of the city. *34 Murray St. ☎ 03/6237-2999. www.grandmercurehadleyshotel.com.au. 87 units. Doubles $175–$285. AE, DC, MC, V. Map p 149.*

★★★ The Harbour Houses BOAT HARBOUR Contemporary self-contained beach houses right on the edge of the sand at Boat Harbour with stunning views. *256 Port Rd. ☎ 03/6442-2135. www.harbourhouse.com.au. 3 units. Doubles $220. MC, V. Map p 150.*

★★★ Henry Jones Art Hotel HOBART The Henry Jones oozes style and history in equal measure. Located right on the waterfront in an old jam factory, it has more than 300 original artworks hung throughout the hotel. Rooms are contemporary but with plenty of historical

Henry Jones Art Hotel.

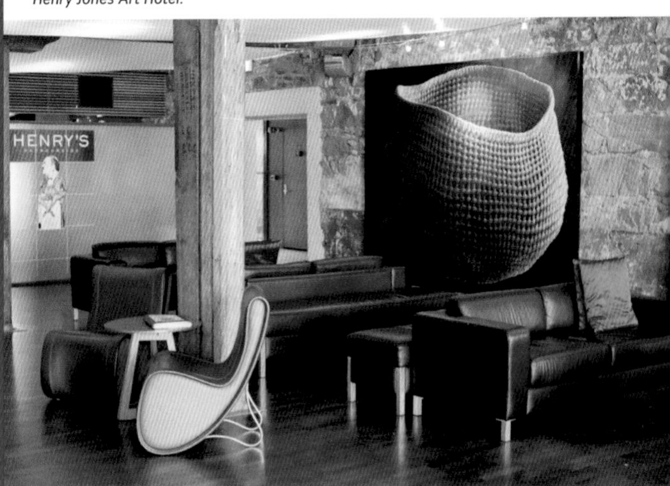

touches, such as the original beams and sandstone walls. *25 Hunter St.* ☎ *03/6210-7700. www.thehenryjones.com. 56 units. Doubles $218–$418. AE, DC, MC, V. Map p 149.*

★ **Hotel Charles** LAUNCESTON Clean and modern, the rooms of this brand-new hotel are brightly decorated and very spacious. It's built on the site of the old hospital—and is just across the road from the new one. It's a stylish place to stay on the fringe of the city but still close enough to walk into town if you want to. *287 Charles St.* ☎ *03/6337-4100. www.hotelcharles.com.au. 100 units. Doubles $198–$290. AE, DC, MC, V. Map p 152.*

The Islington HOBART A gorgeous 1847 Regency-style mansion has been transformed into a stunning boutique hotel, with each room luxuriously fitted out with antiques and original artwork. It's the perfect choice for a romantic weekend away. *321 Davey St.* ☎ *03/6220-2123. www.islingtonhotel.com. 11 units. Doubles $320–$570. AE, DC, MC, V. Map p 149.*

Lake St. Clair Lodge LAKE ST. CLAIR These loft-style cottages right on the shoreline of Lake St. Clair are in a perfect spot to use as a base for exploring the southern end of Cradle Mountain Lake St. Clair National Park. Each cottage has two bedrooms and a fireplace, needed more often than you'd think, even in summer, and there is a restaurant on site. *Lake St. Clair Rd., Derwent Bridge.* ☎ *03/6289-1137. www.lakestclairresort.com.au. 42 units. Doubles $280. AE, DC, MC, V. Map p 150.*

Mercure Hobart HOBART Good-value hotel with nice, if a little dated, rooms in the heart of the city. It's in need of a refurbishment, but rooms are clean and comfortable and staff are friendly. *156 Bathurst St.* ☎ *03/6232-6255. www.accorhotels.com. 140 units. Doubles $107–$170. AE, DC, MC, V. Map p 149.*

MONA Pavilions BERRIEDALE Each of the eight state-of-the-art, high-tech pavilions overlooks the Derwent River on the Moorilla estate, around 15 minutes from Hobart. They are part of the MONA art gallery complex (p 13, ❷), and feature original artwork on the walls. If you like radical design and architectural boldness, you'll love it: if chintz is more your style, stay away. *655 Main Rd.* ☎ *03/6277-9900. www.moorilla.com.au. 8 units. Doubles $490–$720. AE, DC, MC, V. Map p 149.*

Montgomery's Private Hotel & YHA Backpackers HOBART Clean, modern and comfortable, this is one of Hobart's best budget options. The double and family rooms with private bathroom are good value and the hostel is in a great location, just one block back from the waterfront. *9 Argyle St.* ☎ *03/6231-2660. www.yha.com.au. 50 units. Dorm bed $30, double with bathroom $130. MC, V. Map p 149.*

OceanViews GRASSY This simple but comfortable two-bedroom house in the heart of Grassy village has sweeping ocean views when there isn't an impenetrable sea mist, which could put a London pea soup fog to shame. It has a hot tub big enough for four that also has great views—when the fog lifts! You can't miss it (just look for the crayfish fishermen about to be tipped into the brink out the front). *Myrtle St.* ☎ *03/6461-1177. www.kingislandholidayvillage.com.au. 1 unit. Double $220. MC, V. Map p 150.*

★ **The Old Woolstore Apartment Hotel** HOBART There's no prize for guessing that the Woolstore

Hotel was, in a former life, a woolstore, built sometime in the very early 1900s. Much of the original character of the building has been retained in the hotel makeover. The rooms are large, bright and cheerful, and the hotel offers good value in a great location. *1 Macquarie St. ☎ 03/6235-5355. www.oldwoolstore.com.au. 242 units. Doubles $164–$389. AE, MC, V. Map p 149.*

Ormiston House STRAHAN This elegant Federation mansion was the grandest on the west coast when it was built in 1899. The rooms are a bit on the chintzy side, but who can resist snuggling up in a four-poster bed when the rain is bucketing down outside? *1 The Esplanade. ☎ 03/6471-7077. www.ormistonhouse.com.au. 5 units. Doubles $190–$260. MC, V. Map p 150.*

★ Palana Beach House PALANA This family beach house on the northern tip of Flinders Island has stunning ocean views and is just metres from the beach, a wide sweep of white sand perfect for long solitary walks. There are two bedrooms in a separate wing, a double bed in the main section of the open-plan house and a fully equipped kitchen, TV and DVD player, and open fireplace for cold nights. The only downside is that it is full of personal mementoes and photographs of the owners, so you never really feel as at home as you could be. *Palana Rd. No phone. www.flindersislandbeach.com. 1 unit. Doubles $150–$220. No cards. Map p 150.*

Quamby Estate.

Peppers Seaport Hotel LAUNCESTON Built in the shape of a ship on the site of an old dry dock where the North and South Esk River meet to become the Tamar River, this riverfront hotel has stylish contemporary rooms, all with lounge areas and balconies, many with good water views. *28 Seaport Blvd. ☎ 03/6345-3333. www.peppers.com.au/seaport. 60 units. Doubles $219–$304. AE, MC, V. Map p 152.*

★★ Peppers York Cove GEORGE TOWN The one- and two-bedroom apartments are huge, but it's the mesmerising water views from the floor-to-ceiling glass windows that really take the breath away at this riverfront hotel at York Cove on the eastern side of the wide Tamar River mouth. Hotel rooms are also available and offer plenty of room to move, but lack the drop-dead gorgeous views. *2 Ferry Blvd. ☎ 03/6382-9900. www.peppers.com.au/yorkcove. 37 units. Doubles $269–$349. AE, MC, V. Map p 150.*

★★ Quamby Estate HAGLEY It's very easy to make yourself at home in this 1830s' mansion near Launceston—so easy it can be hard to leave. Rooms are decorated with a mix of old and new and some have bathtubs that are so deep you almost need floatation devices. Facilities include a private massage room and nine-hole golf course; there's a

Premium suite at The Saffire.

fully stocked bar that operates on an honesty system, a massive full-size billiard table and extensive gardens. The restaurant menu, however, is limited to just three dishes, so plan to eat elsewhere after your first night. *1145 Westwood Rd. ☎ 03/6392-2135. www.quambyestate.com.au. 9 units. Doubles $190–$368. AE, DC, MC, V. Map p 150.*

Rocky Glen Retreat NARACOOPA These cute little European-style chalets look tiny from the outside but are surprisingly roomy on the inside, although the en suite bathroom is poky. They are metres from the beach and sport great views, as does the adjoining Rocky Glen restaurant (p 137). *1 Lovers Lane. ☎ 03/6461-1103. www.rockyglen.com.au. 3 units. Doubles $150. AE, DC, MC, V. Map p 150.*

Rosevears Vineyard Retreat TAMAR VALLEY Rosevears not only makes great wine; its luxury cabins built high above the vineyard with views across the Tamar River Valley and surrounding mountains are a great place to stay if you are touring the Tamar Valley wine route. *1a Waldhorn Dr., Rosevears. ☎ 03/6330-0300. www.rosevears.com.au. 16 units. Doubles $150–$280. MC, V. Map p 150.*

★★★ **Saffire** COLES BAY One of Australia's few true super-luxe lodges, unless you're rich a stay at Saffire is one of those once-in-a-lifetime experiences, but one you'll never forget. Get back to nature in pure luxury, with million-dollar views of the Hazards at Freycinet Bay in million-dollar architect-designed "beach shacks', gorgeous food, a sublime spa (rates include a 1-hour spa treatment) and incredible scenery. *2352 Coles Bay Rd. ☎ 03/6256-7888. www.saffire-freycinet.com.au. 20 units. Doubles $1,450–$2,450. AE, DC, MC, V. Map p 150.*

The Sebel Launceston LAUNCESTON Conveniently placed in the centre of the city, you can walk to anywhere from this all-suite hotel. All of the apartments have balconies and are self-contained and offer plenty of room to move. *Corner of St. John St. & William St. ☎ 03/6333-7555. www.mirvachotels.com.au. 51 units. Doubles $179–$209. AE, MC, V. Map p 152.*

Shanleys Huon Valley GLENDEVIE This beautiful country home is a self-contained, self-catering luxury couples' retreat overlooking the rolling hills and vineyards of the Huon Valley. It's a good base from which to explore the south and is close to the Huon Valley's vineyards and the Tahune AirWalk. *119 Police Point Rd. ☎ 03/6297-6425. www.shanleys.com.au. 1 unit. Double $280 w/breakfast. MC, V. Map p 150.*

★★ **Shannon Coastal Cottages** KING ISLAND It's almost impossible to tear yourself away from the view from these two fully self-contained houses high on the hill on the northern side of Currie Harbour. There are two cottages to choose from—a one-bedroom and a two-bedroom—although 'cottage' is a bit misleading: the two-bedroom one is larger than the average house. There is a price to pay for the view, though: the lighthouse shines directly in the bedroom window so make sure you pull the curtains at night. ☎ *03/6461-1074. www.shannoncoastalcottages.com.au. 2 units. Doubles $150–$160. MC, V. Map p 150.*

★ **Strahan Village** STRAHAN Motel-style rooms high on the hill overlooking the harbour. It's a bit of a steep walk up from the village centre (and reception, which is also at the bottom of the hill), but there is a car park behind the hotel. The views are fantastic. If you don't fancy the climb, the waterfront cottages are loaded with character and are right opposite the wharf. *The Esplanade.* ☎ *1800/420-155. www.puretasmania.com.au. 141 units. Doubles $110–$248. AE, MC, V. Map p 150.*

Vistas on Trousers Point FLINDERS ISLAND This B&B is in a great spot if you want to explore the southern half of Flinders Island, and is only minutes away from Trousers Point and Mount Strzelecki, two of the island's most popular destinations for bushwalkers and beach lovers. Ask about free yoga classes in the neighbour's 'dance yurt'. No children under 12. *Trousers Point Rd.* ☎ *03/6359-4586. www.vistasontrouserspoint.com.au. 8 units. Doubles $155–$185. MC, V. Closed June & July. Map p 150.*

Woodbridge on the Derwent NEW NORFOLK Built by convicts in 1825, this grand old mansion is Tasmania's only member of the elite Small Luxury Hotel group. Suites are extravagant and full of original art and antiques with ultra-modern bathrooms. Most suites have open fireplaces and all have river views. In-house dining is available. *6 Bridge St.* ☎ *0417/996-305. www.woodbridgenn.com.au. 8 units. Doubles $380–$600. MC, V. Map p 150.*

Zero Davey HOBART If you want to be on the waterfront, this is the place. Colourful and very modern one-, two- and three-bedroom apartments make a welcome change from the heritage themes of much of Hobart's other accommodation options and the location is ideal if you like being in the thick of things: it's right on the edge of Constitution Dock overlooking the boats. Roadside rooms can be noisy. *15 Hunter St.* ☎ *03/6270-1444. www.escapesresorts.com.au. 34 units. Doubles $165–$340. MC, V. Map p 149.* ●

Strahan Village waterfront cottages.

The
Savvy Traveller

Before You Go

Government Tourist Offices

Tourism Tasmania is the best source for information on Tasmania. The website, www.discovertasmania.com, has details on attractions, hotels, events, transport and more and there is a phone service where you can talk to Tasmanian travel experts: ☎ **1300/827-743** (for the cost of a local call from anywhere in Australia), or email information@tourismtasmania.com.au. If calling from overseas ☎ **+61 3/6230-8235.** Tourism Australia (www.australia.com) is another good source of information.

The Best Time to Go

Any time is a good time to visit Tasmania—just make sure you have 2 weeks to make the most of the island. Surrounded by oceans, it never gets unbearably hot, but then again, neither does it get freezing cold, although it certainly gets colder than what most coastal Australians are used to. Unlike much of mainland Australia, Tasmania has four distinct seasons. The warmest months are December, January, February and March, and winter extends from May through to August. One of the best times to visit is **autumn** when the fagus (or *Nathofagus gunnii*, Australia's only native deciduous beech) cloak the mountainsides with a covering of gold and red and the grand European trees in the stately parks and gardens around the country are also ablaze with colour. The mild days are ideal for hiking. **Spring** is also glorious, with gardens across the island in bloom, including the tulips at Table Cape near Wynyard and the roses at the National Rose Garden near Launceston. **Summer** has lots of festivals in full swing (see below) and long lingering twilights (perfect for penguin-watching), thanks to Tassie's location below the 40th parallel (or the circle of latitude 40 degrees south of the Earth's equatorial plane). **Winter** often brings snow in the highlands and on Mount Wellington near Hobart, and the crisp sunny days and cold nights are perfect for curling up beside an open fire in heritage accommodation with a platter of good Tasmanian cheese and wine. It's also a great time to see whales cruise by the coastline.

The only time you should try to avoid Tassie, if you can, is during the summer school holidays (last two weeks in Dec and all of Jan, as well as Easter), when it can get busy, although not nearly as busy as the popular tourist destinations on mainland Australia. In fact, Tassie is a great place to go during these times to escape the crowds if that's the only time you can travel. If you do travel during school holidays, make sure you book well ahead, and be aware that some places, such as camping and caravanning in Freycinet National Park, are decided by ballot for the period from late December to mid-February and again over Easter. The ballot is drawn in August and you will need to apply well before then. See www.parks.tas.gov.au/natparks/freycinet/activities.html. There are also school holidays in July and late September through to early October, and while they are certainly busy they are not nearly as busy as the summer holidays. For school term dates, see www.australia.gov.au/topics/australian-facts-and-figures/school-term-dates.

Previous page: Watch out for Tasmanian Devils.

During winter, many tourist attractions will have shorter operating hours or may be closed.

Festivals & Special Events

SUMMER. One of Tassie's largest annual festivals, **The Taste** (Dec 28–Jan 3; www.tastefestival.com.au) is a week-long carnival of Tasmanian food and wine that attracts nearly 250,000 people to Hobart each year, although part of the attraction may be that the festival coincides with the arrival of the 100 or so yachts racing (or sometimes limping) to the finish of the **Sydney-to-Hobart Yacht Race,** which departs Sydney on Boxing Day (Dec 26); most yachts complete the 630-nautical-mile race in 2 days. The waterfront near Salamanca Place buzzes with activity as yachts come and go, fishing boats head off into the Southern Ocean or return laden with crayfish, finfish or squid, and buskers, musicians and performers entertain the crowds. There are usually outdoor movies, kids' events, special exhibitions and outdoor concerts, and most events are free. Another great summer festival is **The Falls Festival** (Dec 29–Jan 1; www.fallsfestival.com; p 145), a 2-day and 2-night music festival that kicks in the New Year with a fantastic line-up of local and international bands on two stages. Launceston parties in February with **Festivale** (mid-Feb; www.festivale.com.au) with 3 days of food and wine and free entertainment in City Park, and around the same time Hobart celebrates all things nautical at the biennial **Australian Wooden Boat Festival** (every 2 years, next one Feb 2013; www.australianwoodenboatfestival.com.au). One event not to miss is the **National Penny Farthing Championships,** the most competitive penny-farthing races in the world. They are held every February at Evandale near Launceston (www.evandalevillagefair.com).

AUTUMN. The biggest event in autumn is the biennial **Ten Days on the Island** (every 2 years, next one late Mar 2013; www.tendaysontheisland.com), a fabulous 10 days of indoor and outdoor theatre, dance, visual arts, music, film, opera and literature, all across the island. Another uniquely Tasmanian annual arts event is the **John Glover Festival** (Mar; www.johnglover.com.au). The main event is the announcement of the winner of this year's Glover Prize for the best new painting depicting the Tasmanian landscape. It's the richest landscape prize in Australia. You can see the finalists at the Falls Park pavilion in Evandale over the long weekend in mid-March. In April, more than 300 rally cars, including Lamborghinis, Ferraris and Porsches, race around the island for 6 days in **Targa Tasmania** (www.targa.org.au).

WINTER. In June, Cradle Mountain Lodge hosts **Tastings at The Top** (www.cradlemountainlodge.com.au), a 3-day culinary carnival with everything from degustation dinners to cooking demonstrations, while a festival to warm the heart of every chocoholic is Latrobe's annual 2-day **Chocolate Winterfest** (mid-July; www.chocolatewinterfest.com.au).

SPRING. Blooming Tasmania (Sept & Oct; www.bloomingtasmania.com) is a flower festival held across the island with open gardens, flower shows, community fairs and guided garden walks. Special events include the **Spring Tulip Festival** at the Royal Tasmanian Botanical Gardens and the **Colours of Wynyard** festivals. Also in October is the annual **Derby River Derby** (www.neriversfestival.com.au), a madcap river race of lilos, dinghies, canoes, tyre inner tubes and just about anything else that floats. It's a highlight of the 10-day **North East Rivers Festival** (mid-Oct; www.nerivers festival.com.au). The 4-day **Tasmanian Craft Fair** (early Nov; www.tascraftfair.com.au) attracts more than 250 artisans and stallholders to Deloraine each year, making it the biggest craft fair in the country. If handicraft is not your thing, you might prefer the craft beers on offer at **Tasmanian Beerfest** (mid-Nov; www.tasmanianbeerfest.com.au), where you can taste hundreds of different beers from around the world, learn how to brew your own or just enjoy the live music in Australia's biggest waterfront beer garden.

The Weather

Tasmania tends to get a bad rap for its weather, but that's usually only by Australian mainlanders who have never been there. Tassie has a temperate maritime climate, which means that temperatures are fairly stable throughout the year, so you don't really get the extremes that you encounter in central Australia. Tasmania does have four distinct seasons, and winter is cold by the standards of northern Australians. Spring and autumn are cool and crisp, and summer is mellow; temperatures rarely rise above 25°C (73°F). December is the wettest month, but the west coast is wet all year and gets, on average, 2,400mm (95 in.) of rain a year. It would be a mistake, however, to visit Tasmania at any time of the year without being prepared for all weathers; it can, and does, change quickly—you can wake up in crisp sunshine and go to bed with snow on the nearby hills.

Useful Websites

- **www.discovertasmania.com:** where to go and what to see from Tourism Tasmania.
- **www.eatability.com.au/au/hobart:** another good site with lots of restaurant reviews and tips and comments from diners.
- **www.hobart.citysearch.com.au:** for events, entertainment, dining and shopping.
- **www.hobarttravelcentre.com.au:** information and accommodation and tour bookings for Hobart and Tasmania.
- **www.ract.com.au:** everything you need to know about motoring in Tasmania.
- **www.whereis.com:** online maps and driving directions.
- **www.yourrestaurants.com.au:** restaurant and bar reviews.

Mobile phones (cell phones)

Australia is on the GSM (Global System for Mobiles) network, so as long as your mobile phone is world-capable (most phones from the UK, Ireland and Europe are) and you have activated global roaming (contact your service provider to check), you should be able to make and receive calls pretty much anywhere in Hobart, Launceston and most larger towns, although reception is almost non-existent away from urban areas, and even then, you'll often need a phone with 3G coverage. Telstra has the best coverage; Optus is OK; Vodafone hardly works at all outside Hobart or Launceston. Not all North American phones are GSM, but you can rent one before leaving home from **InTouch U.S.A.** (☎ **800/872-7626;** www.intouch global.com) or **RoadPost** (☎ **888/290-1606** or 905/272-5665; www.roadpost.com). InTouch will also, for free, advise you on whether your existing phone will work overseas; call ☎ **703/222-7161** between 9am and 4pm EST, or go to http://intouchglobal.com/travel.htm. If you plan on making a lot of calls, consider buying a pay-as-you-go phone or sim card in Australia for

TASMANIA'S AVERAGE TEMPERATURE & RAINFALL (HOBART)

	JAN	FEB	MAR	APR	MAY	JUNE
Daily High (°F/°C)	73/23	75/24	72/22	66/19	61/16	55/13
Daily Low (°F/°C)	54/12	54/12	50/10	46/8	43/6	41/5
Rrainfall (in/mm)	1.6/42	1.4/36	1.5/37	1.8/45	1.4/36	1.2/31
	JULY	**AUG**	**SEPT**	**OCT**	**NOV**	**DEC**
Daily High (°F/°C)	54/12	55/13	59/15	64/18	66/19	70/21
Daily Low (°F/°C)	37/3	39/4	43/6	45/7	48/9	50/10
Rrainfall (in/mm)	1.8/45	1.9/48	1.6/40	1.9/48	1.8/45	2.1/54

more attractive call costs, as global roaming rates can be extortionate. There are outlets at all major airports and in most shopping centres.

Car Rentals

Most of the major sights and attractions in Hobart and Launceston are readily accessible by public transport or on foot, so if you are just exploring the city don't bother with a hire car. However, the best of Tassie is to be found outside these two cities, and while there are some intercity coach services that also service regional centres, you really do need your own transport. Remember: Australians drive on the left.

All major car rental companies operate in Tasmania, and cars can be picked up at the airport and some hotels. **www.vroom.com.au** is a great place to compare costs across all major companies. **Avis** (☎ **13 63 33;** www.avis.com); **Budget** (☎ **1300 362-848;** www.budget.com.au); **Europcar** (☎ **1300 131-390;** www.europcar.com.au); **Hertz** (☎ **13 30 39;** www.hertz.com.au); **Thrifty** (☎ **1300 367-227;** www.thrifty.com.au). **Flinders Island Car Rentals** (☎ **03/6359-2168;** www.ficr.com.au.) **King Island Car Rentals** (☎ **03/6462-1282;** www.kingisland.org.au.)

Getting **There**

By Plane

Tasmania has two main airports: **Hobart International Airport** (www.hobartairpt.com.au) and **Launceston Airport** (www.launcestonairport.com.au), plus the smaller regional airports of Devonport and Burnie (which is actually within walking distance of the town of Wynyard). Despite being called Hobart International Airport, no international flights fly in or out of Hobart (apart from the occasional charter flight). If coming from overseas, you must connect with a domestic flight in Sydney or Melbourne.

Virgin Blue (☎ **13 67 89;** www.virginaustralia.com) has daily services to Launceston from Melbourne, Sydney and Brisbane and to Hobart from Melbourne, Sydney, Brisbane and Canberra. **Qantas** (☎ **13 13 13;** www.qantas.com.au) flies daily into Hobart from Melbourne and Sydney, and Launceston from Melbourne. Qantas subsidiary **Qantaslink** flies into Devonport. Qantas's budget subsidiary, **Jetstar** (☎ **13 15 38;** www.jetstar.com), operates low-cost services to Hobart and Launceston from Melbourne and Sydney. **Regional Express** (**REX** ☎ **13 17 13;** www.regionalexpress.com.au) operates daily services to Burnie and King Island from Melbourne. **TasAir** (☎ **03/6248-5088;** www.tasair.com.au) flies into King Island from Devonport and Burnie and **Sharp Airlines** (☎ **1300 556-694;** www.sharpairlines.com.au) provides regular, daily services to Flinders Island from both Launceston and Melbourne.

The **Hobart Airport Shuttle** (☎ **1300 385-511;** www.tasredline.com.au) meets all scheduled flights into Hobart Airport and drops off at hotels, motels, bed and breakfast accommodation, and hostels in central Hobart and inner-city suburbs. Tickets are $15 per adult one way ($25 return), $10 children 3–15. A taxi fare will cost $35 to $40, depending on traffic.

In Launceston, there is also an **Airporter Shuttle** (☎ **03/6343-6677**) that meets all scheduled flights. Tickets cost $14 one way, $25 return. A taxi fare will cost between $32 and $36.

In Devonport **North West Shuttles** (☎ **1300 659-878**) runs a shuttle between the city and airport for $15 per person; transfer to the ferry is also $15. There is also a shuttle from **Burnie** airport at Wynyard (**Wynyard Airport Services;** ☎ **0427/158-196**) to Burnie; $22 per adult or $20 per person if two. Bookings are essential for both the Devonport and Burnie services.

By Ferry

The ***Spirit of Tasmania*** (☎ **1800 634-906;** www.spiritoftasmania.com.au) has two ships that cross Bass Strait between Station Pier in Port Melbourne and Devonport on Tasmania's north coast every day in both directions. The journey takes around 10 hours and departs from both ports at 7:30pm and arrives at 6am; during peak holiday time (mid-Dec to mid-Mar and during Easter) there is also a daytime sailing departing at 9am and arriving at 6pm 4 days a week.

It's a car ferry so you can take your car, motorbike, campervan or caravan, and kennels are available on request if travelling with your pet. You can also bring a bicycle along with you as well. If you'd prefer to fly but still want the freedom of having your own car or caravan once in Tasmania, you can book your vehicle on as freight. On-board accommodation ranges from airline-style reclining seats to private cabins, as well as two-berth and four-berth cabins, which you can book for exclusive use or opt to

Quarantine: What You Can & Can't Bring In

Tasmania is strict about its quarantine laws, and if you're travelling by car you will be searched by quarantine officers as you depart the ship. Processed (dried, cooked or canned) food is OK, but no fresh fruit or vegetables are allowed. Many plants and cut flowers are prohibited, and your fishing equipment and any hiking and camping gear must be clean. Dogs must have been treated for tapeworm. For more information, see www.dpiw.tas.gov.au.

share with other passengers. All cabins are air-conditioned and have private bathroom facilities and there are two restaurants and a bar, as well as a cinema, tourist information centre and a very well-stocked gift shop on board.

One-way passenger fares range from around $100 per adult for a recliner chair to around $550 for a deluxe porthole cabin, but there are lots of options in between. An average-size car (up to 5m/16½ ft. in length) costs an additional $83 each way. The website has details of fares and latest specials. Bookings are essential.

Getting **Around**

By Bus

Getting around Tasmania by public transport is possible, but slow and circuitous. The most comprehensive service is offered by **Tassielink Coaches** (☎ **1300 300-520;** www.tassielink.com.au) with terminals in Launceston (Cornwall Sq. Transit Centre, corner of St. John St. & Cimitiere St.) and Hobart (Hobart Bus Terminal, 64 Brisbane St.). The Explorer Pass, valid for 7, 10, 14 and 21 days, allows unlimited travel in all directions and has links to more than 50 destinations throughout Tasmania. Prices range from $208 for the 7-day pass up to $329 for the 21-day pass.

Redline Coaches (☎ **1300 360-000;** www.tasredline.com.au) has daily services from Smithton west of Stanley (where Tassielink does not go) to Hobart via Burnie, Devonport, and Launceston. **Metro Services** (☎ **13 22 01;** www.metrotas.com.au) operates commuter bus routes in and around Hobart, Launceston and Burnie. The minimum fare (which covers most short hops in the city) is $2.60 for adults and $1.30 for children for a 4km (2½-mile) 'section'. Sections are marked on bus-stand signs, but if in doubt just tell the bus driver your destination and he or she'll work out the fare. Tickets are available from the driver. A Day Rover ticket ($4.60) allows unlimited travel after 9am on Monday to Friday or all day Saturday, Sunday and public holidays.

By Car

The best way to really explore Tasmania is by car. You'll find car rental agencies in all major towns and regional centres offering competitive prices (see Car Rentals, p 165).

Driving in Tassie is lots of fun and generally hassle-free. Parking in towns is relatively easy. Outside of Hobart and Launceston you won't find much traffic, and serious traffic jams in the cities are rare. However, Tassie's narrow, winding roads do present some challenges: driving at night is best avoided; if you do, watch out for animals—the roadsides are littered with roadkill; many roads are unsealed and some can be icy and large log trucks are common in remote areas—give them plenty of room.

Petrol is available 24 hours in larger regional centres, but petrol stations will operate limited hours in more remote areas and may even be closed on Sundays.

The speed limit in built-up areas is 50km (31 miles) per hour unless otherwise indicated. Most other roads have a maximum speed limit of 100km (62 miles) per hour, although there are a couple of short highway stretches that allow 110km (68 miles) per hour. On all open roads, however, lower speed limits are frequently indicated, and these limits must be adhered to.

The wearing of seat belts is compulsory. Speed cameras and random breath-testing units operate throughout Tasmania.

The **RACT** (Royal Automobile Club of Tasmania) provides reciprocal roadside service for members of affiliated automobile clubs, including all Australian clubs (NRMA, RACV, RAA, RACWA, RACQ, RANT) and most clubs across North America, the UK and Europe. It also has the best range of up-to-date roadmaps. If you break down, and are in mobile phone range, call ☎ **13 11 11.**

By Motorbike

The same road rules apply to motorbike riders as drivers of cars and you'll need a valid motorcycle rider licence. It is compulsory to wear a helmet. And bring wet-weather gear—you'll need it. You can hire motorcycles from **Tasmanian Motorcycle Hire** ☎ **03/6391-9139;** www.tasmotorcyclehire.com.au) in Evandale near Launceston and **Moto Adventure Tasmania** (☎ **0447 556-189;** www.motoadventure.com.au) in Hobart, but you'll need to supply your own riding gear and helmet.

By Taxi

All taxi journeys are metered, although you may have to book ahead if you want a taxi outside of the main urban centres of Hobart, Launceston and Devonport. **Central Cabs** ☎ **13 10 08; Hobart Yellow Water Cabs** ☎ **047/036-268; Maxitaxi Service** ☎ **13 62 94; Taxi Combined** ☎ **13 22 27; Yellow Cabs** ☎ **13 19 24.**

Fast **Facts**

ATMS/CASHPOINTS ATMs are everywhere and most use global networks such as Cirrus and PLUS. Australian ATMs use a four-digit PIN code, so check with your bank and make sure you change yours before you leave home. Many banks impose a fee every time you use a card at another bank's ATM, and that fee can be higher for international transactions (up to $5 or more) than for domestic ones (where they're rarely more than $2).

BANKING HOURS Banks are open Monday through Friday from 9:30am to 4pm.

BIKE RENTALS Rent bikes from **Derwent Bike Hire,** 20 McVilly Dr., Regatta Grounds, Queens Domain, Hobart (☎ **0428/899-169;** www.derwentbikehire.com).

BUSINESS & SHOP HOURS Shopping hours are usually from 9am to 5pm daily, with extended shopping hours until 9pm on Friday nights. Smaller retail stores may close on Saturday afternoons and Sundays, although most large supermarkets are open from 7am to 9pm daily.

CLIMATE See The Weather, p 164.

CONSULATES & EMBASSIES All foreign embassies are based in Canberra. There is a **British Honorary Consul** in Hobart (1A Brisbane St. ☎ **03/6213-3310**) but otherwise you'll need to contact the following consulates on the mainland: **Canada,** Level 5, 111 Harrington St., The Rocks, Sydney (☎ **02/9364-3000**); **Ireland,** Level 26, 1 Market St., Sydney (☎ **02/9264-9635**); **New Zealand,** 55 Hunter St., Sydney (☎ **02/9223-0144**) or Level 10, 454 Collins St., Melbourne (☎ **03/9642-1279**); and **United States,** Level 59, MLC Centre,

19–29 Martin Place, Sydney (☎ **02/9373-9200**).

CREDIT CARDS Visa and MasterCard are universally accepted in Australia; American Express and Diners Club are less common and usually attract a surcharge; and Discover is not used. Always carry a little cash, because many merchants will not take cards for purchases under $15.

CUSTOMS The duty-free allowance in Australia is $900 or, for those under 18, $450. Anyone over 18 can bring in up to 250 cigarettes or 250 grams (8.8 oz.) of cigars or other tobacco products, 2.25 litres (41 fluid oz.) of alcohol and 'dutiable goods' to the value of $900. 'Dutiable goods' are luxury items such as perfume, watches, jewellery, plus gifts of any kind. Because Australia is an island, it is free of many agricultural and livestock diseases. To keep it that way, strict quarantine applies to importing plants, animals and their products, including food. Sniffer dogs at airports detect these products (as well as drugs). Amnesty trash bins are available before you reach the immigration counters in airport arrivals halls for items such as fruit. Don't be alarmed if, just before landing, the flight attendants spray the aircraft cabin (with products approved by the World Health Organization) to kill potentially disease-bearing insects. For more information on what is and is not allowed, contact the **Australian Quarantine and Inspection Service** (☎ **02/6272-3933;** www.affa.gov.au). Its website has a list of restricted or banned foods, animal and plant products, and other items. In addition, Tasmania has its own quarantine rules. It is the only Australian state free of fruit fly, and quarantine officials are very strict about not allowing fresh fruit and vegetables on to the island. See box Quarantine, p 166.

ELECTRICITY The current is 240 volts AC, 50 hertz. Sockets take two or three flat prongs, and international visitors will need an adaptor, best bought before you leave home as most Australian stores only stock adaptors for Australian appliances to fit other international outlets. Power does not start automatically when you plug in an appliance; you need to flick the switch beside the socket, and turn it off before pulling the plug.

EMBASSIES See Consulates & Embassies above.

EMERGENCIES Dial ☎ **000** to call the police, the fire service or an ambulance. Both the Hobart and Launceston public hospitals have emergency sections. Call the **RACT** for car breakdowns (☎ **13 11 11**). If you are not a member of an auto club at home that has a reciprocal agreement with the RACT, you'll have to join on the spot before they will tow or repair your car. This usually costs around $150, but includes a 12-month membership.

EVENT LISTINGS ***Tasmanian Travelways*** is a free bimonthly tourism magazine with a wealth of Tasmanian travel and tourism services and products, including accommodation, restaurants, wineries, tours and an events section. It's available at tourist information offices and many hotels and attractions across the state and has an online version at www.travelways.com.au. There is also an events section at www.discovertasmania.com. For details of what's on in Hobart, see www.liveguide.com.au/Hobart.

FAMILY TRAVEL To locate accommodation, restaurants and attractions that are particularly kid-friendly, refer to the 'Kids' icon throughout this guide. Most Tasmanian hotels accommodate families; all but the most expensive restaurants are child-friendly, although not all offer specific children's menus.

GAY & LESBIAN TRAVELLERS Tasmania was one of the last Australian states to revoke anti-gay laws (as recently as 1997). However, the state seems to have made up for its past and became the first Australian state to recognise overseas same-sex marriages as official partnerships under state law in late 2010. While overt demonstrations of gay affection are not always tolerated on the street, there are many businesses that welcome gay travellers—look out for the rainbow Tasmania map that signifies gay-friendly venues. For more information, see www.gaytasmania.com.au or get a free copy of the Tourism Tasmania's *Discover Tasmania Gay & Lesbian Visitor's Guide* (☎ **1300 827-743;** www.discovertasmania.com/about_tasmania/gay_and_lesbian_visitors). The **TasPride** festival is held at various locations across the state in early November. See www.taspride.com.

HOLIDAYS The 10 public holidays in Tasmania are New Year's Day, Australia Day (Jan 26), Royal Hobart Regatta (second Mon in Feb in southern Tasmania), Eight Hours Day (second Mon in Mar), Good Friday, Easter Monday and Tuesday, Anzac Day (Apr 25), Queen's Birthday (second Mon in June), Recreation Day (first Mon in Nov in northern Tasmania), Christmas Day, and Boxing Day (Dec 26). Almost everything is closed on Christmas Day and Good Friday. On all other major public holidays, banks and businesses are closed, but larger stores and some tourist attractions may remain open.

INSURANCE Check your existing insurance policies before you buy travel insurance to cover trip cancellation, lost luggage, medical expenses or car rental insurance. Australia has Reciprocal Health Care Agreements (RHCAs) with Finland, Italy, Malta, New Zealand, Norway, Republic of Ireland, Sweden, The Netherlands and the United Kingdom, which allow restricted access to health care services. See www.medicareaustralia.gov.au.

INTERNET CAFES There are a few dedicated Internet cafes in Hobart, but many cafes and hotels offer free Wi-Fi for paying customers. Public libraries also offer Internet access. For details of public online access centres, see www.tco.asn.au.

LOST PROPERTY Call credit card companies the minute you discover your wallet has been lost or stolen and file a report at the nearest police station. Your credit card company or insurer may require a police report number or record.

MAIL & POSTAGE Stamps for standard-size mail inside Australia are 60¢; to send a postcard outside Australia will cost $1.45 and will usually take between 5 and 7 working days to reach the destination. Stamps are available from post offices and some newsagents if there are no post offices in the vicinity, and you can post a stamped letter or postcard at any red post box, which are plentiful around the cities and towns. The **General Post Office (GPO)** in Hobart is at 9 Elizabeth St. (☎ **13 13 18**). It's open Monday to Friday 8:30am to 5:30pm. General-delivery letters can be sent c/o Poste Restante, GPO Hobart, TAS 7000, Australia, and are collected at the GPO.

MONEY The Australian dollar is divided into 100¢. Coins are 5¢, 10¢, 20¢ and 50¢ pieces (silver) and $1 and $2 pieces (gold). Even though prices often end in a variant of 1¢ and 2¢ (for example, 68¢ or $1.99), prices are rounded to the nearest 5¢—so 97¢ rounds down to 95¢, and 58¢ rounds up to 60¢.

Bank notes come in denominations of $5, $10, $20, $50 and $100. Most major bank branches offer currency-exchange services. Most larger stores will accept traveller's cheques, but they may be hard to cash at smaller stores and restaurants, so always ask first.

OPTICIANS Eyeglasses can be repaired and contact lenses purchased at any optometrist in Hobart, Launceston and larger regional centres; if possible, take your prescription with you.

PARKING Compared to mainland cities, such as Sydney and Melbourne, parking is both cheap and easy in Hobart and Launceston. You can often find free on-street parking and there are a number of parking stations throughout the city centre. There are some parking meters. All meters accept 10¢, 20¢ and $1 coins, some also accept 50¢ and $2 coins. Parking meters operate Monday to Saturday from 8:30am to 6pm and Sunday 9am to 4pm. Parking fines are issued to anyone who parks over time or illegally and the minimum fine is around $25. Most hotels offer free parking.

PASSES The **See Tasmania Card** gives free entry to more than 50 attractions and discounts at many more, but in my experience it offers little real value unless you are planning on visiting an awful lot of attractions, more than is realistic. Prices range from $189 to $365 per adult for 3, 7 and 10 days, $131 to $255 kids. Order at **www.seetasmaniacard.com.** Much better value is the **National Parks Pass** (see box, p 115), which will save you serious money if you are planning on visiting three or more parks during your stay.

PASSPORTS & VISAS Along with a current passport valid for the length of your stay, the Australian government requires a visa from visitors of every nation (except New Zealand) to be issued before you arrive. Short-term tourist and business visas (up to 3 months) are issued instantly online, and called an **Electronic Travel Authority (ETA).** This is an electronic visa that takes the place of a stamp in your passport and is electronically recorded on Australian government systems. To apply online, see **www.eta.immi.gov.au;** the $20 charge is payable by credit card. Applications for ETAs can also be submitted through travel agents or airlines. Apply for non-ETA visas at Australian embassies, consulates and high commissions. For more information, see **www.immi.gov.au.**

PHARMACIES Most often called 'chemist shops', Australian pharmacists may only fill prescriptions written by Australian doctors, so carry enough medication with you for your trip. You can also buy common over-the-counter medications such as headache tablets and cough syrups at supermarkets.

SAFETY Tasmania is a safe place, but, just like anywhere else, it pays to be careful and use common sense. Keep your wallet hidden, don't wear money belts, 'bum packs', or 'fanny packs' outside your clothing. For most visitors, the most dangerous thing they encounter is the surf—always swim or surf at patrolled beaches between the red and yellow flags, which mark the safest area for swimming—or the possibility of having a car crash trying to avoid a collision with an animal on the roads at night.

SENIOR TRAVELLERS Visiting seniors (often called 'pensioners' in Australia) from other countries don't automatically qualify for the discounted entry prices to tours, attractions, transport and events that Australian seniors enjoy, but it is always worth asking. Carry ID that shows your age.

SMOKING Smoking is banned in all enclosed public places, including public transport, offices, hospitals, hotels, bars and restaurants, and in some busy pedestrian areas in Hobart. Some hotels have outdoor sections where smoking is permitted, often called 'beer gardens'. It is illegal to smoke in cars carrying children under the age of 16.

TAXES Australia imposes a 10% **Goods and Services Tax (GST)** on most goods sold in Australia and most services. The GST applies to most travel-related goods and services, including transport, hotels, tours and restaurants. By law, the tax has to be included in the advertised price of the product, though it doesn't have to be displayed independently of the pre-tax price. The **Tourist Refund Scheme** (TRS) enables you to claim a refund of the GST paid on purchases of more than $300 (GST inclusive) in the one store (as long as they are all on the one tax invoice) in the 30 days before you leave the country. You must wear or carry the goods on board the aircraft or ship and present them along with your original tax invoice, passport and international boarding pass to a Customs Officer at a TRS facility at the international airport or cruise terminal. A departure tax of $38 is payable by all persons 12 years or older upon leaving Australia, and it is generally included in the airline or cruise ticket price.

TELEPHONES Most of Tasmania's public phone boxes take coins, and many also accept credit cards and $10 phone cards available from newsagents. Local calls cost 50¢, no matter how long you talk, but don't return unused coins (you won't get any change back if you use a $2 coin to pay for a 50¢ local call). Numbers beginning with 1800 within Australia are toll-free; numbers starting with 13 or 1300 in Australia are charged at the local fee; numbers beginning with 1900 (or 1901 or 1902 etc.) are pay-for-service lines, and you will be charged as much as $5 per minute.

To make international calls from Australia: first dial 0011 and then the country code (US or Canada: 1; UK: 44; Ireland: 353; New Zealand: 64), then the area code and number. **For directory assistance:** dial ☎ **12455** for a number inside Australia and ☎ **1225** for numbers to all other countries. The international calling code for Australia if calling from overseas is 61.

TIPPING Tipping is not expected anywhere, but certainly appreciated; most Australians leave tips for good restaurant service, but usually only in expensive restaurants. Ten per cent is the usual figure, with more for exemplary service, and tips are often pooled and shared out amongst all staff. In hotels, if you want to tip luggage porters, $1 to $2 is plenty, as is a small gratuity of $2 for delivery room service, but never more than 10% of the bill. Most people tip taxi drivers any small change left over from the fare and $5–$10 for tour guides.

TOURIST OFFICES **The Hobart Travel Centre,** 20 Davey St., Hobart (☎ **1800 990-440;** www.hobarttravelcentre.com.au) is a good place to pick up maps, brochures and general tourist information about Hobart as well as towns throughout Tasmania. Open Monday to Friday 8:30am to 5:30pm, Saturday and Sunday 9am to 5pm. The **Launceston Visitor Information Centre** is on Cornwall Square, 12–16 St. John St. and open weekdays 9am to 5pm, weekends 9am to 3pm (☎ **03/6336-3133;** www.visitlauncestontamar.com.au), and the **Devonport Visitor Information Centre** is at 92 Formby Rd. (☎ **03/6424-4466;** www.devonporttasmania.travel) is open daily from 7:30am to 5pm.

TOURS The Hobart Travel Centre (see Tourist Offices above) is the best place to go for information (and bookings) about tours.

TRAVELLERS WITH DISABILITIES Most hotels, major stores, attractions and public toilets in Australia have wheelchair access, although the entrance or access may not be obvious and it may pay to call ahead. Some (but not all) buses and taxis (it's a good idea to book 24 hours in advance for taxis) have wheelchair access facilities. Call to check access facilities on your intended metro bus route (☎ **1800 654-184**). Wheelchair rental is available from **Red Cross** offices in Hobart, Launceston and Burnie. ☎ **03/6235-6031.**

If you wish to visit Australia with your guide dog, remember that animals must satisfy certain health requirements and may need to undergo quarantine after arrival (see **www.daff.gov.au** for more information). Text telephone (TTY) facilities are still limited largely to government services.

WEATHER For the local forecast, call ☎ **1900 955-364** ($.77 per minute) or see **www.bom.gov.au/tas.**

Tasmania: **A Brief History**

C. 10,000 B.C. The land mass now known as Tasmania is cut off from mainland Australia by rising sea levels, isolating the population of 4,000 to 6,000 Tasmanian Aborigines.

1642 Dutch explorer Abel Tasman charts the west coast, naming it Van Diemen's Land after the governor of Batavia.

1770 Then Lieutenant (later Captain) James Cook arrives at Botany Bay (in present-day Sydney) and takes possession of the mainland east coast for England, naming it 'New South Wales'. Van Diemen's Land is still thought to be an extension of the mainland.

1788 The penal Colony of New South Wales is established with the arrival of the first fleet of 11 convict ships under Governor Arthur Philip.

1793 French explorer Bruni D'Entrecasteaux charts the channel that bears his name, as well as the Huon River and Bruny Island.

1797 The *Sydney Cove* is wrecked on Preservation Island near Flinders Island. Miraculously, survivors make it back to Sydney to launch a rescue mission, travelling by longboat to what is now Ninety Mile Beach in Victoria and trekking 600km (370 miles) overland to Port Jackson (Sydney). Their reports of large numbers of fur seals result in sealers quickly settling the outer islands of the Furneaux Group.

1798 Explorers George Bass and Matthew Flinders circumnavigate Tasmania, proving it is an island.

1802 French explorer Nicolas Baudin and his cartographers, the Freycinet brothers, chart large sections of the east coast.

1803 Fears of the French claiming Van Diemen's Land prompt the British to form a convict settlement at Risdon Cove on the eastern shore of the River Derwent. In 1804, Lieutenant-Governor David Collins moves the settlement across the river and calls it Hobart Town.

1825 Previously governed by New South Wales, Van Diemen's Land becomes a colony in its own right.

1830 Lieutenant-Governor George Arthur decides to remove all Aborigines from the settled areas in order to end the escalating raids upon settlers' huts. His plan, called the Black Line, entailed the use of a human chain that swept across the settled districts. Only two Aborigines were captured, but three were killed.

1833 The convict prison for repeat offenders is established at Port Arthur.

1834 George Augustus Robinson starts his mission to protect Aborigines and takes the remnants of the population to Flinders Island. By 1847, the settlement at Wybalenna is abandoned, and most of the 135 Aborigines who lived there are dead.

1842 Hobart Town becomes a city; convict transportation is at its highest—5,329 are transported to Van Diemen's Land that year.

1853 End of convict transportation to Van Diemen's Land, 3 years after the end of transportation of convicts to New South Wales. More than 74,000 convicts had been sent to the island since 1802.

1856 The name of the colony is formally changed to Tasmania, in honour of Abel Tasman.

1876 Truganini, once widely (but erroneously) believed to be the last Tasmanian Aborigine, dies on Bruny Island.

1877 The penal settlement at Port Arthur is closed.

1901 Australia becomes a Commonwealth. Tasmania is one of the six states of the new nation.

1936 The last known Tasmanian tiger (thylacine) dies at Hobart's Beaumaris Zoo.

1975 On the night of January 5, a ship travelling up the Derwent River in Hobart strikes two pylons of the Tasman Bridge, bringing down the concrete central spans. Twelve people are killed, including the occupants of four cars on the bridge that went over the edge. It takes nearly 3 years to repair the bridge.

1982 The Tasmanian government plans to build a hydroelectric dam on the Gordon River 40km (25 miles) from Macquarie Harbour, near Strahan. Over 3 months, about 6,000 protesters blockade the river and construction roads, most at Warners Landing 6km (3.7 miles) from the junction of the Franklin and Gordon Rivers. Many (1,272) people are arrested, including Bob Brown, who, after serving 19 days in gaol, was voted into parliament on the day of his release. He is now the leader of the Australian Greens and was the first openly gay member of the Parliament of Australia.

1983 On July 1, the High Court of Australia rules in favour of the Federal Government (and conservationists) and prevents the Tasmanian government's proposed Franklin River Dam.

1996 A lone gunman, Martin Bryant, murders 35 people at Port Arthur, resulting in new gun-control laws that are among the strictest in the world.

2003 State Parliament provides legal recognition to de facto and same-sex relationships by

Accommodations

Restaurants

Photo **Credits**

Note: l= left; r= right; t= top; b= bottom; c= center

Cover Photo Credits: Front Cover (l to r): Bushwalker on beach, Bay of Fires Walk, Mt William National Park, Tasmania. © Holger Leue / Lonely Planet Images / Alamy Images. Tasmanian Devil, sarcophilus harrisi, single adult sitting on a rock. © Gerry Pearce / Alamy Images. Hiker Atop Cradle Mountain In Tasmanias Central Highland. © Axiom Photographic / Alamy Images. Back cover: Port Arthur Historic Site Tasman Peninsula Tasmania. © Marc Anderson / Alamy Images.

Interior Photo Credits: All pictures © James Horan with the following exceptions: © Lee Atkinson: p 57; 61 (t); 63; 64; 65 (t); 65 (b); 68 (t); 68 (b); 69; 103 (t); 104 (b); 105 (t); 111 (b); 119; 125

Port Arthur Ghost Tour: © Photo by Simon Birch / Courtesy: Port Arthur Historic Site Management Authority (PAHSMA): p 31

Peppermint Bay: © Courtesy Peppermint Bay: p 136

Mud Bar, Peppers Seaport Hotel: © Mantra Group Digital Library: p 140

@VDL © Photo by: Adam Johnson / Courtesy @VDL: p 148

Saffire © Photo by: George Apostolidis / Courtesy Saffire / Federal Group: p 159

Notes